FOOD
GURUS

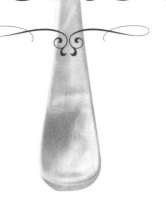

20 People who changed The Way We Eat and Think about Food

FOOD GURUS

STEPHEN VINES

Marshall Cavendish
Editions

This edition published in 2012 by Marshall Cavendish Editions
An imprint of Marshall Cavendish International
1 New Industrial Road, Singapore 536196
genrefsales@sg.marshallcavendish.com
www.marshallcavendish.com/genref

Other Marshall Cavendish offices:
Marshall Cavendish Corporation. 99 White Plains Road, Tarrytown NY 10591-9001, USA
• Marshall Cavendish International (Thailand) Co Ltd. 253 Asoke, 12th Flr, Sukhumvit 21
Road, Klongtoey Nua, Wattana, Bangkok 10110, Thailand • Marshall Cavendish (Malaysia)
Sdn Bhd. Times Subang, Lot 46, Subang Hi-Tech Industrial Park, Batu Tiga, 40000 Shah
Alam, Selangor Darul Ehsan, Malaysia

Marshall Cavendish is a trademark of Times Publishing Limited

A CIP record for this book is available from the British Library
ISBN 978-981-4361-07-1

Cover design by Cover Kitchen
Book design and illustrations by TeamAsia

Printed and bound in Great Britain by TJ International

Table of Contents

Introduction

*W*hat is a food guru? The simple answer to this question is that it is a person who has changed the way we eat and think about what we eat, for better or for worse. The food gurus on these pages are not merely good cooks, or great food writers, or even people who run some of the world's most popular restaurants—they are much more than that because each one has had a transformative influence on the food we eat. This is a very big claim to make and I trust that the stories of these extraordinary people will justify the expectations made by such an assertion.

Of course, making judgments about who qualifies for this accolade is subjective and it is quite possible that some readers will be dissatisfied with the selection of gurus in this book and have views on others who should have been included. However, this work does not claim to be definitive; it is a subjective selection in a field where claims of objectivity are suspect because food rightly excites passion and controversy and there are no absolute standards. Thus, there is plenty of room for lively debate and I hope this book contributes to the dialogue.

In making this selection of just twenty food gurus, I have attempted to strike a balance between chefs, food writers and other influential people in the food industry who have left an enormous legacy, and in some cases continue to do so. There is, admittedly, a bias in this book towards personalities from Britain and the United States, leaving an opportunity to consider other personalities from other nations. To be frank, the bias emanates from the limitations of my knowledge and access to information. It seems far better to write as much as possible on the basis of what you know best and so that is what I have done.

Writing this book has sent me on a fascinating journey through history; the more I researched this subject, the more I realized that social development is very much reflected in the way we eat and think about food. This is hardly a novel observation but I was struck by the extent to which this proved to be the case. Changes in eating habits provide early indications of the transformation of society and food thus emerges as what economists call a *leading* indicator as opposed to being a *lagging* one. A vivid example of this can be found in Britain where, in the 1970s a version of chicken tikka masala from the Indian subcontinent, became the nation's most famous dish. The enthusiasm of British people for Indian food was one of the important forces pushing forward the embrace of multiculturalism.

What is striking is that it is only in the twentieth century that food really rose beyond being a means of subsistence for the mass of the people. It is true that in earlier periods a variety of special foods, not regularly consumed, were only produced for particular occasions; but in the day-to-day lives of ordinary working people, the choice of food was limited and eating associated more with sustenance rather than enjoyment. Only the affluent could contemplate food as a regular part of their leisure activities. Almost without exception, the rich played no role in food preparation. However, as we shall see in the chapter on Catherine de Medici (Chapter 12), the rich and powerful had a considerable supervisory influence on the production of meals and ways of eating.

Now everything has changed as wealthy people willingly and enthusiastically enter kitchens with their sleeves rolled up and ready to cook, while in the industrialized world, it is often those with less money who are less inclined to cook and tend to rely almost exclusively on convenience foods that are merely reheated or simply unpacked before being served. There are other paradoxes in a world where discussion of food has reached new levels. Indeed this is a world where entire television channels are devoted to the subject, yet fewer meals are being cooked from scratch, families no longer eat together and basic knowledge of how to cook has ceased to pass from one generation to another. These developments and many others are reflected in these pages through the lives of the food gurus.

Because interest in food as a subject has mushroomed in the last 50 years, it has ceased to be a specialist concern reserved for chefs and food producers. Now that food has become a mainstream preoccupation and is discussed among people in much the same way as, say sport, it has become a sometimes obsessive subject of interest. Television has played a major role in easing the way of food into the mainstream of popular culture and so there was a temptation to focus on those who are best known through this medium. However, I think this would have been a mistake, not because there are not a great number of highly influential television chefs but because it is often hard to pin down the precise nature of their contribution to the development of food and eating.

But this is not a book about culinary celebrities, not least because of the transience of fame. Yet some of the people in this book are very big celebrities, such as Gordon Ramsay, who was a well-established chef before being caught up in the whirlwind of television. Jamie Oliver, on the other hand, had never run his own kitchen before his engaging personality propelled him forward to the TV screen and made him into a personality who could use his fame to open restaurants. However, it would be a mistake to think that the concept of celebrity chefs started with television. For example, Antonin Carême, who rose to fame in the mid-eighteenth century, was certainly a celebrity in his day. He was courted by influential people and the publication of his books had the public rushing to the bookshops. The famous author in the Victorian age, Isabella Beeton, became well-known through magazine articles and only wrote one book but such was her fame that after she died books appeared under her name, making her something of a brand.

I would also like to admit that at the onset, I had intended to write only about chefs. However, the more I studied the subject, the more I realized that, although they needed to occupy a major place in this work, there are many other people associated with the world of food who do not cook for a living yet have made a major impression on the way we eat. Some of them, notably Ray Kroc (the man who transformed the McDonald's hamburger chain into an international behemoth) might well be considered to have devalued the world of food but it is very hard to argue that he has made no impact. The same can be said of Robert Atkins, whose advocacy of a high protein, low carb diet has millions and millions of adherents who follow it religiously. Occasionally and maybe only in part, Atkin's work has left an enormous impression even on people who do not know his name. Both Kroc and Atkins are something of an anathema for foodies (apologies for using this terrible term but it is surprising how many people are happy to be described in this way). Much more acceptable to food connoisseurs is Carlo Petrini, the founder of the Slow Food Movement, who could be considered the antithesis of Ray Kroc. But he too has critics that question advocating an approach to food primarily designed for those with the leisure and means to indulge in the higher reaches of the culinary world. In other words, he is decried as an elitist yet this is a strange criticism because striving for perfection and improvement is something that unites all those included in this book. Although I myself actively dislike McDonald's hamburgers and remain skeptical over Atkin's views, it is quite impossible to not recognize the considerable achievements of these two people.

As for the chefs who populate these pages, well, what can I say? Anyone who has worked closely with chefs as I have is likely to tell you that they are a very distinctive group of people, living a life that most of us would not dream of living. Think about it – do you know anyone else who is still predictably hard at work even on holidays and rest days when everyone else should be relaxing? Who else rarely eats what they cook and is forced to have their meals at irregular times and odd hours? And how many other people work under the kind of pressure that prevails in commercial kitchens where, in the space of a couple of hours, they are required to turn out a succession of dishes according to a timetable which would send the average domestic cook into a state of apoplexy?

It should also be pointed out that most chefs have a rather limited formal education, typically they enter the trade at a young age and may have endured years of arduous apprenticeships in the kitchen but they tend to be lacking in the wider sense of education. This reinforces the very confined world they inhabit, largely populated by other chefs and people in the food business following a set of norms and behavior that is particular to their trade. To say they are a class apart is therefore no exaggeration.

In this very high pressure environment, it comes as no surprise that chefs often have drinking, drugs, gambling and personal relationship problems that can make them less than charming human beings but quite wonderful masters of the culinary art. To mention that some of the world's most famous chefs have enormous egos is akin to the revelation that movie stars tend not to be modest. Sure, they have enormous egos and can be very awkward to deal with but this may well be the price of stellar achievement.

The best chefs are people driven to a remarkable extent. Take the example of Carême, one of the great French master chefs. His daily routine required him to rise before dawn to get to the market to find the best produce and saw him retiring around midnight after his day's work was done and his kitchen was cleaned to a state matching his high standards. In the modern age, Fernand Point provides another example of this extraordinary work ethnic as he too rises at dawn and is unlikely to leave his kitchen much before 11 pm. Throughout the day, he consumes vast amounts of champagne – a regime few of us could manage. Very long working days are the rule not the exception in kitchens and these are places where conditions tend to be harsh; there is the heat, the noise and the ever present danger of injury from knives, burns or slipping on wet floors. It's no wonder that chefs are not the most placid of people.

It is out of these circumstances that the chefs on these pages emerge, not as wonderful human beings but as exemplary cooks who have pioneered new ways of eating.

Some very good cooks in this book, such as Marguerite Patten and Elizabeth David, have never worked full time in a commercial kitchen. However, this does not make them any less driven, working like demons to discover new recipes and more information about food and many aspects of eating. It is hard to believe that they were any less obsessive than the chefs in the kitchens and maybe it was precisely because cooking was not their trade that they had the time to cover a far wider area of gastronomy than that explored by those required to cook food for customers.

There are seven women featured in this book, which is a minority, and this reflects the reality that, until very recently, most of the really recognized and influential people in the world of food were men. The exceptions from an earlier period, such as Catherine de Medici, appear in these pages. Yet she was very much an exception, as was Mrs Beeton in the Victorian era and even Marguerite Patten who started to become famous in the 1950s. Many people have observed the irony of the situation in which most of the cooking in the world is done by women, but the superstars of the culinary world are men. This is definitely changing and some of those who are responsible for this change, such as Alice Waters, also appear in these pages. It is however fair to say that even now professional kitchens are dominated by men and that female cooks have to work that bit harder to gain recognition.

One of the things that struck most forcibly while research for this book was underway was how little has changed in the way that food styles are hailed as being, say, nouvelle cuisine or fusion food,

because new cooking styles are a constant part of the evoluti
of food. Evolution is the key word here because each 'new' fuu.
revolution borrows from the past and is essentially an improvement
as opposed to something astonishingly new. Even today in the
revolutionary kitchen of Ferran Adrià, he is building on established
styles of cuisine, albeit with some novel cooking methods. The idea
that fusion is something new is frankly absurd because all developed
forms of cuisine borrow from other forms. Were it otherwise, we
would never see the variety of food that we see today, where the
significant difference is improved means of transportation. This
means that, for example, a spice from Morocco is readily available in
Paris and can be included in a 'French' dish, whereas fifty years ago,
access to this variety of ingredients was simply unthinkable.

My interest in food is long-standing and reached a new level almost
two decades ago, when my partners and I opened a small café,
followed by restaurants, coffee shops and canteens. I am well aware
of the folly of thinking that just because you imagine you know
something about food you can make the leap into the restaurant
business. A widely quoted statistic is that 90 percent of restaurant
start-ups fail. More recent research suggests that this is a wildly
exaggerated figure. Nonetheless, the failure rate is high and I am
grateful to have started in a very modest way. The business remains
demanding and it is definitely not recommended for anyone
looking for a quiet life. What I have discovered is that the most
interesting end of the business is the food itself. Although when
you are running a restaurant, it is surprising how little time is solely
devoted to food and how much is spent dealing with everything
else. What all this has taught me is that serving food to the public
is quite an extraordinary endeavor. From there, I developed a
fascination with the people who have been most successful in both
producing the food, writing about it, and influencing the way we
eat because it takes extraordinary people to be so successful in this
extraordinary business. That is the genesis of this book and I hope
that readers will be as interested as I have been in learning about the
personalities who appear on these pages.

To use a food analogy, some readers might treat this book like a Spanish tapas or a Chinese dim sum, in other words a collection of small delicacies that can either be enjoyed as single dishes or combine to make a really tasty meal. Each chapter is self-contained but there is a pattern here and by looking at the lives of individual food gurus we can see how the history of food develops. In all events, if this book is half as tasty and fulfilling as the best tapas or dim sum, its objective will have been achieved.

Most of the chapters in this book contain recipes which serve to give an idea of the kind of food produced by the gurus. They are either in original form or, on occasion, modified for ease of reproduction in domestic kitchens. I have added measurement conversions which are as close as possible to the original recipes.

Chapter 1

The Alchemist in the Kitchen

Ferran

Adrià

Ferran Adrià i Acosta, the Catalonian Spanish chef from the world famous El Bulli restaurant, which closed for business in July 2011, has been showered with accolades to an extent that makes it hard to know where to start in describing him. *Gourmet* magazine has Adrià as "the Salvador Dalí of the kitchen." The *New York Times* piled on the praise by calling him "the Elvis of the culinary world." Rafael Anson, president of the International Academy of Gastronomy and a fellow Spaniard, is an avid fan, saying, "Ferran is the Picasso of the modern kitchen. Just as Picasso revolutionized art with cubism, Ferran has changed the history of cooking. He has changed all the rules — just like challenging the social norm that says you should have sex at night with the lights off. He has brought an incredible creativity and liberty to the kitchen."

This level of recognition is not to be lightly dismissed, but the real reason Adrià can be considered a food guru is that he has invented an entirely novel cooking style widely known as molecular gastronomy. However, he has adamantly disowned this title, insisting that it is a meaningless term and preferring to describe his style of cooking as deconstructionist. Adrià has defined what he means by this in his heavyweight work called *El Bulli 1994-1997*. Deconstructionism, he wrote, means: "Taking a dish that is well known and transforming all its ingredients, or part of them; then modifying the dish's texture, form and or its temperature. Deconstructed, such a dish will preserve its essence... but its appearance will be radically different from the original's."

The temple of deconstructionism is Adrià's El Bulli restaurant in Roses on the Spanish Costa Brava, about 100 miles from Barcelona. El Bulli has had three Michelin stars and been ranked best restaurant in the world five times by the influential *Restaurant* magazine.

Yet the restaurant lost money and before it closed only opened in the evenings, limiting service to 8,000 seats per year. Adrià decided to transform it into a non-profit culinary institute dedicated to devising new cooking techniques and new dishes. Before it closed, El Bulli attracted around two million enquiries for tables; allocation was made by lottery and, as with all lotteries, the chances of success were minimal. Yet Adrià himself was skeptical of his best restaurant ranking: "The best restaurant in the world does not exist," he insisted. "It's stupid to talk of El Bulli as the best. It's not something you can measure. It's not like winning a 100-meter race. You can only talk about the most creative, the most influential."

Diners at El Bulli who were lucky enough to come more than once were unlikely to find themselves presented with a familiar menu because the kitchen was in a state of permanent revolution, one that is throwing up hundreds of new recipes every year. The emphasis was on the new but as Fernan freely concedes it was also about "spectacle." He said that eating at his restaurant was like "a night out at the theatre."

The theatre generally centered on Adrià's culinary foam creations designed to extract the maximum flavor out of food basics. The intrinsic flavors of the food are mixed with a natural gelling agent, then placed in a siphon bottle and squeezed out with the help of nitrous oxide.

A very good example of how this works was given in an article published by the London-based *Guardian* newspaper which dissected how he prepares one of Spain's most famous dishes - Tortilla Española, the Spanish omelet. "First, he reduces the old-fashioned tortilla to its three component parts: eggs, potatoes and onions. Then he cooks each separately. The finished product, the deconstructed outcome, is one-part potato foam (food-foaming is another technique Adrià has given the world), one-part onion purée, one-part egg-white sabayon. One isolated component is served on top of the other in layers, and topped with crumbs of deep-fried potatoes. The dish, minuscule, comes inside a sherry glass. Adrià, with the playful irony that exists in practically everything he does, names this dish... Tortilla Española." And then there's the paella fashioned out of Rice Krispies and the foie gras turned into frozen dust. Some of this sounds simply unbelievable. This is cooking that employs liquid nitrogen and calcium chloride chemical processes that do not somehow seem to belong in the kitchen.

But the hard-to-imagine lies at the core of Adrià's technique. Equally important are his general views on food production. These views were encapsulated in what might be described as a manifesto published in 2006 by Adrià and a distinguished group of his disciples. They included the British chef Heston Blumenthal (who may well vigorously question this description), alongside the equally influential American chef Thomas Keller and the food writer Harold McGee, who has championed the kind of cooking originated by Adrià. This rather pompous and immodest document sets out, with unusual clarity, a defined approach to their cuisine. They believe that their approach to food has "been widely misunderstood, both outside and inside our profession. Certain aspects of it are overemphasized and sensationalized, while others are ignored." They therefore set out the three basic principles which guide their approach to cooking.

In summary, they are: "Excellence, openness, and integrity. We are motivated above all by an aspiration to excellence. We wish to work with ingredients of the finest quality, and to realize the full potential of the food we choose to prepare, whether it is a single shot of espresso or a multicourse tasting menu." They point out that there are now fewer restraints on ingredients and ways of transforming them.

"Paramount in everything we do is integrity. Our beliefs and commitments are sincere and do not follow the latest trend." This means building on culinary traditions and respecting them but also embracing innovation. They insist that they "do not pursue novelty for its own sake. We may use modern thickeners, sugar substitutes, enzymes, liquid nitrogen, sous-vide, dehydration, and other nontraditional means, but these do not define our cooking. They are a few of the many tools that we are fortunate to have available as we strive to make delicious and stimulating dishes."

And they emphasize that what they call "the fashionable term" – molecular gastronomy –"does not describe our cooking, or indeed any style of cooking."

The manifesto ends with a call for cooperation: "We believe that cooking can affect people in profound ways, and that a spirit of collaboration and sharing is essential to true progress in developing this potential." They urge fellow cooks to share ideas, techniques and information.

This joint statement of intent or manifesto is unusual in as much as it is a self-conscious attempt by practicing chefs to define their work. Most chefs simply don't bother, although in 2006, Adrià delivered his own 23-point culinary manifesto to the Madrid Fusion conference. This is a somewhat longer version of the joint statement summarized above. It was very much in the spirit of the manifesto for nouvelle cuisine written in 1973 by Henri Gault who defined what he meant by the term and produced guidelines for this cuisine which enjoyed a profound but relatively short-lived prominence, although its influence lingers.

It remains to be seen how long deconstructionism will exert an influence although, like nouvelle cuisine, it is likely to form part of the gastronomic canon influencing food production, even among those who do not fully embrace its methods.

Ferran Adrià has written a great deal about his work and is unusually self-analytical but his background does not suggest a great concern for the written word. He was born on 14 May, 1962, and had an undistinguished school record followed by a failed attempt to study business administration which ended when he was 18. This left him "qualified" to be nothing more than a dishwasher at the French restaurant of the Hotel Playfels in Castelldefels, saving up for money to go on a holiday to Ibiza. He was told that the island of Ibiza was a fun place with plenty of girls and so he managed to get a job at the Club

Cala Lena. Fortunately, the chef took him under his wing and started to teach him Spanish cooking based on the definitive reference to Spanish cuisine, *El Practico*. From there he worked in a number of restaurants in Barcelona, ending up in the respected Finisterre restaurant as an assistant chef.

Called up for military service in 1982, Adrià became a cook in the navy and was soon sent to work in the captain general's kitchen where he had to think up new menus every day. He took this opportunity to introduce the fashionable nouvelle cuisine dishes, something of a departure from standard naval fare. At this young age, he became head of the kitchen and on one occasion had to cook a meal for the King of Spain. It was here he met a fellow Catalan, Fermi Puig, now a well-known chef in Barcelona. Puig suggested that he should use his August leave to secure a temporary job at El Bulli restaurant in the small town of Roses on the Costa Brava where Puig had worked. By then, the restaurant already had a high reputation and was awarded two Michelin stars, making it the highest ranked restaurant in the country.

El Bulli was owned by Doctor Hans Schilling, a German homeopathic doctor, and his wife, Marketta. She initially did the cooking when the restaurant was established in 1961 as part of a mini-golf course complex. They named their restaurant after their bulldogs, known colloquially as El Bulli. By the 1980s, it had evolved into one of Spain's best restaurants.

But Adrià was more attracted by what he thought was the restaurant's beachside location rather than its cuisine of which he knew nothing. However, he discovered to his dismay that it was located up a winding track and not on the beach, a disappointment that soon evaporated when he discovered the haute cuisine being turned out in the kitchen under the management of Juli Soler and Jean-Paul Vinay, the chef de cuisine. Soler was to become his right-hand and partner when he eventually took over the restaurant. Soler liked the brash naval chef and told him he could have a full-time job when he completed his naval service, an offer he did not take up until some months after his departure from the navy at the end of 1983. Within seven months of joining the staff, he was promoted as one of the joint heads of the kitchen with Christian Lutaud. Vinay was leaving to open his own restaurant and Adrià, Lutaud and another colleague, Toni Gerez, were also mulling an offer to open a restaurant of their own. Soler was determined to keep them at El Bulli and made Adrià and Lutaud an offer they could not refuse — full control of the kitchen. The chefs were serious about their work and spent time visiting as many restaurants as they could afford and toured markets to source new suppliers.

In 1985, Soler encouraged Adrià to go to France to experience French restaurants and obtain in-service traineeships with the famous chefs Georges Blanc and Jacques Pic. In 1987, on a visit to the Côte d'Azur, Adrià had a chance encounter with another famous chef, Jacques Maximin, who told him "creativity is not copying". This remark stuck forcibly in Aria's mind. He recalled, "This simple sentence was what brought about a change in approach in our cooking, and was the cut-off point between 're-creation' and a firm decision to become involved in creativity. After getting back to the restaurant, we were convinced that we needed to use major cookery books less and less and try to find an identity of our own. This was the start of our plunge into creativity in El Bulli."

The French influence lingered but Adrià, now joined in the kitchen by his younger brother Albert, began working on transforming Spanish dishes. Here they were influenced by visiting the Currito restaurant in Madrid, serving simple but compelling Spanish food, which was less complex than the French cuisine he was accustomed to cooking.

In 1987, Lutaud left the restaurant to open his own establishment, leaving Adrià in sole charge of the kitchen. It was a heady moment for Adrià who had dreamed of running his own kitchen. Yet one of the first decisions he took was to close it for a half a year during the quiet winter months. He wanted time to plan and create something quite different. It was not immediately obvious what this would be, but Adrià was determined it would be different. He now believes that the year 1990 was the time when he discovered the avant-garde, heavily influenced by the work of Michel Bras and Pierre Gagnaire, who demonstrated that there were few borders to creativity in cooking and that what mattered were flavor and the purity of the food. Adrià was determined to create a cuisine "that had no roots," abandoning his previous attachment to French and Spanish styles. This was also the year when the restaurant's owners decided to retire, allowing Adrià and Soler to form a partnership to buy them out. Adrià graciously acknowledges that the Shillings, the former owners, had given him considerable autonomy in the kitchen but, as is the way with chefs, Adrià sought total control.

Things started to move fast at this stage. The restaurant regained its second star from the Michelin Guide, and a third Michelin star in 1997. However, Adrià handed back his stars two years later and declared a lack of interest in accolades of this kind, including that of the Gault & Millau guide, the pioneers of nouvelle cuisine who had championed his cuisine. This public flaunting of highly coveted awards served as a timely reminder that at his core Adrià is a chef and fits of temperament are hardly strangers to professional kitchens, especially at the upper levels of this occupation.

In 1992, Adrià had the idea of starting a cooking workshop in his restaurant; he was attracted to the notion of using his kitchen for food creativity without having to cook for customers. The following year saw the publication of *El Bulli: El sabor del Mediterráneo,* or *El Bulli: The Taste of the Mediterranean* in which Adrià says he did more than provide recipes and methods but ambitiously attempted to codify the restaurant's cooking style from what he describes as "a theoretical point of view".

The following year, Adrià was determined to take this process a step further. He describes his intentions in this way: "We would need to expand our idea of creativity and orientate our search not so much towards mixtures of products or variations on concepts that already existed in order to create new recipes, but to create new concepts and techniques. From then on, the technique-concept search was our main creative pillar, without abandoning other styles and methods, and this gave rise in subsequent years to our foams, new pasta, new ravioli, the frozen savory world, new caramelization, and so on. Technique-concept creativity almost certainly marks the most important difference between a cuisine that is merely creative and one that is constantly evolving."

Adrià's worldwide fame was now firmly established and although the restaurant remained at the heart of his operations, all pretense of operating the restaurant alone as a profit center had been abandoned. It only made money from 1998 to 2000. So the restaurant itself was not designed to make a profit, it should be more accurately viewed as something akin to a laboratory from which experiments emerged. In fact, they emerged both from the restaurant kitchen itself and from what more humble caterers would call a food factory established in nearby Cala Montjoi. In 2001, it was decided to abandon lunchtime opening because Adrià wanted more time for his creative work and saw meal service in the middle of the day as an unnecessary and time-consuming distraction. It certainly did not mean he was relaxing because he still claimed to be putting in a 15-hour day.

El Bulli had been transformed into an innovative food industry with an impressive output of books published by his own company, not least the so-called "catalogues" of the restaurant's work whose annual publication began as early 1998. There is also a range of supermarket books and, believe it or not, some simple recipe works. In addition, he has produced a DVD cooking series, which was distributed with the *El Periódico de Catalunya* newspaper; it was called *Cocina Fácil* or *Easy Cuisine,* demonstrating again that this infinitely complex chef is quite capable of reducing the complex to the perfectly intelligible.

Aside from what might be described as the advanced recipe book business, there is a hotel; a clutch of fast food outlets, pointedly called Fast Good; a range of cookware and tableware; a range of own label food products; a complex web of endorsement deals (including some with vast food companies generally more associated with the lower end of the market such as Pepsi and United Biscuits); and a fixed place at the top of the lucrative lecture circuit.

In summary, Adrià has transformed himself into a food industrial complex. For a man who says he is not interested in profit or luxuries, he has proved remarkably adept at money-making.

Yet one thing Adrià will not do is follow in the footsteps of other celebrity chefs such as Gordon Ramsay or Joel Rubichon who have opened restaurants in their names around the world. He insists that if a restaurant bears his name, customers expect him to be in the kitchen. Yet he is the first to admit that the produce of his kitchen rests very strongly on his famous team. The team still includes his brother Albert, who started his culinary life as a pastry chef. Adrià's second in command is Oriol Castro, who has created many of the El Bulli signature dishes and then there is Marc Cuspinera and Eduard Bosch. Adrià stresses the teamwork that exists in his kitchens and is generous in attributing credit to his colleagues. He says, "To have such a collection of talent is absolutely abnormal in this business. We have the best team in the world and the reason I can say this, in all confidence, is that it is measurable. Tell me what new ideas there have been in the world in the last decade and then look at what we have come up with here." As ever, the modesty of the great chef is qualified.

No one reaches the position Adrià enjoys without controversy. The bulk of the criticism surrounds allegations of pretentiousness and unnecessary complexity, plus a feeling that Adrià gets carried away with trying to be novel at the expense of making food taste good. One of his most vociferous critics is Santi Santamaria, who has also earned Michelin 3-star recognition for his work. He alleges that, "Adrià's dishes are designed to impress rather than satisfy and use chemicals that actually put diners' health at risk."

This criticism of health risk has been echoed by the German food writer Jörg Zipprick, who accused Adrià of more or less poisoning his customers with the additives he uses. According to Zipprick, Adrià's menus should carry health warnings: "These colorants, gelling agents, emulsifiers, acidifiers and taste enhancers that Adrià has introduced massively into his dishes to obtain extraordinary textures, tastes and sensations do not have a neutral impact on health."

Adrià has responded to his critics but seems hardly troubled by their views. Neither are his followers, who tend to be more vehement in denouncing those who question his work. Yet the great chef has set himself a daunting task of constant innovation, something that has not really been achieved by any other chef in history. Traditionally, the great chefs have produced a novel form of cuisine and added refinements along the way but have been satisfied to rest on their laurels. Adrià appears to want to do more and remains in a state of permanent revolution

It is China and what he calls the Orient where Adrià is looking for aspiration. He says, "The impact of the Orient on Western food has barely hit 50 percent of what it might be. Chinese food, save for what you find in a few London restaurants, does not come close to what you get in China itself. Japan has so many concepts still to offer us, especially in their spiritual relationship with food. But its China in particular that excites me. China, with its millennial gastronomic tradition, with its minute attention to the health value of each dish, has a terrain of which we've barely scratched the surface."

He is also excited by Brazil and Argentina and then throws in a reference to the Maghreb – a region in Northwest Africa, as another source of inspiration – that's three continents in total. No one can fault Adrià for lack of ambition; maybe he really can pull it off and innovate to the end of his days.

Adrià Recipes

Something as conventional as rack of lamb would never, ever find its way into Ferran Adrià's ultra-experimental kitchen at El Bulli. But in his book Cocinar en Casa, he converts it into an unexpected, wonderful dish that anyone can make. Who else would think to coat a rack of lamb with a pistachio pesto, then wrap it in pancetta to keep it nicely moist and make it even richer as it roasts?

Pistachio-Crusted Rack of Lamb with Pancetta

Total time: 1 hour 10 minutes
Serves 4

Ingredients
⅓ cup (1.5oz./15g.) unsalted pistachios
1 tablespoon chopped thyme
1½ teaspoons chopped rosemary
⅓ cup (2.6oz/83ml) extra-virgin olive oil
salt and freshly ground pepper
one 1½ pound rack of lamb,
frenched (8 chops)
6 oz. thinly sliced pancetta or bacon
8 scallions, white and tender green parts only

Method
Preheat the oven to 280°F (140°C/Gas 1). In the bowl of a mini processor, finely chop the pistachios with the thyme and rosemary.

Add half of the olive oil and process to a paste; season with salt and pepper. Scrape half of the pistachio paste into a small bowl and stir in the remaining olive oil.

Coat the lamb with half of the remaining pistachio paste. Wrap the pancetta slices around the lamb, between the bones, leaving the bones exposed. Spread the remaining pistachio paste over the pancetta and set the rack in a small roasting pan. Roast the rack for about 40 minutes, or until an instant-read thermometer inserted in the centre of the meat registers 130°F for medium-rare. Transfer the lamb to a cutting board and let rest for 5 minutes. Reserve the pan drippings.

Meanwhile, spoon 1 teaspoon of the rendered pancetta fat from the roasting pan into a medium skillet and heat until shimmering. Add the scallions and cook over high heat until softened and browned in spots, about 4 minutes. Carve the lamb rack into four 2-chop servings and transfer them to plates along with the scallions. Drizzle the pistachio pesto all around and serve right away.

Make ahead
The pesto can be refrigerated overnight.

Cigala con quinoa (langoustine with quinoa)

Kefir is a fermented milk product from the Caucasus region.
Serves 4

Ingredients
4 x 140 grams (5oz.) langoustines

For the langoustine essence:
langoustine heads (already prepared)
olive oil

For the puffed quinoa (this is the seed of the Chenopodium or Goosefoot plant. It is commonly used as a grain and substituted for grains because of its cooking characteristics):
50 grams quinoa (1.8oz.)
250 grams olive oil (8.8oz.)
salt

For the cooked quinoa:
50 grams quinoa (1.8oz.)
200 grams water (7oz.)
salt

For the Metil solution:
3 grams Metil
100 grams (3.5oz.) water

For the quinoa-coated langoustine:
4 langoustine tails, previously prepared
100 grams (3.5oz.) cooked quinoa, previously prepared
4 teaspoons (3.5oz.) Metil solution, previously prepared

For the spring onion (scallion) rings:
2 x 50 grams (1.8oz.) spring onions (scallions)
ice cubes

For the diced tomato:
1 x 100 grams (3.5oz.) ripe tomato

For the lime cubes and chopped zest:
2 x 150 grams (5.3oz.) limes

For the chili oil:
1 gram dried chili
50 grams (1.8oz.) sunflower oil

For the quinoa shoots:
60 grams (2.1oz.) quinoa shoots
4 teaspoons water
salt

Extras:
160 grams (1.8oz.) kefir
16 fresh small coriander leaves
extra-virgin olive oil
salt

Method
Remove the heads from the langoustines, and set these aside for
preparing the essence. Peel the tails up to the last ring of the shell.
Remove the intestinal tract and store the tails in the refrigerator.

To make the langoustine essence, sauté the langoustine heads
in a little olive oil in a frying pan. Crush the heads one by one
to obtain their juice. Add a few drops of olive oil to the essence
obtained, without emulsifying it. The preparation should be made
immediately before presentation and finishing.

To make the puffed quinoa, boil the quinoa for 25 minutes in
plenty of water. Drain, rinse in cold water to stop the cooking
process, then drain well. Spread the cooked quinoa out over trays
lined with parchment paper; ensure the grains are not overlapping.
Leave the quinoa in a warm place for 24 hours until it is completely
dry. Once dry, cook the quinoa in oil at 180ºC (350ºF) until it
puffs up. Drain, soak up the excess oil on paper towel and season
with salt while still hot.

For the cooked quinoa, boil the quinoa in lightly salted water for
14 minutes. Drain and lay out on a tray to cool. Refrigerate.

To make the Metil solution, blend the ingredients together at room
temperature in a liquidizer until they form a smooth, even mixture.
Strain and leave in the refrigerator for 24 hours.

For the quinoa-coated langoustine, mix the cooked quinoa with the
prepared Metil solution. Coat the langoustine tails with this mixture
so that only the tail shell remains uncovered. Lay out on parchment
paper and put in the refrigerator.

Pine-nut Marshmallows

And just to prove that Adrià can suggest something really simple,
here is a snack anyone can make.
Serves 10

Ingredients
500 milliliters (1 pint) milk
9 x 2 grams gelatine leaves, rehydrated in cold water
40 grams (1.4oz.) virgin pine-nut oil
75 grams (2.6oz.) toasted pine-nut powder
salt

Method
Place 400ml milk in the freezer until it cools to 3°C (37°F).
Meanwhile, mix the gelatine with the remaining milk in a pan.
Dissolve the gelatine at 40°C (104°F) and pour into a mixing bowl.
Start to whip the mixture. After 30 seconds, add all the cooled milk
in one go. Continue to whip for 3 minutes. Add the pine-nut oil.
Keep whipping for another 30 seconds, then spread out over
a transparent sheet to a thickness of 2.5cm.

Refrigerate for two hours. Cut into 2.5cm. cubes. Refrigerate in an
airtight container. Before serving, lightly salt the cubes and coat four
sides with toasted pine-nut powder, leaving two uncoated sides.

Recipes from *Cocinar En Casa (Cooking at Home)* by Ferran Adrià,
Juli Soler and Albert Adrià. El Bulli Books, 2003

Chapter 2

The Dieter's Guru

Robert

Atkins

*R*øbert Coleman Atkins (1930 – 2003) is arguably the twentieth century's most famous dietician and, as such, has had an enormous influence on the way we eat. He is very much a man of his time because for most of the history of mankind eating, or prosaically, the process of avoiding hunger, he has characterized man's relationship with food. Finding ways to reduce and refine our consumption of food is something that only came to prominence in the latter part of the twentieth century.

As civilization developed, this relationship became more complex, moving well beyond mere sustenance into the realms of taste and presentation. However, for most people in the world, the consumption of food remained at the sustenance level. The food revolution of the later nineteenth century and beyond signified that the provision of food for the masses in more developed nations had moved well beyond this sustenance level. What happened next, in terms of historical development, was very rapid because the previous problem of food scarcity was transformed into a range of problems caused by abundance. Attention started to turn towards ways of reducing food consumption and creating diets to prevent obesity and disease. Dieting was known before the twentieth century, but it had not become a mass phenomenon. It was not until as recently as the 1970s that dieting became a mass mainstream activity; some would say an obsession, both for reasons of health and appearance.

The paradox of our time is that, although interest in dieting is now significant, health problems associated with bad diets and obesity are increasing. A series of three research studies, based on 2008 data, published in the medical journal the *Lancet* in 2011, shows that worldwide obesity levels have doubled since 1980. In 2008, almost 10 percent of men and 14 percent of women were estimated to be obese. This compares with five and eight percent, respectively, in 1980.

Measurements using the standard gauge of the average body mass index (BMI) – which compares height and weight – showed that the people of the United States had the highest BMI measurements in the developed world, although the problem is most acute in some Pacific Island nations. Australia and New Zealand were also close to the top of the BMI bad league.

The problems in America were additionally reflected in a 2009 Gallup-Healthways Well-Being Index, which found that 63.1 percent of Americans were either overweight or obese. This breaks down as 36.6 percent being overweight and 26.5 percent being obese.

However, there are some crumbs of comfort to be found amidst this alarming news on the diet front. In 2011, the *Lancet* reported that high blood pressure problems were showing modest improvement and cholesterol levels were falling slightly. This indicates that although there is no place for complacency in tackling the obesity problem, there are some signs that people are becoming somewhat more careful in their dietary habits. Yet it cannot be denied that countries, like America and Britain, which seem to be most obsessed with dieting are also home to some of the worst effects of bad eating habits.

It is not an exaggeration to say that dieting greatly preoccupies hundreds of millions of people. As a result, some of the world's most prominent culinary experts are focused on finding ways of helping people to eat less, or to eat in ways that do not damage their health. It's interesting to note that practically all of the world's leading chefs now pay at least lip service to dietary concerns, although James Beard (Chapter 3), the American culinary guru who rose to fame in the 1950s, wittily remarked that: "A gourmet who thinks of calories is like a tart who looks at her watch." It is hard to imagine such a cavalier attitude towards dieting being expressed by today's leading culinary personalities.

This interest in healthy diets spreads far beyond those who consciously follow a prescribed eating regime and has made an impact on the consciousness of more or less everyone who is not faced with the grim task of eating for survival. Inevitably, the interest in diets has spawned an enormous industry and given risen to the emergence of dieting gurus. None are more famous or more influential than Robert Atkins.

Atkins, who has the distinction of developing a diet bearing his name, pulled off the seemingly remarkable feat of demolishing myths about what made people fat and then developed a regime which he claimed made it easier for people to lose weight. Inevitably, his claims and methods have been greeted with an enormous volume of controversy, a controversy which continues unabated even after his death, which itself remains a source of much dispute.

The essence of Atkins' approach to dieting is his belief that carbohydrates, not fat or high protein, are responsible for most weight gain. The Atkins Diet or the Atkins Nutritional Approach, as he first called it, prescribes a lifetime of weight control based on the limited consumption of simple carbohydrates and protein and the establishment of controlled portion sizes, accompanied by a not too demanding exercise regime.

It is not possible to give an accurate estimate of how many people follow this program but the number is certainly in the tens of millions. Fifteen million people alone have purchased various versions of Atkins' bestselling book *New Diet Revolution*. At the Atkins Centre for Complementary Medicine, he claimed to have treated over 50,000 patients and a number of Atkins' former employees have spun off their own treatment centers and publications. The Atkins Diet appears to have overtaken all other dieting regimes in terms of adherents. It is certainly more popular than the Harvey and Marilyn Diamond Food Combining Diet which also advocates avoiding eating proteins and carbohydrates at the same time and it has displaced the highly influential position once held by the Audrey Eyton F-Plan Diet, which, in essence, recommends eating a large amount of fiber.

Atkins managed to climb to the top of the dieting tree by preaching that the reduction of carbohydrates, found in such basic foods as grains, pastas, potatoes and, counter-intuitively, fruits, were the key to weight loss. He targeted white flour and refined sugar as the prime villains in the battle against obesity.

His research led him to believe that the body tends to absorb carbohydrates quickly provoking a hyperinsulin response that speeds up the conversion of calories to fats. In addition, Atkins argued that hyperinsulin is responsible for inducing hunger pangs and thus encourages more eating. He recognized that carbohydrate elimination was impossible but that intake could be greatly reduced if people stopped eating commonplace items such as bread and potatoes.

Yet, and this is where he made life easier, followers of his plan were permitted to continue consuming previously forbidden items for dieters such as big steaks or even dairy foods because they in his view were far less likely to produce weight gain.

The diet allows its followers to eat all manner of foods that appear to be highly inconsistent with a weight loss regime, including cheese hamburgers, chocolate truffles and salads with rich creamy dressings. Indeed Atkins was a fan of these high protein foods.

The Atkins diet seemed too good to be true. Robert Atkins famously claimed that "If you believe that weight loss requires self-deprivation, I'm going to teach you otherwise." This seemingly impossible claim led many people, a large number of them in the medical profession, to set out to prove that the diet not only did not work but had the potential to cause problems with the heart alongside ailments such as constipation, fatigue and bad breath. Many controlled studies of the Atkins Diet have been conducted by medical specialists but none of them are truly definitive. For example, doctors from Yale and Stanford universities undertook a study, the results of which were published in the *Journal of the American Medical Association.* The study found that followers of the Atkins Diet lost weight but this was because they consumed fewer calories not fewer carbohydrates.

The American Heart Association is among critics of the diet and maintains that it simply does not work as a means of long-term weight loss. The Association argues that the diet restricts the intake of healthy foods that provide essential nutrients and that it requires the consumption of high cholesterol and fat with high protein content. This, it says, presents a risk of many types of disease. More extreme critics of the diet allege that following the Atkins regime incurs the risk of ailments such as osteoporosis, strokes, coronary heart disease, liver disorders and diabetes. There is also a view among many nutritionists that the central premise of the diet, namely that of reducing carbohydrates, is flawed because they question whether carbohydrates are the central cause of weight gain. They insist that it is the over-consumption of calories which is to blame. Atkins' critics display remarkable zeal; there is even a website called *AtkinsDietAlert.org* which carefully tracks all the allegations against the diet.

However, both critics and advocates of the diet seem to agree that in its initial stages the Atkins Diet can cause significant weight loss. But the critics maintain that this is due to water loss, not fat loss. They believe that once the body restores its water and sodium balance, the rate of weight loss is reduced and the beneficial effects of the regime are confined to the reduced intake of calories.

Atkins and his defenders are not even slightly persuaded by these arguments and insist that a lot of the criticism emanates from a basic misunderstanding of how the diet works. First, they point out that there is a popular misconception that this diet focuses on meat consumption and entirely eliminates carbohydrates, which it does not. Atkins' followers believe it is perfectly reasonable to reduce consumption of sugar and processed foods, which are the main sources of "bad" carbohydrates. Secondly, they emphasize that the diet is not a license to eat what you want on the list of acceptable foods and drinks because the plan prescribes reducing portion sizes and balanced dishes. Finally, the program's advocates are aggrieved that critics overlook Atkins recommendation to take regular exercise and include nutritional supplements in their eating regime.

As for the risk of disease, the diet's advocates point to research showing that weight loss, lower cholesterol and reduced triglyceride levels achieved by this regime also raise the level of so called "good" cholesterol, high-density lipoprotein (HDL) and this reduces the risk of cardiovascular disease, hypertension and diabetes.

This debate is unlikely to disappear any time soon but the lasting, and possibly less controversial impact of Robert Atkins work has been to create greater awareness of carbohydrate intake and to modify diets accordingly. Many people, who do not consider themselves to be followers of the Atkins Diet, have opted to reduce potatoes or rice with their meals and are eating less bread as a means of reducing their weight. The Atkins philosophy has therefore consciously or otherwise permeated the mass consciousness, at least in western nations, and made a permanent impression on the way we eat.

Robert Atkins told an interviewer that when he set out in the dieting arena he simply wanted to reduce his own weight, "I didn't realize I was going to be fighting the whole world." He was always aggressively defensive about his work and insisted on its sound medical basis. Behind this insistence lay a medical degree from Weill Cornell Medical Colleges and experience as a physician specializing in cardiology and complementary medicine.

Moreover, Atkins came from a family with a professional food background. He was born in 1930 in Columbus, Ohio and when he was 12, moved with his parents to Dayton, Ohio where his father owned a chain of restaurants. Robert Atkins showed little interest in this business; on the contrary, at the age of 16, he appeared on a youth radio show and thought he had the talent to be a comedian. While at college, his inclination towards the entertainment industry was developed by spending the summer as a waiter and entertainer at resorts in the Adirondacks, a mountain range area in Northeast New York State.

Atkins appears to have been striving to be as well-liked as his father was. He told an interviewer, "I will never be as nice as him, I wish

I were. I try. But I'm not nearly as nice as my dad was." Both his parents went on their son's diet but he jokingly criticized his mother for her failure to adhere to the regime, "My mom cheats too much," he said, "but she tries."

The fame from dieting was to come; meanwhile, Atkins graduated from the University of Michigan and headed for medical school. At first, he seemed destined to become a traditional doctor. His wife, Veronica, said "He was a blue-blood at first; he believed in medical orthodoxy wholeheartedly." Although he trained in cardiology, Atkins felt that this made him more of a technician than a doctor. By 1959, he opened a medical practice on New York's Upper East Side but it was not a great success and Atkins was depressed over his lack of patients.

The turning point came four years later in 1963 when Atkins was 33 years old but according to him: "I appeared to be 45, I weighed 193 pounds and had three chins. I couldn't get up before 9 a.m. and never saw patients before 10. I decided to go on a diet. He later told Larry King on CNN, "I was gaining a lot of weight. Yes, I was practicing cardiology, but I was gaining weight. And there was an article in the AMA journal that said, by the way, you don't have to go on a low-calorie diet, you can go on a low-carbohydrate diet. And I thought, oh, how wonderful that is. So I went on a diet. It was very, very exciting. And I not only lost a lot of weight very easily, but I needed a lot less sleep. I used to need eight and a half hours sleep, and by the end of two months, I needed five and a half hours sleep, which, by the way, for the last 40 years, that's about all I needed." This was the birth of the Atkins Diet.

Atkins acknowledged that he based his work on that of Alfred W. Pennington who had shown great success with 20 patients while working at DuPont after the Second World War. Pennington's subjects lost an average of 22 pounds in just over 100 days by eliminating sugar and starch. Atkins built on this to formulate his more comprehensive diet plan aimed at minimizing carbohydrates. He was hired as a medical consultant by the American Telephone and Telegraph Company, the old behemoth known as AT&T. He treated 65 patients with the same regime he had been following. Within a couple of years, news of the success of this diet spread and he was invited to appear on the influential television show *The Tonight Show Starring Johnny Carson* with another guest Buddy Hackett, who made fun of the diet. However, this did not deter viewers and Atkins fame steadily grew.

By 1970, his diet was heavily featured in *Vogue* magazine and such was its impact that it became known as the Vogue Diet. Bantam Books quickly moved in to sign up the new dieting guru and got him together with an experienced writer Ruth West to produce a book squarely aimed at the popular market, stripped free of medical jargon and footnotes. The hardcover rights were sold to David McKay who published the book in September 1972. By Christmas, it had sold 200,000 copies and by the following April total sales had risen to 900,000. The book went on to sell millions of copies.

Then came a second book, which Atkins claimed he was reluctant to write. He described it as a "been there, done that situation. But people in this country had to be warned. The people in power have created an obesity epidemic." Asked who these people were he responded, "Partly government, partly media. They are pushing a high-carbohydrate diet with the misnomer of low fat. A diet should be named after what you do eat, not what you don't eat." He went on to write or co-author another 15 books, some of which contained recipes based on his diet but most of them are derived from the original work. As Atkins' publishing activity multiplied so did the claims of the books. A couple of these works claim to show how diet increases energy levels and another is devoted to dieting as a means of preventing aging.

As his fame spread so did the controversy. In 1973, he was summoned to a Congressional Hearing on fad diets and lambasted for damaging people's health and being impudent. One senator asked him how he could dare to impugn the reputation of noted doctors who had shown that the way to reduce weight was to avoid fatty foods. Atkins was hardly meek in response; he seemed to revel in the controversy. According to his wife Veronica, he decided to be "the best enemy you ever had."

It was an invitation taken up by many people including a number of his clients who sued him. In 1993, this led to the temporary suspension of his medical license following a complaint that he treated a patient with ozone which he said would kill cancer cells in her blood. She went to another doctor who treated her for an embolism, an air bubble blocking a blood vessel. Atkins appealed to the courts against his suspension and was vindicated. He insisted that alternative healing techniques had their place in medicine. However, not that many people were interested in this side of his work and for almost two decades he fell out of the limelight. Atkins moved away from focusing on dieting and established the Atkins Center for Complementary Medicine which blended Western medicine with practices found in other cultures. The Center had some success and at one point claimed to be the largest alternative medicine practice in the world with 90 employees.

However, it seems that Atkins' real interest remained in the field of nutrition and in 1992, he published *Dr Atkins' New Diet Revolution,* which caught yet another wave of interest in dieting. The timing was good because high-protein diets came back into fashion. This work was not significantly different from previous books but it gained attention and became a best seller because public attitudes were changing. The success of this book persuaded the entrepreneurially minded doctor to establish a company called Atkins Nutritional in 1998. The company sold food products for people following the Atkins Diet and it flourished.

In 2002, Atkins got another major boost from an article in the *New York Times* by Gary Taubes entitled *'What if it's all been a big fat lie',* arguing that low-fat diets had failed and provided some scientific data for this assertion. Taubes, a science writer with a healthy appetite for demolishing scientific myths, went on to produce other books, notably *Good Calories, Bad Calories,* which gave intellectual ballast to Atkins' arguments.

Atkins' was clearly pleased by Taubes intervention and in the same year of the *Times* article he was invited to speak to the American Heart Association, which had a history of criticizing his work. He also managed to raise his profile by going back on television chat shows.

But all was not that well and in April 2002, he had a heart attack while eating breakfast but an aide revived him with mouth-to-mouth resuscitation. Great efforts were made to emphasize that this attack had nothing to do with his diet.

However, a year later, at the age of 72, he died after slipping on an icy pavement in New York. He suffered severe head trauma and spent nine days in intensive care before finally succumbing.

Even in death, Atkins was pursued by controversy, with his opponents keen to prove that his demise was a consequence of his diet. It is claimed that at the time of his death he was obese and that his heart condition contributed to his demise. However, the hospital which treated him said that the immediate cause of his death was the fall and the injuries that followed. Much acrimony surrounds this subject and continues to this day.

Robert Atkins was not a man greatly troubled by self-doubt or lack of conviction. He told one interviewer, "'It is obviously clear that I am right, and the rest of the world is wrong. In two weeks, through your own personal experience, you will determine that you feel better, are less hungry, enjoy what you're eating and have lost weight. If they are right, none of the above would happen. Since we've learned from our experience that it works, then I must be the one that's right." There was never a chance that he would persuade his critics of the veracity of his belief that all they needed to do was to try his diet and realize the error of their ways. However, there are a great many skeptics out there who would not dream of going on his diet yet have modified their eating behavior by cutting down on carbohydrates.

Atkins' remarkable influence on the way we eat surely justifies his status as a food guru but he is certainly one of the most controversial personalities in this book. Many people with a passion for food will object to his inclusion in a work on this subject but they will have a hard job denying his influence.

Atkins Recipes

The recipes which follow are taken from the *www.atkins.com* official website. Although Robert Atkins may have provided nutritional advice for these dishes, it seems unlikely that he produced the recipes himself. The selected recipes deliberately focus on dishes which are most unlikely to appear in other diets but serve to illustrate the Atkins approach of dieting without pain and sacrifice.

Beef Fillet with Bacon and Gorgonzola Butter

Prep Time: 15 mins. Cook Time: 20 mins
Serves 2

Nutritional Information
Per Serving:
Net Carbs: 2.0 grams
Fiber: 2.0 grams
Protein: 41.0 grams
Fat: 35.0 grams
Calories: 480

1 small scallion
2 tablespoons (1oz./30g.) butter, softened
2 tablespoons (1oz./30g.) crumbled Gorgonzola cheese
   (or any blue cheese)
2 (6oz.) fillet mignons
¼ teaspoon (150g.) salt, divided
¼ teaspoon (150g.) freshly ground pepper, divided
2 slices bacon
2 teaspoons virgin olive oil
½ pound (200g.) mixed mushrooms (such as oyster, cremini,
   shiitake or portobello), sliced

Method

1. Arrange rack in center of oven. Heat oven to 425°F (220°C/Gas 7).
2. Thinly slice white portion of scallion; set aside.
3. To make the Gorgonzola butter, finely chop green portion of scallion, and place in a small bowl. Add butter and cheese; stir to combine.
4. Sprinkle each beef fillet with 1/8 teaspoon salt and pepper. Wrap a slice of bacon around side of each filet, and secure with toothpicks.
5. In a 10-inch nonstick skillet, heat oil over medium-high heat. Add filets, and cook on all sides, turning frequently with tongs, until browned, about 5 minutes. Transfer to a rimmed baking sheet. Roast 7 to 10 minutes for rare. Or roast until an instant-read meat thermometer inserted in center of each filet registers 135°F (57°C) for medium-rare, 145°F (62°C) for medium, 160°F for (63°C) medium-well or 180°F (71°C) for well done.
6. While filets roast, heat same skillet over medium—high heat, add mushrooms, reserved white portion of scallion and remaining $1/8$ teaspoon each salt and pepper. Reduce heat to low, and cook, stirring frequently, until mushrooms are tender, about 4 minutes.
7. Spoon mushrooms onto 2 serving plates, and top each with a filet. Serve with Gorgonzola butter.

Chicken Pot Pie

Prep Time: 15 mins
Cook Time: 50 mins
Serves 6

Nutritional Information
Per Serving:
Net Carbs: 9 grams

Fiber: 5 grams
Protein: 36 grams
Fat: 28 grams
Calories: 460

Ingredients

1 Atkins Cuisine pie crust dough, rolled out to a 10 circle or
  9x13 (23x33cm.) inch rectangle
1½ pounds (680g.) boneless, skinless chicken breast halves,
  cut into 1½-inch (3.8cm.) pieces
2/3 cup (156ml.) chicken broth
1 small yellow onion, chopped (½ cup/75g.)
1 carrot, thinly sliced (½ cup/75g.)
2 stalks celery, thinly sliced (3/4 cup/5.3g.)
½ teaspoon (110g.) fennel seeds, crushed
½ cup (120ml.) heavy cream
2 tablespoons Thick-It-Up Low Carb Thickener
2 tablespoons fresh parsley, chopped
salt and freshly ground black pepper, to taste

Method

1. Preheat oven to 350°F (180°C/Gas 4).
2. Place chicken, broth, onion, carrot, celery and fennel seeds in
   a medium saucepot. Bring to a boil. Reduce heat and simmer
   15 minutes, until chicken is cooked through and vegetables are
   tender. Strain stock into a small saucepan.
3. Mix in cream; bring to a boil. Stir in thickener; cook 2 minutes
   until mixture thickens. Pour sauce over chicken and vegetables;
   stir to coat. Mix in parsley. Season to taste with salt and pepper.
4. Spoon chicken mixture into a deep 9-inch (23cm.) diameter pie
   plate or 7x11 inch (18x28cm.) casserole dish. Lay dough over
   filling; press down edges with tines of a fork to adhere to rim.
5. Bake 25 to 30 minutes, until crust is golden and baked through.
   (Cover edges of dough with aluminum foil if browning too
   quickly.)

Chocolate Cake with Chocolate Mint Mousse

Prep Time: 30 mins
Cook Time: 20 mins
Serves 8

Nutritional Information
Per Serving
Net Carbs : 9.9 grams
Fiber : 4.4 grams
Protein : 12.5 grams
Fat : 60.9 grams
Calories : 689

Ingredients
For chocolate mint mousse:
1 ½ cup (375ml.) heavy cream
3 chocolate whey protein powder scoops
½ teaspoon mint extract

For chocolate cake:
1 cup (240ml.) heavy cream
1 tablespoon decaffeinated espresso powder
1½ teaspoons vanilla extract
2 tablespoons chocolate extract
1 ¼ cups (190g.) soya powder
½ cup (150g.) unsweetened cocoa
½ cup pecans, toasted and finely ground
1 teaspoon (4g.) baking powder
½ teaspoon salt
2 sticks unsalted butter
24 packets sugar substitute
4 eggs, separated
½ cup raspberries, for garnish
mint leaves, for garnish

Method for Chocolate Mint Mousse

1. Beat cream with an electric mixer until thickened.
2. Add protein mix and extract; continue beating until smooth and firm. Chill 30 minutes.

Method for Chocolate Cake

Heat oven to 325°F (160°C/Gas 3). Grease two 8-inch (20cm.) cake pans, dust with cocoa. In a small saucepan over medium heat, combine cream and espresso. Cook, stirring occasionally, until espresso dissolves. Cool slightly; stir in vanilla and chocolate extracts.

In a medium bowl, whisk soya mix, cocoa, pecans, baking powder, and salt. In a large bowl, with an electric beater on medium, beat butter until fluffy, about 5 minutes. Add egg yolks, one at a time, beating well after each addition. Add dry mixture one third at a time, beating just until combined. Beat in espresso cream mixture.

In a clean bowl, beat egg whites until almost stiff; add sugar substitute. Whip until stiff. In three additions, fold egg whites into chocolate mixture, until thoroughly combined. Divide batter in prepared pans; smooth tops.

Bake 20 minutes or until cake spring backs when lightly touched in the middle. Cool in pans on racks 5 minutes; invert onto racks to cool completely. Place one cake layer on a serving plate. Spread with ½ mousse filling, leaving a ½ inch border. Top with remaining cake layer and mousse. Garnish with raspberries and mint leaves.

Chapter 3

The Dean of American Cuisine

James Beard

$\mathcal{T}$his description of James Andrew Beard (1903–1985) as the Dean of American Cuisine was bestowed on the famous food writer, chef and man about restaurants in 1954. When he died, Craig Clairborne, a Beard protégé, wrote in the *New York Times* that his mentor was "an innovator, an experimenter, a missionary in bringing the gospel of good cooking to the home table."

Beard is rightly regarded as the man who helped America's more affluent citizens develop a taste for fine cuisine with the distinctive flavor of their own country. But he did more than that and his influence spread well beyond his wealthier followers who were the first to benefit from his work. This is often how food revolutions work. They start with the better off because that's where food innovation always starts, and then the revolution moves on with a trickle-down effect that has a far more widespread impact.

The food writer David Kamp pinpoints the 1950s as the time when Beard came to prominence. He wrote, "It was in this decade that Beard made his name as *James Beard,* the brand name, the face and belly of American gastronomy." He was a large man, six feet, two inches tall and perpetually overweight, he peaked at around 310 pounds. He also, incidentally, had markedly big hands.

Beard's large size was combined with a large personality and as he became known to a wider public through television and to food devotees through his books and cookery lessons, he came to epitomize the true epicurean. He probably would not have liked this description and often demurred when described as a gourmet, preferring a more down-to-earth description.

The James Beard Foundation, an organization established to preserve and develop Beard's legacy, makes these sweeping claims about him: "He was a pioneer foodie, host of the first food program on the fledgling medium of television in 1946, the first to suspect that classic American culinary traditions might cohere into a national cuisine, and an early champion of local products and markets. Beard nurtured a generation of American chefs and cookbook authors who have changed the way we eat." These claims are not without justification.

It is important to understand the context of the period in which Beard rose to prominence. The privations and hardships of World War II were over, Americans were anxious to put all this behind them, get on with their lives and benefit from a new era of prosperity. The end of the war also brought new influences to American cuisine; it came in part from GIs or general infantry members who had traveled abroad for the first time in their lives. They didn't necessarily want to eat all the foreign food they had experienced overseas but were looking for American versions of it. This meant modified types of Italian pizzas and lasagna, versions of Chinese food such as egg foo yung and chow mein – or fried noodles – and then there were the barbecued meats with spicy Polynesian sauces.

In addition, a social revolution was underway with more married women going out to work, leaving them with less time to cook labor-intensive meals for their families. They wanted gadgets to make their kitchen work easier and they wanted convenience foods which could conjure up a meal in minutes. This also, incidentally, was the era of casseroles when such favorites as the tuna noodle casserole and the green bean bake were served in millions of American households.

Developments flowed thick and fast. In 1951, the first cake mix appeared; the following year, Lipton launched an onion soup mix, and in the following year, the ubiquitous Cheez Whiz made its appearance accompanied by frozen waffles. In 1954, Swanson introduced the first frozen TV dinner. This meant that not only could an entire meal be conjured up without cooking but it could be eaten on a convenient tray away from the dining table.

In 1954, Burger King made its debut, followed by McDonald's the following year. The first microwave ovens appeared in 1955, followed by the electric can opener catering to the growing number of Americans who produced meals out of cans. Food innovation was all the rage, some of it in ways that make gourmets shudder. But in general it was a revolution of an increasingly prosperous society which wanted to eat, didn't want to wait for its food and just loved all these new and enticing tastes.

While convenience and new tastes were all the rage with the mass of the people, middle class Americans turned their attention to eating better and discovering new kinds of food. James Beard was the ideal guru to guide them. He had a depth of knowledge and an understanding of food combined with an instinctive showmanship that enabled him to spread his ideas.

Judith Jones, the famous cook book editor who worked with Beard, recalled his splendidly irreverent American attitude towards his work. She wrote: "if anyone ever questioned the direction he was taking the recipe, he'd say, 'We're Americans, we can do as we please.'"

James Beard, born in Portland, Oregon in 1903, was middle aged by the time the post-war food revolution took hold but in many ways he had led a life preparing for this eventuality. He seems to have had an extraordinary memory of his very earliest eating experiences. In his memoir *Delights and Prejudices,* Beard said that he recalled his first eating experience at the age of two when he was taken to the Lewis and Clark Exposition; "I think it marked my life — watching Triscuits and shredded wheat biscuits being made. Isn't that crazy? At two years old, that memory was made. It intrigued the hell out of me." Beard was famous for being able to recall meals he had eaten, even at a very young age. However, when he was three, he had something far more unpleasant to recall as he was struck down with malaria and confined to bed. While convalescing he was fed on a careful diet prepared by his mother and a Chinese maid, Jue Let, whose cooking from her home country had a profound influence on him. She made Chinese broths and other easy to digest foods. Beard later said that "the Chinese have the perfect palate."

Beard wrote that "both my parents had sensitive palates" but his mother Mary Elizabeth Jones, who was raised in Ireland, "had an uncanny sense of food." She was an unusually independent woman who emigrated to the US via a first stop in Canada and travelled widely in France and Italy, developing knowledge of these cuisines. She ran what was essentially a boarding house but had the fancy name of the Gladstone Hotel. His father, John Beard, was an importer and a keen gambler who could also cook and was famous for his brunches. They married late in life and produced only one child who was precocious and spoiled.

So the young Beard had an interesting childhood in which food figured prominently and drama was to be had from the lodgers at the boarding house. It was the drama rather that captivated Beard in his youth and had him hustling around the local dramatic societies for roles. He had been a student at Reed College in Portland but was expelled in 1922 for homosexual activity. In his later years, Beard was quite open about his homosexuality but in the period when he rose to fame, tolerance of different sexual orientations was minimal and he was forced to keep quiet. In his 1964 autobiography, he wrote, "By the time I was seven, I knew that I was gay. I think it's time to talk about that now."

The expulsion from Reed gave Beard an opportunity to join a traveling theatre troupe. He then moved to Britain to study at the Royal Academy of Music in London and from there, he travelled around Europe, principally France where he acquired his taste for French cuisine. However, he was making little progress in attempts to launch a career in the theatre and so returned to the United States in 1927. New York seemed to be the place for aspiring actors so Beard went there. But more frustration greeted him as competition among performers was heavy and he was making little headway. By 1935, after seven years of trying to establish himself in the theatre, Beard started supplementing his meager income with a fledgling catering business.

In 1937, in partnership with his friend Bill Rhodes, the business was established on a proper footing as Hors d'Oeuvre Inc., a small enterprise selling highly innovative cocktail food. At last, Beard had come up with something that was successful.

It rapidly became clear that his future lay in the food business. Three years after establishing the food shop, he wrote *Hors d'Oeuvre and Canapés,* a pioneering work on the subject. The book was successful and his business flourished. *Hors d'Oeuvre and Canapés* was followed in 1942 with *Cooking Outdoors,* another pioneering work because no one else had tackled this subject in such a comprehensive manner.

America's entry into the Second World War meant the demise of the food shop and Beard enlisted. He had a brief spell as a cryptographer, but for most of the war, he was with the United Seamen's Service, setting up sailors' canteens in Marseilles, Panama, Puerto Rico and Rio de Janeiro. By the time the war ended, Beard and the entire American nation were ready for something different to take the collective mindset away from the problems the nation had been facing. Although it was not presented as such, there was a search for people who could lead Americans into this new hedonism.

Beard's culinary reputation had started to build before the War and started to attract attention again shortly afterwards. In 1946, he was invited to appear on NBC's television cookery show *I Love to Eat.* This was followed by more television and radio appearances and a proliferation of articles in influential publications such as *Women's Day and Gourmet.*

In the decade stretching from 1945 to 1955, he wrote or co-wrote seven more food books. As if this was not enough to keep him busy, he was taken on as a consultant by a number of restaurants and food companies and launched his own restaurant. Beard also broke new ground by endorsing food products on television, beginning in 1946 when he appeared as Elsie the Cow to promote the products of the Borden Company. He went on to do a number of other endorsements, explaining that he needed the cash to pay for his cooking schools.

However, he was promoting the kind of processed food that he really despised and proclaimed himself to be "the world's greatest gastronomic whore" for so doing. But he was a realist who could get paid around US$500 for writing an article in a food magazine, which involved a fair amount of work, whereas he could get US$10,000 for endorsing food products, which involved very little work indeed.

The first of Beard's schools – The James Beard School of Cooking – was established in New York City in 1955, followed by two others in Seaside and Oregon. Alongside these schools, Beard traveled widely throughout the country lecturing and giving lessons for the next three decades. It was in these circumstances that he built up a network of devoted followers, some of whom, like Julia Child (Chapter 7), became very famous themselves. His message was consistent, telling Americans to be proud of their nation's culinary heritage and the ingredients produced at home. He did not want to scare off people by stressing the complexity of food preparation; on the contrary he reveled in that which was simple and honest but with no compromises on quality.

He famously said, "There is absolutely no substitute for the best. Good food cannot be made from inferior ingredients masked with high flavor. It is true thrift to use the best ingredients available and to waste nothing." Fortunately, Beard did not take himself as seriously as some of his followers. Here are his thoughts on cannibalism, "I believe that if ever I had to practice cannibalism, I might manage if there were enough tarragon around."

Not surprisingly for someone who loved food, Beard was an avid restaurant guest. In 1956, he published a list of America's best restaurants, revealing a preference for upmarket and rather clubby male establishments. There was also a degree of misogyny or discrimination in Beards' attitude towards female cooks but in later life he came to appreciate the work of people like Alice Waters at Chez Panisse in California (Chapter 20) and Suzy Nelson, co-owner of The Fourth Street Grill in New York.

Beard also had firm views on what customers should expect of restaurants and on the respect that customers should show towards the restaurants themselves. He wrote in a magazine column, "The only way to combat the stupid treatment of food in many restaurants is to be firm about sending food back to the kitchen whenever it is not right."

He told restaurant customers not to be cowed by their hosts into saying the food was good if it was nothing of the kind. But Beard was insistent that customers also had responsibilities when dining out. He abhorred the "mannerless" practice of making multiple restaurant bookings pending a decision on where to eat and told his readers that no-shows in restaurants could be very damaging to their business. Having been a consultant to restaurants in New York and Philadelphia he knew what he was talking about.

Sometimes, however, Beard seemed to be a bit of a tease. He most certainly enjoyed restaurants but in later life reflected that "after endless luncheons in smart restaurants, endless tastings, endless talk about food one inevitably develops a certain antipathy toward elegant cuisine. How I have longed, after a week of rich and complicated foods, for the exquisite pleasure of a simple piece of boiled meat!"

Beard also demonstrated a desire to use his association with food for social purposes. Very close to the end of his life in 1981, he helped found the City Meals-on-Wheels in New York City with his friend Gael Greene. The project helped feed destitute elderly people.

Beard died on 21 January, 1985 in New York. He was 81 and had suffered a fatal heart attack. His cremated ashes were taken back to his home state of Oregon where they were scattered on the beach at Gearheart, a place he had enjoyed summers in his childhood. Beard was no longer at the height of his fame when he died but there was an enormous response from America's food community and glowing obituaries proliferated.

Julia Child was among those who were most keen to preserve Beard's legacy. She suggested preserving his home in Greenwich Village as the gathering place it had been during his life. The renovated building serves as a culinary center open to the public. Peter Kump, a former Beard student who went on to establish the Institute of Culinary Education, was instrumental in arranging the purchase and helping to found the James Beard Foundation. The object of the foundation is to honor Beard's memory by providing scholarships to aspiring food professionals and to champion the cause of America's culinary tradition.

The annual James Beard Foundation Awards, held on the great man's birthday, honors a range of chefs, restaurants, food writers, restaurant designers and food connected online media people. It is a major event in the culinary calendar, accompanied, as may be expected, by fine food produced by the foundation's scholarship winners. The foundation also publishes a quarterly magazine, a restaurant directory and a directory of chefs who have cooked at the Beard House.

Despite the Foundation's noble aims and the work it has done, it has been plagued by scandal. In 2004, its head Leonard Pickell was imprisoned for grand larceny or wrongful acquisition of another person's property and in the following year the foundation's board of trustees was forced to resign. Things have improved since then but the stain remains on the foundation's reputation and creates great difficulties for those now running the body.

None of this detracts from James Beard's legacy as one of America's outstanding food gurus. A man who taught contemporary Americans how to eat.

Beard Recipes

Cheddar-Chili Spread

James Beard began his professional food career making canapés, bite-size bread with fillings or spreads. So it is fitting to begin with one of his recipes in those early days.
Yields 3 cups

Ingredients
2 cups (8oz./110g.) sharp Cheddar cheese at room temperature, grated
2 canned peeled green chilies, chopped
½ canned pimiento, chopped
1 small garlic clove, grated
½ cup (1 stick) butter, softened
3–4 tablespoons brandy, sherry, or bourbon
¼ teaspoon Tabasco sauce (to taste)
salt to taste
cream or whole milk (optional)

Method
Mix all ingredients (except the cream or milk) in the bowl of an electric mixer or food processor, or mash with a fork, until it has a good spreading texture. If it is still too stiff, add cream or milk, a few teaspoons at a time, until it has the right consistency.

Serve the spread in a crock, or form it into a large ball or log and roll in chopped toasted nuts or chopped parsley or chives. Serve with crackers, Melba toast, or sliced French bread and provide a knife to spread it with.

From *Beard on Food, Knopf,* 1974

Braised Beef

James Beard was keen on this kind of simple comfort food.
Serves 6–8

Ingredients
5-pound (2.25kg.) boneless chuck roast
3 tablespoons vegetable oil
salt and pepper to taste
2 tablespoons fresh or dried thyme, or a combination of thyme,
    rosemary, and or summer savory
1 bay leaf
pinch cinnamon
2 onions, stuck with 2 cloves each
3 cloves garlic, peeled and left whole
2 sprigs parsley
1 leek
2 cups (473ml.) red wine, beef stock, beer, or water

Method
In a braising pan or large heavy enameled cast iron casserole,
brown the roast on all sides in the oil until the outside is slightly
charred and richly colored. Remove all but 2 tablespoons of the
remaining fat.

Salt and pepper the meat to taste, and sprinkle with herbs. Thyme
is a favorite because it has a pungency that is most effective with
beef, but you could use rosemary or summer savory, which would
give an entirely different quality. Add the bay leaf, cinnamon,
onions, garlic, parsley, and leek. Pour in the liquid of your choice
and bring to a boil. Reduce the heat, cover the pot, and either
simmer on top of the stove over very low heat, allowing 30 to
35 minutes per pound, or cook in a 325°F (160°C/ Gas 3) oven,
allowing 35 minutes a pound, about 3 hours, until the meat is quite
tender. Add more liquid if needed.

Remove the meat to a hot platter to rest for about 15 minutes and skim the fat from the pan juices. If you want more gravy, strain the liquid, pour additional wine or beef stock into the pan and bring to a boil. Thicken the juices with little balls of butter and flour, kneaded together. Let it reduce until it lightly coats a spoon.

Serve the sliced roast with onions which have been braised separately in a little beef fat and red wine or Madeira, or with buttered carrots, boiled potatoes, the glorious gravy, and red wine.

From *Beard on Food, Knopf,* 1974

Banana Bread

This very American recipe can be served as a dessert or snack. Yields 1 loaf

Ingredients
½ cup (1 stick/115g.) butter, at room temperature
1 cup (130g.) sugar
2 eggs
1 cup (230g.) mashed, very ripe bananas (2 large or 3 medium)
2 cups (200g.) all-purpose flour
1 teaspoon baking soda
½ teaspoon salt
⅓ cup milk
1 teaspoon (5ml.) lemon juice
½ cup (60g.) chopped walnuts or pecans

Method
Preheat oven to 350°F (180°C/ Gas 4). Lavishly butter a 9-inch x 5-inch x 3-inch (23x13x8cm.) loaf pan.

Cream the butter and gradually add the sugar. Mix well. Add the eggs and mashed bananas and blend thoroughly.

Sift together the flour, baking soda, and salt. Combine the milk and lemon juice, which will curdle a bit. Slowly and alternately fold in the flour mixture and milk mixture, beginning and ending with the dry ingredients.

Blend well after each addition. Stir in the nuts. Pour batter into the pan and bake for 45-50 minutes, or until the bread springs back when lightly touched in the center.

From *Beard on Bread, Knopf,* 1995

Chapter 4

The Household Manager

Isabella Beeton

$\mathcal{I}$sabella Mary Beeton (née Mayson), better known simply as Mrs Beeton, is one of the most influential cookery writers in British history. Born in 1836 and dying in 1865 at the cruelly young age of 28, she was a celebrity before the age of celebrity cooks and an inspiration to a generation of Victorians. Her influence persisted after her death, which was not well-publicized, allowing her publisher to trade on her name without acknowledging that she had died. In effect, her name became an early version of the kind of brand that is commonplace these days. Such was Mrs Beeton's influence that it extended well into the twentieth century, giving new generations of readers an opportunity to marvel at the scope of her sage advice.

Her reputation is almost entirely based on one book, *Mrs Beeton's Book of Household Management,* often known simply as *Mrs Beeton's Cookbook.* The book began life as a series of magazine articles in the *Englishwomen's Domestic Magazine* and was published in October 1861. Over 60,000 copies were quickly sold and by 1868, an astonishing two million copies were in circulation.

Mrs Beeton's Book of Household Management is a massive work of 1, 112 pages, containing over 900 recipes, but is more than a recipe book, as the title implies. The book provided the mistress of a middle-class Victorian household with a full armory of advice on everything from the management of servants to some sage directions for the use of poisons, to tips on fashion, childcare and even animal husbandry, plus some passing words on religion and popular science. The recipes themselves were

Isabella Beeton

revolutionary in their format, providing a template for the way recipes are typically presented these days, beginning with a list of ingredients, which had previously been buried in the middle of the recipe.

Mrs Beeton gave what were, at the time, rather precise instructions for preparation, cooking times and costs. Modern readers will likely be appalled by some of her cooking times, such as allowing 45 minutes for the cooking of cabbage, but this is how British people of the Victorian era liked their vegetables cooked.

Recipe books now typically contain the level of detail she provided and we are accustomed to having recipes set out with considerable clarity. It was not so in Mrs Beeton's time, indeed some of her measurements can be seen as frustratingly vague by today's standards.

Yet she was a great believer in leaving nothing to chance. She wrote: "In order that the duties of the Cook may be properly performed, and that he may be able to reproduce esteemed dishes with certainty, all terms of indecision should be banished from his art. Accordingly, what is known only to him, will, in these pages, be made known to others. In them all those indecisive terms expressed by a bit of this, some of that, a small piece of that, and a handful of the other, shall never be made use of, but all quantities be precisely and explicitly stated. With a desire, also, that all ignorance on this most essential part of the culinary art should disappear, and that a uniform system of weights and measures should be adopted."

This groundbreaking work was helpfully accompanied by colored engravings of sufficient utility to be employed in subsequent editions appearing decades after her death.

It now seems to be accepted that Mrs Beeton's recipes were not her own. This lack of originality, or plagiarism - to put it more strongly - was first noticed by Elizabeth David (Chapter 8) but has more recently been elaborated in Katherine Hughes's biography of Mrs Beeton, called *Cooking Up a Storm*. Hughes found that the bulk of her recipes came from a cookbook by Eliza Acton and that she also copied from the work of other cooks such as Alexis Soyer, Anthelme Brillat-Savarin and Antonin Carême (Chapter 6).

The charge of plagiarism seems harsh in many ways because recipe adaptation is the lifeblood of cookbooks. Indeed, cookbook authors are inveterate readers of other writer's cookbooks and they tend to be avid collectors of recipes, which they adapt to some degree or other, quite often without any acknowledgment. Mrs Beeton gave no acknowledgment at all but did test all her recipes with her cook and kitchen maid and presented them in a user-friendly form. Moreover, a great deal of space in the book is devoted to general guidelines on, for example, baking or frying.

Mrs Beeton furnishes general advice that may well be derivative but is delivered in a thoroughly practical and clear way, giving readers a one-stop destination for learning all the cooking basics. She was careful to exclude anything she deemed to be too fancy or beyond the capabilities of the averagely competent domestic cook. Hughes is among those who do not judge her too harshly for what amounts to borderline cheating. "Although she was a plagiarist", says Hughes, "she was adding value. She was an extraordinary innovator."

This seems reasonable because her achievement was not just to present recipes but to provide a whole package of advice and specific instructions which gave confidence to domestic cooks and made them venture more boldly into the kitchen than they would otherwise have done.

But there is more to Mrs Beeton than a single book and as is the case for many of the food gurus discussed in these pages. Her short life's work is also a telling reflection of her times and the changes in society, which she had a hand in creating.

Sam Beeton, Isabella's husband, was a man with a keen eye for an opportunity and played an essential role in his wife's success. He had founded a printing and publishing company to cater for growing demand among a newly literate working class looking for cheap books. Then he realized that no other publisher was specifically targeting children or women and so established his company in both these market niches. One of his most successful ventures was the *Englishwomen's Domestic Magazine,* founded in 1852; by 1856, it was selling 50,000 copies per year.

The key to its success was providing advice to women, like Mrs Beeton, who were no longer living with or near their families as had been the pattern for earlier generations, and were bereft of the advice that comes with such arrangements. These women had to establish their own households, often on less than adequate resources and they had to keep up appearances. Moreover, many consciously strove to be modern in tackling their new lives. Therefore a printed and reliable source of advice was most welcome, especially from someone as well organized and systematic as Mrs Beeton.

The social background of mid-nineteenth century Britain also explains why Mrs Beeton and her innovative husband were so astute in capturing the popular mood. This was a period in which the pace of change was accelerating: in the world of communications the railways had transformed transportation and stimulated an unprecedented degree of movement around the country.

Britain, with its large empire, was importing exotic goods from the colonies and the industrialization of the big cities gave rise to a wave of consumerism that had not existed before. This meant many new products and services, which had hitherto been the exclusive preserve of the upper class, were now trickling down to the middle class and some parts of the urban working class. In fact, the whole class system was in transition as the middle class expanded, giving rise to a population of nouvelle riche who had money but remained socially insecure and constantly sought guidance on what was the 'right' thing to do.

Mrs Beeton herself was an exemplar of this transition. Her mother was the granddaughter of domestic servants, married to a second husband, Henry Dorling, who grew rich by making race cards for the Epsom racecourse. Mrs Beeton, therefore, had a comfortable childhood, a better education than was customary for girls of her time and was given encouragement to develop her talents. These did not include cooking but did include an ability to speak French and German and play the piano. She was sent for two years to Heidelberg in Germany to develop her musical talent. Her father Benjamin Mayson died young and her mother married to Henry Dorling afterwards. Between them they had an extraordinarily large family with 21 children, an impressive number even by Victorian standards. Managing this vast household was quite a job and by her late teens Isabella was helping her mother supervise the staff, manage the household's accounts and assist in the care of her younger siblings.

Isabella Mayson married Sam Beeton in 1856 at the age of 21. Her first baby must have been conceived during her honeymoon but died shortly after birth. Then there were a string of miscarriages. Hughes was given access to the family papers in 1999 and believes it is more than likely that Sam Beeton infected his wife with syphilis. At the time, this was an incurable disease and shrouded in a cloud of shame which accounts both for the secrecy surrounding her illness and her persistent ill health. Her early death however was caused by puerperal fever, a genital infection, which was a common ailment in Victorian times. Sam Beeton, who is believed to have contracted the sexually transmitted disease from prostitutes before he married, lived until the age of 47, which seems to be wretchedly unfair as his wife died shortly before her 29th birthday.

However, her lack of children in the initial stages of her marriage (although she subsequently had four children) had one very positive effect, which was to persuade her to join her husband's business, a relatively unusual decision for a Victorian housewife. She became a contributor to her husband's magazines and in 1857, started work on the cookbook. The precise details of her life at this time are not known, although Mrs Beeton is the subject of several biographies. What is clear is that she must have been a woman of considerable determination and dedication to hard work. In 1858, for example, she was not only working for her husband and maintaining her other duties as a housewife, she also found time to open a soup kitchen at her home catering to poor children suffering the harsh winter of that year. By then she was writing a monthly supplement for the *Englishwoman's Domestic Magazine,* these pieces were later incorporated into her famous book. The Beetons were not only successful with their publishing formula but determined to build upon this success. In 1860, they visited Paris to gather new ideas and establish contacts with fashion houses but not, it seems, restaurateurs. As a consequence the magazine was revamped, color fashion plates were added and the whole outlook of the publication became slicker. As a result they felt confident enough to raise its cover price.

As the magazine gathered strength, Isabella Beeton started to think about incorporating her work into a book. It took her four years to complete the work, which was published in October 1861. In the preface she wrote: "I must frankly own, that if I had known, beforehand, that this book would have cost me the labor which it has, I should never have been courageous enough to commence it. What moved me, in the first instance, to attempt a work like this, was the discomfort and suffering which I had seen brought upon men and women by household mismanagement. I have always thought that there is no more fruitful source of family discontent than a housewife's badly-cooked dinners and untidy ways. Men are now so well served out of doors at their clubs, well-ordered taverns, and dining-houses, that in order to compete with the attractions of these places, a mistress must be thoroughly acquainted with the theory and practice of cookery, as well as be perfectly conversant with all the other arts of making and keeping a comfortable home."

The book was promoted as: 'Comprising information for the Mistress, Housekeeper, Cook, Kitchen-Maid, Butler, Footman, Coachman, Valet, Upper and Under House-Maids, Lady's-Maid, Maid-of-all-Work, Laundry-Maid, Nurse and Nurse-Maid, Monthly Wet and Sick Nurses, etc. etc.—also Sanitary, Medical, & Legal Memoranda: with a History of the Origin, Properties, and Uses of all Things Connected with Home Life and Comfort.'

Mrs Beeton insisted that, "Excellence in the art of cookery, as in all other things, is only attainable by practice and expertise." The scope of her book, as noted above, is quite daunting; on the cookery front alone there are 82 recipes for soups, 200 recipes for sauces and 128 recipes for fish. And then there are the didactic explanations for how to do this, that and the other. Mrs Beeton subsequently earned a quite undeserved reputation for extravagance. For example, she is widely misquoted as having instructed her readers to "take ten eggs" but her focus remained firmly on economy and value for money. She advised the mistress of the house to take charge of household purchases to eliminate waste and unnecessary expense and commented that "the best articles are the cheapest may be laid down in a rule." She also gave cheaper alternatives for expensive ingredients and relentlessly suggested money saving ways of recycling and keeping down costs.

The accusation of plagiarism in the recipes has emerged as a major issue in the reassessment of Mrs Beeton's work but it should also be noted that in other parts of her book she refers to the "scientific expertise" of her husband's colleagues such as John Sherer who subsequently produced *Beeton's Dictionary of Universal Information,* an example of a book bearing her famous name, produced after her death.

Within four years of the appearance of her book, Mrs Beeton had died. Her husband, apparently, never got over her death and following her demise his business acumen seemed to desert him. However, he was sufficiently aware of the phenomenon they had created to appreciate that he needed to keep her name alive. So he pretended that she was still penning articles and works that appeared under the Mrs Beeton brand name. It is, incidentally, a testimony to the strength of this brand that, according to Hughes, more than a century after her demise, Ginsters, the British pie manufacturers, thought the brand sufficiently valuable to pay £1 million for the right to use the name Mrs Beeton on their products.

Immediately after his wife's death, Sam Beeton commissioned a string of journalists to keep her name alive with updates of the famous book and to produce new titles such as *Beeton's Book of Needlework,* which appeared in 1870, implying his wife was the author. Then there was a gardening book also using her name and as time went on instead of dropping the pretense that she was still alive, the deceit increased as the author was identified not merely as Beeton but specifically as Mrs

Beeton. No wonder most of her readers had no idea she was dead and an image evolved of a somehow comforting middle-aged woman who never existed.

While Mrs Beeton's name flourished, her husband's business did not and as Sam Beeton's debts mounted, a merchant bank called Overend, Gurney & Co bought many of them. This bank famously collapsed in 1866 provoking an enormous financial scandal. It was the end of the road for Sam Beeton who was forced to sell his publishing business to Ward, Lock & Tyler, which included the rights to his wife's work. He was kept on to run the business but died of tuberculosis in 1877. The new owners of the publishing house showed themselves to be unscrupulous and unrestrained in the exploitation of the Beeton name.

Elizabeth David carefully chronicled how they changed the book, beginning in 1888 when much new material was added, some of which would never have been penned by the original author, yet no acknowledgement was given to the source of these changes. The changes mounted and by the 1960s, David found that not a single Mrs Beeton original recipe had survived. More recently however, the original 1861 edition has been revived and is available in print and online. Nicola Humble, the editor of the Oxford version of the original book explains why, over a century since first publication, it was decided to re-issue the original and why it deserved to be such a success: "Ultimately, *Household Management* is so much more than a cookery book. It tells a story of a culture caught between the old world and the new, poised between modernity and nostalgia. It tells of kitchens in which meat is still roasted on spits over open fires, but where many of the bottled sauces and condiments we take for granted today were already available."

Alan Davidson, Britain's foremost culinary historian, wrote of Mrs Beeton that her book had something "which was necessary to make it great…that intangible quality which is hard to pin down but which radiates almost palpably from the finest cookery books, an emanation that tells the readers that the author really knows what she is about."

This is no small claim and it is amply justified.

Beeton Recipes and General Advice

The following items are reproduced in their original form, the first is a recipe for a typically simple and wholesome dish, the following sections on eggs and roasting meat give a sense of Mrs Beeton's wonderful practicability.

Baked Apple Dumplings (a Plain Family Dish)

Ingredients
6 apples
¾ pounds (350g.) of suet-crust
sugar to taste

Mode. Pare and take out the cores of the apples without dividing them, and make 1/2 pound of suet-crust; roll the apples in the crust, previously sweetening them with moist sugar, and taking care to join the paste nicely. When they are formed into round balls, put them on a tin, and bake them for about 1/2 hour, or longer should the apples be very large; arrange them pyramidically on a dish, and sift over them some pounded white sugar. These may be made richer by using one of the puff-pastes instead of suet.

Time. From ½ to ¾ hour, or longer. Average cost, 1–½ d. each.
Sufficient for 4 persons.

Seasonable from August to March, but flavorless after the end of January.

Eggs

The eggs of different birds vary much in size and color. Those of the ostrich are the largest: one laid in the menagerie in Paris weighed 2 lbs. 14 oz., held a pint, and was six inches deep: this is about the usual size of those brought from Africa. Travelers describe *ostrich eggs* as of an agreeable taste: they keep longer than hen's eggs. Drinking-cups are often made of the shell, which is very strong. The eggs of the *turkey* are almost as mild as those of the hen; the egg of the *goose* is large, but well-tasted. *Duck's eggs* have a rich flavor; the albumen is slightly transparent, or bluish, when set or coagulated by boiling, which requires less time than hen's eggs. *Guinea-fowl eggs* are smaller and more delicate than those of the hen. Eggs of *wild fowl* are generally colored, often spotted; and the taste generally partakes somewhat of the flavor of the bird they belong to. Those of land birds that are eaten, as the *plover, lapwing, ruff*, &c., are in general much esteemed; but those of *sea-fowl* have, more or less, a strong fishy taste. The eggs of the *turtle* are very numerous; they consist of yolk only, without shell, and are delicious.

Roasting Meat

The difference between roasting meat and baking it may be generally described as consisting in the fact, that, in baking it, the fumes caused by the operation are not carried off in the same way as occurs in roasting. Much, however, of this disadvantage is obviated by the improved construction of modern ovens, and of especially those in connection with the Leamington kitchener, of which we give an engraving here, and a full description of which will be seen at paragraph No. 65, with the prices at which they can be purchased of Messrs. R. and J. Slack, of the Strand. With meat baked in the generality of ovens, however, which do not possess ventilators on the principle of this kitchener, there is undoubtedly a peculiar taste, which does not at all equal the flavor developed by roasting meat. The chemistry of baking may be said to be the same as that described in roasting.

Should the oven be very brisk, it will be found necessary to cover the joint with a piece of white paper, to prevent the meat from being scorched and blackened outside, before the heat can penetrate into the inside. This paper should be removed half an hour before the time of serving dinner, so that the joint may take a good color.

By means of jar, many dishes, which will be enumerated under their special heads, may be economically prepared in the oven. The principal of these are soup, gravies, jugged hare, beef tea; and this mode of cooking may be advantageously adopted with a ham, which has previously been covered with a common crust of flour and water.

All dishes prepared for baking should be more highly seasoned than when intended to be roasted. There are some dishes which, it may be said, are at least equally well cooked in the oven as by the roaster; thus, a shoulder of mutton and baked potatoes, a fillet or breast of veal, a sucking pig, a hare, well basted, will be received by connoisseurs as well, when baked, as if they had been roasted. Indeed, the baker's oven, or the family oven, may often, as has been said, be substituted for the cook and the spit with greater economy and convenience.

Chapter 5

The Chef's Chef

Paul

Bocuse

*P*aul Bocuse, born 1926, has been described by Alain Ducasse, another prominent French chef, as "the grumpy pope of French cuisine". Bocuse is generally known as "Monsieur Paul," bestowing on him the kind of first name recognition attached to an honorific title which is the mark of the truly famous and the greatly respected. Ducasse adds: "Monsieur Paul is a classical chef. Being classical means he hates unnecessary artifice—in fact, he considers all artifice unnecessary. And he's right. By insisting on the quality of produce and rigor of technique, Bocuse discovered a surefire recipe for excellence."

It is tempting to see Bocuse as the quintessential French chef fulfilling every cliché about people in his position. He comes from a long line of chefs and was steeped in the culinary tradition almost literally from birth. And he looks the part: a large man who has only slightly diminished in his eighth decade. He wears with ease the full chef regalia, topped by the white toque, a large cylindrical chef's hat. He has an ego impressive even by chef standards; large murals and posters depicting the great chef are displayed inside and outside his restaurants and include a tableau showing a new interpretation of Da Vinci's *Last Supper* in which Bocuse is to be found seated at the center of the table, a place normally occupied by Jesus Christ.

Bocuse can be temperamental; he is a fanatic for perfection and is known to have the chef's trademark outbreaks of bad temper but also a wicked sense of humor to mitigate this reputation for ferocity. Most importantly, he's a sublime cook admired by his colleagues and recognized as having had a profound influence on the development of modern French cuisine and the role played by chefs producing it.

Away from the caricatures is a seemingly contradictory man tied firmly to the great traditions of French cuisine yet embracing change and playing a leading role in the evolution of a new cuisine. His roots and life are firmly planted in the Lyons region of France but he was one of the first modern French chefs to branch out to America and further afield. Bocuse is a great lover of all things American and mischievously claims to have American blood, after benefiting from a blood transfusion in an American hospital following a bullet wound received while fighting the Germans in the Second World War. Americans have reciprocated this affection and showered him with honors.

In California, the city declared a Paul Bocuse Day and both New York and Chicago have bestowed honors on the French chef. More recently, in 2011, the Culinary Institute of America (CIA) named Bocuse as "Chef of the Century."

"He is one of the greatest, most significant chefs of all time," said Tim Ryan, the institute's president. This accolade joins a long list that includes being named as Chef of the Century in the French restaurant guide book by Gault & Millau back in 1969 and he has three French Legion of Honour awards culminating in the 2004 Commander of the Legion of Honor award.

Bocuse has added to the already considerable reputation of French cuisine and has made two distinctive contributions to the world of food. He is one of the creators of the nouvelle cuisine movement, a product of the late 1960s and 1970s which came as something of a revolt against what many saw as the stultified state of French cooking with its emphasis on heavy sauces, reliance on a relatively limited range of ingredients and a general resistance to change in the kitchen.

Bocuse revolutionized his own kitchen in Lyon while Henri Gault assumed the role of propagandist for the movement with an article he wrote in 1973 that served as a manifesto for nouvelle cuisine. As we shall see in Chapter 17, Bocuse's mentor, Fernand Point started the ball rolling in this direction but it was his protégé who made it happen.

The essence of this new cooking is to rely on the perfection of the ingredients to speak for themselves, allowing the true flavor to shine through with less cooking, lighter sauces, less fat and flour while meat and fish are often served "pink at the bone." This, now widely accepted idea, has been taken further by chefs like Alice Waters (Chapter 20) who believes that the best ingredients need to be organic but Bocuse is no fan of this trend. "I would rather eat an apple that has been treated than a rotten one that was grown organically," he has declared.

Some caution should be exercised in using the term nouvelle cuisine because this idea has had sporadic periods of eruption in France since the early eighteenth century when Vincent La Chapelle believed that his more simple style of cooking started a new cooking trend. As we shall see in Chapter 6, Antonin Carême also described his far more complex culinary style as nouvelle cuisine. Bocuse himself has expressed unease over the use of the term. He told a news agency reporter that "they always talk of nouvelle cuisine, but for me each generation had a nouvelle cuisine."

Bocuse also built on the practice begun by his mentor Fernand Point, which involved emerging from the kitchen to greet guests and becoming his own best publicist. Bocuse maintains that chefs should get out of the kitchen because they need direct contact with the restaurant's most important people — its customers. He also thinks that chefs need to keep an eye on the details of the service and the state of the area where the customers are to be found.

The food sociologist Claude Fischler has argued that Bocuse's real achievement has been to turn the chef, once little more than a scullery worker never credited for his culinary achievements, first into a boss, then a star. This claim goes a little too far because by the twentieth century many chefs were already established as being more than scullery workers although they were not stars in the way they are today. Bocuse has recalled, in his father's day, "The chef was a slave. He lived in a stinking, hot kitchen underground while the owners walked around the dining rooms. The cooks, usually ended up cretins and drunks by the time their careers were over. Now the cooks own the restaurants."

One of France's leading chefs, Jacques Pépin, has said, "I've known Paul for 50 years or more. I am from Lyon, too. Certainly he did more than any other chef in the world that I can think of to bring the chefs into the dining room and to make the profession respectable and to make us who we are now. Now the chefs are stars and it's because of Paul Bocuse. We are indebted to him."

Thomas Keller, chef at New York's Per Se restaurant, has argued that Bocuse helped create the modern cult of the cook. "He's the one who brought chefs out of the kitchen," Keller said. "He set us free in many ways… We were allowed to have an interpretation, a point of view about food." Many other chefs have not only been inspired by Bocuse but are grateful to him for sharing his recipes and methods in a manner not previously seen in the secretive and highly competitive world of French chefs.

Bocuse, who as we have seen is not given to modesty, gladly accepts his place among the pantheon of leading chefs. He is careful to nurture his image and, through his foundation, training institute, and a prize in his name, promotes the culinary trade and contributes to its development.

Although an innovator, Bocuse is suspicious of claims that chefs are, or should be seen, as inventors: "There are too many cooks trying to do new things and you know when one reads cookery books one always finds something which has already been done." He told another interviewer he believed that "in cooking as in music, one doesn't invent much. One makes interpretations but the word 'invention' for me is a bit pretentious."

He is particularly skeptical of some of the more recent culinary innovations. He has complained about the complexity of some modern cuisine and believes that in place of complicated cooking methods, chefs should be concentrating on finding the best suppliers. "I think that finding the best – the best butcher, the best fishmonger, the best vegetable vendor, that's important."

There are few cooking methods more complicated today than that of the deconstructionist school, using the laboratory techniques which are discussed in Chapter One about Ferran Adrià. Bocuse declares, "it's not my cuisine, but I have lots of admiration for him because he brought something." And he works on the principle that the chef is always right if he can fill his restaurant, "El Bulli (Ferran's restaurant) is always full, so he's right," he says.

Bocuse is also deeply suspicious of fusion, particularly the mixing of Asian and European food cultures. He said, "To mix chocolate with tomatoes or tomatoes with jam - that's not an invention . . . a sole with chocolate - the sole is a good product, chocolate is a good product, the two mixed together - gives you shit."

To describe Bocuse as coming from a rich culinary tradition is an understatement. He comes from a family that has been producing chefs for over three centuries. Very close to the restaurant in which Bocuse made his name is the site of a former corn mill at Collonges-au-Mont-d'Or where the miller's wife, an ancestor of Bocuse, was famous for her cooking in the 1760s. The mill was demolished in 1840 and the family moved downstream to a farm that had been run by the monks of the Ile Barbe where the first Restaurant Bocuse was established.

In 1921, Joseph Bocuse, grandfather to Paul, was forced to sell the restaurant. The new owner had no hesitation in calling his acquisition The Restaurant Bocuse. Thanks to the marriage of Paul's father Georges Bocuse to Irma Roulier, he was able to get back into the restaurant business as Roulier's family owned the Hotel du Pont de Collonges. This was a modest bistro, which they renamed as Restaurant Bocuse, although legally the name belonged to the buyers of Joseph Bocuse's restaurant.

Bocuse began his career in 1941 during the German occupation of France and entered the time-honored tradition of becoming an apprentice, working for Claude Maret at Restaurant La Soierie in Lyon. The war was a seminal experience for people of Bocuse's generation. He later said, "It forges the character. You no longer have the same idea of life."

Two years later, he was conscripted to work in a Vichy work camp but escaped and joined the Free French Army and was wounded. He subsequently took part in the famous Victory March through Paris when the war ended.

Before enlisting, Bocuse had begun another apprenticeship with Eugenie Brazier at La Mere Brazier, the first restaurant run by a woman to acquire three Michelin stars. After the war, he went back to her restaurant where the tough life of a soldier was replaced by a less than easy life for apprentices like Bocuse. He recalled that, "at La Mere Brazier you had to wake up early and milk the cows, feed the pigs, do the laundry and cook … it was a very tough school of hard knocks. Today, the profession has changed enormously. There's no more coal. You push a button and you have heat."

The turning point in Bocuse's career came when he left Lyon and travelled to Vienne to work for Fernand Point for eight years. Point had also employed his father and treated the new recruit as a member of his extended family.

In 1959, Bocuse took over his father's ailing restaurant which was later reborn as L'Auberge du Pont de Collonges. His father, Georges Bocuse had died leaving behind some large debts. Within three years of reviving the restaurant, Bocuse had his first Michelin star and then won the Meilleur Ouvrier de France title. In 1965, the restaurant gained its third star, which Bocuse has proceeded to hang onto for an astonishing four decades. This was also the year in which Bocuse managed to buy his grandparent's former restaurant, then called the Abbaye de Colonges.

What followed has been a career of stellar achievements with Bocuse clinging to France's culinary traditions while never being afraid to change. He is the quintessential chef who works like a dog and loves to eat, eschewing current views of what is good for you and what is not. "I am a not a doctor," he said, "so if you ask me if it is good to drink red wine, I will say yes because I have a vineyard in Beaujolais. And if you ask about cuisine, I will say it is about butter, cream and wine because I am a chef."

He comes from the mold of typically driven and unrelenting chefs, claiming that he needs only four to five hours sleep per day and that even in his eighties he can chop faster and do everything his younger employees can do. Although he keeps rather quiet about it these days, he has the chef's typically misogynistic view of women in the kitchen.

In an interview conducted back in 1976, he said, "I would rather have a pretty woman in my bed than behind a stove in a restaurant. I prefer my women to smell of Dior and Chanel than of cooking fat. Women are good cooks, but they are not good chefs. Women who systematically want to do what men do just end by losing their femininity, and what I adore most of all is a feminine woman."

More recently he has written about his complicated love life and seems to revel in the disclosure of his many sexual conquests. When he wrote about this in 2005, he said in an interview, "Food and sex have much in common, we consummate a union, we devour each other's eyes, we hunger for one other." According to Bocuse he has been sexually active since the age of 13 and even a triple heart bypass only succeeded in slightly curbing his sexual appetite.

Bocuse says he has "three wives." The first is Raymonde, the woman he married after the war and with whom he has one daughter, Francoise. His wife worked with him at the front of house in the restaurant and has given no public indication of discomfort with the mistresses.

Then there is Raymone Carlut and Patricia Zizza with whom he has had very long relationships and, according to Bocuse, this menagerie gets on well together. There is a son, Jerome, from the relationship with Carlut and he runs Bocuse's US restaurant in Disneyland. Zizza has a daughter but not from Bocuse but he treats her as his own.

The Disneyland venture is a an example of Bocuse's shrewd business ability where he has established a Chefs de France restaurant inside the French pavilion at the Walt Disney World EPCOT in Orlando, Florida. This association with Disney has taught him much about marketing and leveraging his name into a business brand.

He also has a small chain of brasseries in Lyon, serving various French regional specialties at modest prices and in far less lavish surroundings than his mother restaurant. In 2008, he opened a fast food restaurant, Ouest Express.

There are a large number of products bearing the Bocuse name, including his own label wines and champagne. This proliferation of products and ventures is sufficient to encourage criticism for becoming more of a brand than a chef. Bocuse insists that his proliferation of business interests does not detract from his prime interest as a chef and that he is working in his kitchen every day.

He was one of the first major French chefs to recognize the potential of the Japanese market in the 1970s and has exported French products while undertaking consultancies and cooking classes in Japan. He also has a high profile in Germany and appeared in one of Germany's first television cookery programs in 1988. In neighboring Austria, his legacy is reflected in the fame of Eckart Witzigmann, a three-star Michelin chef, trained by Bocuse. In France itself he had a long running consultancy with Air France which saw him join the team of chefs preparing food for the 1969 maiden flight of the Concorde aeroplane where the term nouvelle cuisine was first used to describe his cuisine.

In 1987, the Bocuse d'Or cooking competition was launched with the participation of some of the world's leading chefs, presided over by Bocuse. This contest is now one of the most important chef's competitions in the world and has launched many notable careers.

Then there is the Institut Paul Bocuse World Alliance, founded in 2004, which trains chefs and has a series of links with famous universities who send students on a four-month intensive course to learn his techniques. This organization is the culmination of various chef training endeavors in which Bocuse has been involved since 1990.

Bocuse has also written nine books with recipes and reflections on his life and his views of food. Unsurprisingly, they are all best sellers.

If there is anyone who can be called the "chef's chef," it is Paul Bocuse. The American chef Charlie Palmer says "I think we all have mentors. But I think Paul Bocuse was much more than that. He was something to aspire to, something to think if we could ever come close to that. He's the chef of the century and there won't be more of those, if ever, in the next century."

Bocuse Recipes

The following recipes are taken from: *La Cuisine du Marche* by Paul Bocuse, Editions Flammarion. The first two are very famous indeed and the third is less complex but nevertheless an absolute classic.

Truffle Soup Elysée

This soup is also sometimes known as Soupe Aux Truffles VGE, the initials refer to former French President Valéry Giscard d'Estaing for whom this soup was created at a lunch which marked Bocuse's award of the Cross of the Légion d'Honneur for being an ambassador of French cooking on 25 February 1975.
Serves 1

Ingredients

2 tablespoons matignon: equal parts carrots (without cores), onions, celery, mushrooms all cut into tiny dices and mixed in unsalted butter
1¾ oz. (44g.) fresh raw truffles
¾ oz. (19g.) fresh foie gras
1 cup (250ml.) strong chicken consommé
2 oz. (50g.) flaky pastry
1 egg yolk, beaten

For the flaky pastry dough:

5 cups sifted flour
¾ tablespoon salt
1 cup (236ml.) water
¾ pound (350g.) unsalted butter

Method

Into each individual ovenproof soup bowl (called gratinée lyonnaise), put 2 tablespoons matignon, 1¾ ounces (44g.) truffles cut into irregular slices, ¾ ounce (19g.) foie gras also cut into irregular slices, and 1 cup (250ml.) strong consommé.

Brush the edges of a thin layer of flaky pastry with egg yolk, and cover the soup bowl with it, tightly sealing the edges. Set the soup bowl in a 425°F (220°C/ Gas 7) oven. It will cook very fast. The flaky pastry should expand in the heat and take on a golden color; that is a sign that it is cooked.

Use the soup spoon to break the flaky pastry, which should fall into the soup.

For flaky pastry dough:

Place the flour on a pastry board, making a well in the middle for the salt and water. Mix and knead the flour with the water until the dough is smooth and elastic. Roll into a ball and let it stand for 20 minutes. Roll the dough out evenly into a sheet about 8 inches (20cm.) square. On top place the butter, which has been kneaded in the same way until it has the same consistency as the dough.

Fold the ends of the dough over the butter so as to enclose it completely. Let it stand again for 10 minutes; then give the dough two "turns." Each "turn" consists of rolling the dough, on a marble slab with a rolling pin, into a rectangle 24 inches by 8 inches (61x20cm.) and 1/2 inch (1.5cm.) thick. Fold the pastry crosswise in three, forming a square again. The second turn is given by rolling the dough, with a rolling pin, in the opposite direction and folding in three.

The purpose of turning and rolling is to distribute the butter evenly in the pastry and to ensure that it expands evenly during the cooking.

Finally, give the dough two more pairs of turns, letting it stand 10 minutes between each pair of turns. The flaky dough is ready to be used and cut after having had 6 turns, which means handled 3 times, 2 turns each time.

Sea Bass in Pastry or de la Loupe Mediterranean en Croute

Serves 8

Ingredients
6-pound (2.7kg.) sea bass
chopped chervil
chopped tarragon
salt
pepper

For flaky pastry dough:
5 cups (1.1kg.) sifted flour
¾ tablespoon salt
1 cup water
¾ pound (350g.) unsalted butter
egg yolk
melted butter or beurre blanc

For the lobster mousse:
½ pound (225g.) raw lobster meat
coral
¾ tablespoon salt
freshly ground pepper
dash of grated nutmeg
1 cup heavy cream
¼ pound pistachios
truffles

Method

Buy a nice, very fresh sea bass; gut it carefully, and remove the skin without hurting the meat; leave the head and the tail intact.

Cut the fish along the back to the backbone. In this long cavity, place freshly picked chervil and tarragon, chopped, salt, and pepper; close the fish. Do the same thing on the belly.

Next, roll out 2 thin sheets of flaky pastry dough the length of the sea bass. Place the fish on top of one of the sheets of pastry; cover it with the other sheet of pastry. Seal the dough by pressing all around the fish to enclose it completely and follow its original shape.

With a very sharp knife, cut off the excess dough, leaving enough to simulate the fins. Make a few lines lengthwise on the fins and tail, and with the remaining dough simulate the gills. Do the same for the eye.

Glaze the dough with an egg yolk, and to make it look more like a fish, reproduce the scales by pressing the dough with a little mold in a half-moon shape. This careful work demands much patience and a certain dexterity.

Place the sea bass thus prepared on a cookie sheet, in a 425°F (230°C/Gas 7) oven. When the dough is firm, reduce the heat to 350° (180°C/Gas 4), so that it cooks evenly, inside as well as outside, without burning the dough. It will take 1½ hours to cook.

To serve: place the sea bass on a long platter and carve in front of the guests. Accompany it simply with melted butter or beurre blanc.

Variation

Before it is wrapped in dough, the sea bass can be stuffed with this excellent lobster mousse:

In a mortar pound the lobster meat. Add the coral seasoned with salt, a turn of the pepper mill, and finely grated nutmeg.

Rub the lobster meat through a very fine sieve into a bowl.

Set the bowl on ice, and beat into the lobster 1 cup very heavy cream and then the pistachios and truffles.

For flaky pastry dough:
Place the flour on a pastry board, making a well in the middle for the salt and water. Mix and knead the flour with the water until the dough is smooth and elastic. Roll into a ball and let stand for 20 minutes. Roll the dough out evenly into a sheet about 8 inches square.

On top place the butter, which has been kneaded in the same way until it has the same consistency as the dough.

Fold the ends of the dough over the butter so as to enclose it completely.

Let it stand again for 10 minutes; then give the dough two "turns." Each "turn" consists of rolling the dough, on a marble slab with a rolling pin, into a rectangle 24 inches by 8 inches (61x20cm.) and ½ inch (1.3cm.) thick. Fold the pastry crosswise in three, forming a square again. The second turn is given by rolling the dough with a rolling pin in the opposite direction and folding it in three.

The purpose of turning and rolling is to distribute the butter evenly in the pastry and to ensure that it expands evenly during the cooking.

Finally, give the dough two more pairs of turns, letting it stand 10 minutes between each pair of turns. The flaky dough is ready to be used and cut after having had 6 turns, which means handled 3 times, 2 turns each time.

Duck Liver Terrine
(Terrine de Foie de Canard)

Serves 16

Ingredients
3 large duck livers, about 1 pound each
4 cups (1ltr.) port wine
2 envelopes gelatin
mixed spices (¾ tablespoon salt, 1 teaspoon pepper, ground
  very fine, clash grated nutmeg)
½ teaspoon salt

Method
Soak the duck livers for 2 hours in tepid water no hotter than
100°F (38°C).

Drain the livers; open each lobe, breaking them with your hands.
Carefully remove any remaining bits of the gall bladder and also
all the blood vessels inside the livers.

Place the duck livers in an ovenproof terrine; season with the
mixed spices.

Dissolve the gelatin in the port wine and add. Let stand in a cool
place for 24 hours.

Cover the terrine and place in a bain-marie. Put in an oven
preheated to 400°F (200°C/Gas 6).

Turn off the oven to cook the livers. Cooking time is 40 to
50 minutes.

Set in a cool place. Using the terrine, serve the duck livers
to guests.

Chapter 6

The King of Chefs

Marie Antoine (Antonin) Carême

*I*n his splendid biography of Marie-Antoine Carême (1784–1833), more usually known as Antonin Carême, Ian Kelly describes the father of haute cuisine as "the first celebrity chef." This is an apt description, although he is more famously known as the "chef of kings and king of chefs." There is a literal meaning here because Carême spent much of his career cooking for royalty and leading European dignitaries and he was most certainly regarded by contemporaries as the reigning king of the kitchen.

To describe Carême as an influential chef is to verge on understatement because in many culinary circles Carême is regarded as the "Master Chef." This view was certainly shared by Carême himself who had the temerity and audacity to write an autobiography immortalizing his achievements. The work, *Notice Biographique Sur Carême,* was not completed; however, it was a groundbreaking endeavor because hitherto biographies of this kind had been confined to great political and social figures, certainly not chefs. But Carême was rarely troubled by self-doubt or modesty. Nor was he slow to acknowledge the extent of his contribution to the culinary arts. "Had any other cook," he wondered, "ever made as many pecuniary sacrifices in order to further the progress of the culinary arts."

The great chef was prone to immodest statements of this kind as he had little to be modest about. In terms of vision, invention of dishes, masterly design of food service and in his writings, Carême set a standard that was arguably not matched until the arrival of Auguste Escoffier (Chapter 10), some half a century later.

A reasonable case can be made for disputing Carême's status as the father of haute cuisine because there was a well-established movement in this direction among French chefs stretching back to the century before Carême's birth. In the mid-eighteenth century, before the great chef had stirred, a small flood of French cookbooks were published by chefs who styled themselves as advocates of the nouvelle cuisine. The same term employed over 200 years later merely demonstrates that the concept of new or nouvelle will always be with us in culinary matters.

These eighteenth-century chefs expressed their modernity in emphasizing the use of indigenous French flavorings, especially members of the onion family, as opposed to the spices from what they called the 'East Indies,' (now called Southeast Asia). They were also in favor of decreasing the reliance on wild fowl and replacing poultry of this kind with domestically reared animals such as woodcocks and larks.

It was in this period that heart-stopping amounts of butter came to be widely used in cooking, replacing a reliance on lard. The previous practice of placing all ingredients in a large pot for stewing was slowly taken over by cooking the various components separately and then combining them without losing the individual flavors. These innovations and others, which are now taken for granted, were hallmarks of this nouvelle cuisine movement and spread beyond France. They went a long way to establishing the primacy of French cuisine over Italian cuisine, which had previously held sway.

Carême became a critic of this movement. He thought that nouvelle cuisine was overblown and lacking in elegance. Too many dishes were served at once in his view and the portions were too large. He also had strong views on the new flavorings employed by chefs of this time. He argued that they were excessive, preventing the true essence of the original foodstuff from emerging. So he set out to codify better ways of preparation, to encourage better organization in the kitchen and to instruct his followers on methods of presentation. Carême also emphasized the need to create whole meals that were greater than their parts, i.e., the individual dishes. These ideas and practices were ultimately incorporated in his seminal five volume work: *L'Art de la*

Cuisine Française au XIXe siècle or *The Art of French Cooking in the Nineteenth Century.* The book ambitiously set out to offer a history of French cuisine and showed how every dish could be classified.

Once contained in a category, Carême guided his readers into the basic methods of preparation, followed by a number of variations emanating from this basic method. Slowly a web of interconnected dishes emerges from this process. The books contain a dazzling number of novel recipes, including 250 meat soups, the same number of fish soups and so on through the sauces, which were to become the signature of classic French cuisine.

Then there are the meat and fish preparations; indeed, more or less everything a chef needs for the production of haute cuisine is to be found in Carême's writing. Some of these recipes might have originated elsewhere but had not been published until Carême embarked on this extraordinarily comprehensive work.

His love of extravagant decoration, founded on his experience as a pastry chef, is central to this work where savory dishes are presented in striking ways, in carefully constructed form, and sometimes complemented with a variety of decorative skewers to create all manner of shapes.

Some of these skewers were of his own design; indeed Carême extended his scope of revolutionary transformation in the kitchen to focus on design issues for a range of utensils, including molds and saucepans. He is even credited with having created the classic chef's distinctive hat or toque.

Carême realized that to be influential he had to magnify his personality and gain recognition for his trade in a way that clearly bore his signature. He also, incidentally, was an early proponent of the idea for a chef's association to encourage sharing of knowledge and the maintenance of standards. Clearly there was a lot of ego operating in this process but it was Carême's ego that propelled the art of cooking into a new stratosphere where it was recognized alongside the other arts.

When Carême embarked on his culinary career, France was in a state of revolution, even his befuddled father, who abandoned him as a boy, appears to have recognized that in these turbulent times there were unexpected opportunities amidst the uncertainty. Maybe in a more settled era someone like the young Carême would have faced greater difficulties in rising above his lowly station.

The revolution spawned many social changes that had a direct impact on the world of food. For a start, more and more people began eating outside their own homes in cafes and restaurants. These restaurants were started by cooks previously employed by members of the upper class who had been stripped of their fortunes and no longer required their services. The highly restrictive guilds that controlled permission to sell various products saw their power diminished, creating opportunities for a whole host of people to establish eating houses.

As the aristocracy fled from France, they often took their chefs with them abroad. Some of these chefs soon saw greater opportunities outside the homes of increasingly impoverished aristocrats and established their own restaurants throughout Europe.

It was also during this period that the social status of chefs underwent a transformation. In the old aristocratic society, chefs were little more than domestic servants working in grand houses. However, on the eve of the revolution, some outstanding cooks began to achieve greater recognition and gained a status above trades such as those of dress makers and dance instructors.

The revolution changed things, not least because it freed chefs to open restaurants and become their own masters. Carême, who cared desperately about status, found himself caught in a dilemma because he believed that great cuisine only emerged from private kitchens, thus ensuring that chefs remained employees. He, however, hovered in the hinterland between employee and individual artisan as he worked mainly in private kitchens preparing banquets but did so as a kind of freelance caterer. He was employed for specific occasions, although he also held down a number of full time posts, most of which were short-lived after he became famous.

Carême insisted that "the master chef has only himself to answer to in his work." He refused to see himself as a servant but recognition of his independent status and artistry largely eluded him and his colleagues.

The Légion d'Honneur created by Napoleon Bonaparte in 1802, never had a chance of heading towards the kitchen in the time of its creator. However, and ironically, it was during the brief restoration of the monarchy under Louis XVIII that Carême was granted the right to be called "Carême de Paris," a form of quasi-ennoblement. The King of Chefs had therefore built a half-finished bridge towards elevating the status of his trade but it took another century before the bridge was completed.

Carême's preoccupation with status was understandable for someone whose beginnings were so inauspicious. His family existed in a state of poverty suggestive of the conditions described by famous British author Charles Dickens. Carême was one of twenty five children whose parents entirely lacked the means to look after them. Such was the obscurity of his birth that even his given name is in question. Carême himself proffered various versions of the name ranging from the most commonly used Antonin to Marie-Antonin, alongside his supposedly correct given name that was Marie-Antoine, the masculine form of Marie Antoinette.

It is not certain what exactly happened when this very poor boy was abandoned by his parents at the age of 11 or 12 and fortuitously found his way into a commercial kitchen. Probably the most comprehensive account comes from his secretary, Frédéric Fayot, who says that the chef told him that his often drunk father took him for a walk and then left him in the street saying: "Go, my little one, go now; there are good trades in the world; leave us, misery is our lot; this will be an age of many fortunes; all that is required to make one is intelligence, and you have that…This evening or tomorrow, perhaps, some good place will welcome you. Go with what God has given you."

This, at any rate, is Fayot's probably fanciful account of how the conversation went. What is more certain is that this was the last time Carême saw his father or any other member of the family.

The young boy was left to wander the streets but was found by a kindly chef who is variously described as a tavern owner, a cook who supplied food to people's homes and a chop house proprietor. The name of his benefactor and his precise business remains unknown but he effectively became Carême's foster father and offered him work as a general kitchen dogsbody.

Fayot implies that the young Carême was barely literate at this time but at the age of 13, he spent his evenings learning to read and write and then discovered the Bibliothèque Nationale, a treasure trove of books. It was said that Carême especially enjoyed the travel books with their vivid and colorful engravings.

It seems that he spent some three or four years at the tavern before moving on to a restaurant at the age of 15. Two years later, Carême got his real break when he was offered an apprenticeship by Sylvain Bailly, a famous *pâtissier* with a shop near the Palais-Royal. Here he embarked on a more formal chef's training for which he was eternally grateful and until he died would maintain that there was no higher calling in the kitchen than that of a pastry chef.

It has to be said this is a distinctly minority view in the hierarchy-conscious world of professional kitchens. But to Carême the confectionary *pièces montées* or centerpieces created by pastry chefs, principally himself, were nothing less than great works of architecture. He wrote: "The fine arts are five in number: painting, sculpture, poetry, music, and architecture—whose main branch is pastry."

Carême remained with Bailly for three years. He became fascinated with sketching and was inspired by drawings of buildings such as temples and pyramids. He often copied their designs to construct the highly fashionable decorative centerpieces that were popular with the wealthy French. These confections, sometimes several feet high, were made of flour, marzipan, sugar and a variety of other pastry ingredients. They were truly spectacular and Bailly displayed Carême's creations in his window.

At Bailly, he continued his vigorous program of self-improvement by studying at the Bibliothèque Nationale in addition to a punishing work schedule. He was rapidly recognized as a valuable member of staff and rose to the position of first pie maker. From there, he moved to another famous patisserie, Gendron's. Here he combined his established culinary skills with a new career as an independent artisan doing "extras" for private clients, usually working on grand banquets. Very quickly, the independent work took over his employment at Gendron and Carême effectively became self-employed. Besides the freedom this gave him, it was also an opportunity to work alongside other master chefs including Boucher, Laguipiere, Robert, Richaut, Bardet, Lasne, Savart, Riquert and Robillard. He described this experience as being admitted to the *grande école* for chefs, echoing the name of the famous schools in other disciplines which were founded at the time.

The grand banquets required the services of many chefs, giving them uncharacteristically large budgets for the food. As a result of this banqueting work, Carême got to know one of France's most famous foreign ministers, Charles Maurice de Talleyrand-Périgord, better known simply as Talleyrand, who hosted the most lavish receptions of the day. Some reports have it that he came into the foreign minister's employment but this seems unlikely although he did a great deal of work for him. Napoleon was ruling France at the time and although the Emperor had little personal interest in food he understood its social function and frequently attended banquets prepared by Carême.

Wanting to create a place where he can entertain and discuss with diplomats, Napolean, in 1804, gave Talleyrand money to buy Château de Valençay which is a large estate outside of Paris. Talleyrand utilized it to the full and brought Carême to the chateau to ensure that it would also be memorable for its food.

It was largely as a result of Talleyrand's patronage that Carême established himself as the chef of choice for the leading figures of the day. Talleyrand, who was very interested in food, took Carême's creative powers to new heights. He challenged the chef to prepare an entire year's worth of menus without repeating himself and using only seasonal foods. Carême easily passed the test. He also continued to work like a fanatic, serving the foreign minister and opening his own patisserie, an establishment which seems to have had the main purpose of providing an auxiliary kitchen for his catering activities.

Carême was also continuing his research into classic food, often making use of the Vatican library (partially founded by the first cookbook writer Platina, see Chapter 15). The first published product of this work was a book called *Histoire de la Table Romaine,* or *History of the Roman Table,* in which he was dismissive of Roman cuisine. All copies of this book have since vanished and it is unlikely that it made much impact at the time. Shortly afterwards, in 1815, Carême completed two other books which commanded a great deal of public attention. *Le Pâtissier Pittoresque (Picturesque Pastry),* and *Le Pâtissier Royal Parisien (Royal Parisian Pastry).* These books contained extensive engravings displaying his famous centerpieces and describing how these extraordinary structures were constructed. As for the recipes, they varied from the very elaborate to the basic – instructing readers how to make cream puff pastry, sponge cakes and Charlotte Russe, which even now has a place at smart dinner tables.

As ever during Carême's lifetime, his preoccupation with food was frequently impinged upon by turmoil in the political world. In 1815, the year the pastry books were published, Napoleon was forced to abdicate and the chef, who was attached to his camp through Talleyrand, thought it wise to leave the country. He moved to London where he served as chef de cuisine for the Prince Regent, later George IV, before moving to Russia to do the same job for Tsar Alexander I. Following that, he went on to Vienna to serve Lord Stewart, the British Ambassador.

Carême wrote: "It is painful for me to admit that foreigners took possession of the most distinguished and most accomplished of our talented young practitioners and sustained the splendor of our calling; I myself, since that time, have traveled in England, Austria and Russia."

He was able to secure positions overseas because of his reputation at the Parisian banquets attended by heads of state and other dignitaries. Each of these post were of short duration. Indeed, even in Paris itself, he did not much care for employment by Russian and Hungarian royalty. The fall of Napoleon appears to have forced Carême into a peripatetic existence, one that is filled with frequent travels and short trips, which he did not like.

In 1824 however, he managed to return to Paris for good, turning down many jobs before accepting a post as chef to the banker James Mayer Rothschild with whom he remained until 1829. He had another four years of life after leaving Rothschild's household. By then he was in poor health as his punishing work schedule took its toll. Carême was known to rise before dawn so that he could select the best products from the market and to retire well after midnight. Conditions in the kitchen itself, although better in the places he worked, remained extremely harsh—the noise was tremendous, the heat considerable and the lack of ventilation practically stifling.

Carême's last years were spent in a frantic scramble to complete his masterwork, *L'art de la Cuisine*. In the end, it had to be finished on the basis of notes that remained after his death. By then, he had a body of published work whose influence extended well beyond his demise. An earlier book, *Le Maitre d'hôtel Français*, was also highly influential and demonstrated Carême's lasting interest in the history of food. As ever, he made the case that modern cuisine far excelled that of previous eras. *Le Cuisinier Parisienne*, published a year before his death, is famous for elaborating on classic dishes still consumed today. It turned out to be something of a forerunner for the vastly more ambitious *Art of Cuisine*.

Carême was much preoccupied by thoughts of his legacy and was pleased that his written work had made a significant impact during his lifetime. Writing about his earlier works on pastry he says, "When I take a look around Paris, I see with pleasure in every neighborhood the improvements and the growth that the pastry shops have undergone since this work appeared." He also drew satisfaction from the appreciation he received from the grand clients who ate his food.

Referring to his time in England, he wrote: "In the space of the eight months that I remained there, for seven of them I did not leave the service of his Britannic Majesty, who had not during that period a single attack of gout, although before my arrival in this royal household, the cooking was so overpowering and spicy that the prince was frequently afflicted for whole days and nights at a time."

He could not have received a higher compliment from one of his other royal patron's, Alexander I, who told Talleyrand, "What we did not know was that he taught us to eat."

Carême died in Paris at the age of 48, and is buried in the Cimetière de Montmartre. He is still revered among chefs and food scholars and there are numerous memorials to his name in the culinary world.

He would be disappointed to learn that his fame has faded but at least when he died, he had the satisfaction of knowing that the dirt-poor child who was literally picked up on the streets of Paris had ended his days as the nation's most revered chef, indeed possibly the best known chef in Europe. His work and the standards he set have become a benchmark for those who followed him in the grand kitchens until, as it always does, the mantle was passed to worthy successors.

Carême Recipes

Here are two recipes adapted for modern use that could be reproduced in a domestic kitchen. By Carême's standards, they are relatively simple. The third recipe is more typical of the elaborate style of his dishes and is given more for reference than in expectation that anyone will try this at home.

Autumn Soup

Ingredients
white part of 3 medium leeks, cut in julienne strips
leaves of 2 celery hearts, cut in julienne strips
½ head of romaine lettuce, cut in julienne strips
3¼ pints / 2 quarts / 2 liters well flavored consommé
5 ounces / 1 cup/150 grams fresh green peas
pinch of sugar
pinch of white pepper
salt (optional)

For the liaison or base:
1 ½ ounces / ½ cup/45 grams flour
6 fl ounces / ¾ cup /175 ml cold consommé

For the croutons:
6 slices bread, crusts discarded, diced
2 ounces / ¼ cup / 60 grams butter
3–4 tablespoons oil

Method

Wash and drain the leek, celery, and lettuce strips. Bring the consommé to a boil

For the liaison: mix the flour with the 6 fl. oz./ ¾ cup / 175 ml. cold consommé and blend until smooth. Add to the boiling consommé, stirring constantly, and simmer until the consommé is thickened and smooth, for 2 to 3 minutes. Add the leek, celery and lettuce strips with the peas, sugar and pepper and simmer, uncovered, until the vegetables are tender, for 15 to 20 minutes. Taste the soup for seasoning, adding more salt and pepper if necessary.

For the croutons:
Heat the butter and oil and fry the diced bread, stirring, until browned on all sides. Drain the croutons thoroughly on paper towels and keep warm. If serving in a tureen, put in the croutons and pour over the soup; if serving in individual bowls, serve the croutons separately.

Butter Sauce A L'Italienne

Ingredients
½ bay leaf
sprig of thyme, or ½ teaspoon dried thyme
1 whole clove
2½ tablespoons butter
2 tablespoons chopped parsley
3 mushrooms, finely chopped1 truffle, finely chopped (optional)
½ clove garlic, crushed
pinch of grated nutmeg
salt and pepper
4 fl. oz. / ½ cup / 125 ml. champagne
double quantity of butter sauce
2 tablespoons olive oil
juice of ½ lemon

Method

Tie the bay leaf, thyme and clove with thread or wrap them in a piece of cheesecloth. In a heavy based pan, melt one tablespoon of the butter and add the parsley, truffle (if using), garlic, tied herbs, nutmeg, and a little salt and pepper. Sauté over medium heat until the mushrooms are soft 1–2 minutes. Add the champagne, simmer five minutes, and discard the tied herbs.

Make the sauce in the top of a double boiler or in a saucepan placed in a water bath *(bain-marie).* Stir in the champagne and mushroom mixture, then gradually stir in the oil. When the sauce is smooth, add the remaining butter in small pieces and stir until incorporated. Add lemon juice to taste with more salt and pepper if needed.

This sauce separates easily and should be made over hot, not boiling, water. The sauce should be served tepid.

Les Petits Vol-Au-Vents a la Nesle

As prepared for Brighton Pavilion and Chateau Rothschild.

Ingredients
20 vol-au-vent cases, the diameter of a glass
20 cocks-combs
20 cocks-stones (testes)
10 lambs sweetbreads (thymus and pancreatic glands, washed
  in water for five hours, until the liquid runs clear)
10 small truffles, pared, chopped, boiled in consommé
20 tiny mushrooms
20 lobster tails
4 fine whole lambs' brains, boiled and chopped
1 French loaf
2 spoonfuls chicken jelly
2 spoonfuls veloute sauce
1 tablespoon chopped parsley

2 tablespoons chopped mushrooms
4 egg yolks
2 chickens, boned
2 calves' udders
2 pints cream
sauce Allemande
salt
nutmeg
truffles
mushrooms
20 lobster tails
4 fine whole lambs' brains

Method

Crumb a whole French loaf. Add two spoonfuls of poultry jelly, one of veloute, one tablespoon of chopped parsley, two of mushrooms, chopped. Boil and stir as it thickens to a ball. Add two egg yolks. Pound the flesh of two boned chickens through a sieve. Boil two calves' udders — once cold, pound and pass through a sieve.

Then, mix six ounces of the breadcrumbs *panada* to ten ounces of the chicken meat, and ten of the calves' udders and combine and pound for 15 minutes. Add five drams of salt, some nutmeg and the yolks of two more eggs and a spoonful of cold veloute or bechamel. Pound for a further ten minutes. Test by poaching a ball in boiling water — it should form soft, smooth balls.

Make some balls of poultry forcemeat in small coffee spoons, dip them in jelly broth and after draining on a napkin, place them regularly in the vol-au-vent, already half filled with: A good ragout of cocks-combs and stones (testicles), lambs' sweetbreads (thymus and pancreatic glands, washed in water for five hours, until the liquid runs clear), truffles, mushrooms, lobster tails, whole lambs' brains

Cover all with an extra thick sauce Allemande.

Chapter 7

Helping America to Cook

Julia Child

$\mathcal{J}$ulia Child, arguably the most famous American cook of the mid-twentieth century, was born in 1912 in Pasadena, California. She is credited with building on the work of James Beard (Chapter 3) in bringing the delights of French cuisine to an initially skeptical American public. She actually did more than that and enticed many of her fellow citizens away from convenience foods, encouraging them to cook and not be afraid of the adventure of preparing dishes with hard-to-pronounce names and seemingly complicated recipes.

Through her television shows and books, Child showed how this could be accomplished with a limited quantity of application combined with a willingness to spend a little time to make something a lot better. "Non-cooks," said Child "think it's silly to invest two hours' work in two minutes' enjoyment; but if cooking is evanescent, so is the ballet." She did not pretend that cooking great food was necessarily simple but insisted it was worthwhile and infinitely rewarding. She urged her followers to: "above all, have a good time."

Child had no background as a chef or indeed in serious cooking, which she only discovered in her thirties. However, she was a willing convert to the cause of good food, which mainly meant French food as far as she was concerned. With the determination and skill which she approached most challenges, she was not satisfied to be a mere gourmet but wanted to know how all this wonderful food was made. Unlike most of the food gurus in this book, she never trained as a chef in the professional sense but was an avid cooking student. The distinction is important because chefs have to know how to make food preparation into a business, whereas cooks are not inhibited by these restraints but are motivated by pleasure and the simple need to provide good food on a daily basis for themselves and their families.

Having discovered what could be done, she was keen to share this knowledge. "Be a fearless cook!" she declared in her typically brisk and enthusiastic way, "try out new ideas and new recipes, but always buy the freshest and finest ingredients, whatever they may be. Furnish your kitchen with the most solid and workmanlike equipment you can find. Keep your knives ever sharp and - *toujours bon appetit!*" This French phrase which means "always keep a good appetite" has been her widely mimicked catchphrase.

Reading her books today and watching her many television cookery programs, Child appears slightly pretentious and not quite credible as a person who could inspire millions of Americans. Her accent was distinctly strange to American ears; her demeanor was one of a woman used to having servants at her beck and call. Indeed her not-suffering-fools-gladly approach should have been enough to turn people off. But what shone through were a tidal wave of enthusiasm and a wealth of knowledge that she willed her followers to share. This is why even today Child is remembered and revered and her name is used to inspire cooks to try that little bit harder.

One of the things most people know about Julia Child is that she was unusually tall; six feet, two inches to be exact. So it was no surprise that she was sporty in her youth, playing tennis, golf and basketball. She was also keen on small-game hunting alongside the youthful preoccupation of being a prankster.

Born into the wealthy McWilliams family, she had a conventional upbringing in comfortable circumstances. She graduated from Smith College, a well-known liberal arts college in Massachusetts. Straining credibility, some sources attribute her first indication of interest in providing food for others as originating at college where she became the chairwoman of the Refreshment Committee for the Senior Prom and Fall Dance. History does not record what culinary delights arose from this position but it is known that, while at college, she wrote a number of plays and unsuccessfully submitted pieces to the *New Yorker* magazine. "There were some famous women novelists in those days," she recalled, "and I intended to be one." It was not to be; her first job after graduation was more prosaic in the advertising department of W. & J. Sloane, a New York-based luxury home furnishing company. She returned to California and continued working in the advertising industry, mainly as a copywriter. The skills learned in these jobs help explain her later proficiency in book writing.

More famous is her wartime experience where she was widely reported to have been a spy. This description is not strictly accurate, although she did work in US intelligence – the Office of Strategic Services (the precursor of the Central Intelligence Agency). Child applied to the OSS after being rejected for military service on grounds of being too tall. However, she was not the type of person to accept the idea of sitting out the war without making a contribution and so took a lowly typist's job at the OSS headquarters in Washington. Clearly underutilized in this position she moved up to being a researcher, dealing with highly sensitive matters, directly under the supervision of the OSS head General William J. Donovan. Later she worked in the section dealing with emergency rescue equipment and was deployed to a special program developing a shark repellent.

In 1944, she was posted to Kandy, Ceylon (now Sri Lanka) a major center for the Allied forces intelligence activity in South Asia. Her job again involved handling highly classified communications. Most importantly for Child, she met her future husband, Paul Child, a fellow OSS officer who, like his wife to be, came from a well-to-do family. They both moved from there to China and then back to OSS Headquarters where she became Head of Registry and was awarded the Emblem of Meritorious Civilian Service. The citation noted her "drive and inherent cheerfulness."

The turning point in Child's culinary career came when her husband, now in the Foreign Service, was posted to Paris in 1948. Paul Child was an enthusiastic gourmet and being stationed in the French capital must have seemed like heaven for the couple who dined out frequently. "After one taste of French food ... I was hooked," Julia recalled. "I'd never eaten like that before; I didn't know such food existed. The wonderful attention paid to each detail of the meal was incredible to me. I'd never really drunk good wine before, and knew nothing at all about it. It was simply a whole new life experience."

Child, rather typically, sought to elevate mere enthusiasm into serious study, besides which being a stay-at-home wife was hardly her kind of thing: "I wanted something that would hold me and sustain me," she said. "Cooking was taken with such seriousness in France that even ordinary chefs were proud of their profession. That's what appealed to me."

She enrolled in the famous Cordon Bleu cookery school. "I was 32 when I started cooking; up until then, I just ate." Child also set about learning French, which she more or less mastered. With the enthusiasm and determination that was her trademark she later studied privately with Max Bugnard and other master chefs and joined the women's cooking club, *Cercle des Gourmettes*.

At the club, she met Simone Beck and Louisette Bertholle, they had the idea of establishing a cookery school aimed at foreign residents living in Paris. They named it *L'Ecole des Trois Gourmandes* (School of the Three Gourmets). From here came the highly ambitious plan to write a definitive guide to French cuisine for American readers. The result was a 734-page encyclopedia of a book called *Mastering the Art of French Cooking*.

The detail and precision which went into its preparation became legendary but its length sent shudders of alarm down the spine of Houghton Mifflin, the publishers who commissioned the work. They paid the princely sum of US$750 to the three authors, and then rejected it. It finally landed with Alfred A. Knopf, which published it in 1961 and helped make it a bestseller. Beck became a lifelong friend to Child and collaborated with her on other works. But, of the three, it was Julia Child who became truly famous as a result of this work.

After the book was published, Child's fame spread through her cooking articles in newspapers and magazines. Around this time, she took part in a book reviewing panel on a television show. This gave the Boston based television station, WGBH, the bright idea of having her host a 30-minute cooking program. Expectations of success for a show hosted by an unknown person tackling a relatively obscure subject were not high. However, when the program first aired in 1962 viewer response was immediately positive. Julia Child quickly graduated from earning a remarkably modest US$50 for each show to the princely sum of US$200 plus expenses. Viewers were captivated by this vivacious woman who cooked on air and clearly had a sense of humor. The show, called *The French Chef,* was syndicated to 96 American television stations and she won an Emmy for her work.

The show spawned another well-received book, The *French Chef Cookbook,* which was published in 1968. More books and more television work flowed from this. Child returned to her original work, collaborating with Simone Beck but not Bertholle with whom relations had soured. The result was *Mastering the Art of French Cooking, Volume Two,* published in 1971. Next came the book *From Julia Child's Kitchen.* This was based on her television program but unlike many of today's TV spin-off cookbooks it was extremely detailed. Child's didactic approached marks her out from these other TV chefs but it is a style followed by the British television chef Delia Smith (Chapter 19), who like Child, essentially views her television work as being educational.

Child also collaborated closely with her husband who took the photographs for the book. He went on to design a studio kitchen for her, making sure it was in harmony with her unusual height. He also designed the kitchen of their home in Massachusetts which was later transformed into an impressive television studio and functioned as the family kitchen. It appeared in her TV shows throughout the 1990s. The set has been preserved and is on display at the National Museum of American History in Washington DC.

Julia Child had become *the* American television chef and had published her seminal work: the *Way to Cook* which appeared in both book and video form in 1989. She also acquired a new collaborator, Jacques Pepin, a famous chef and television personality in his own right. They worked together on television shows and spin-off books.

Child had the distinction of being both populist yet highly regarded by professional chefs. As early as 1966, she appeared on the cover of *Time* magazine under a banner reading: "Our Lady of the Ladle." In 1981, she pursued her campaign to upgrade her fellow countrymen's appreciation of food and wine by co-founding the American Institute of Wine & Food with the famous winemakers Robert Mondavi and Richard Graff.

There was something about Child which captured the popular imagination and was reflected in the way she seeped into popular culture, gaining recognition far beyond the ranks of food enthusiasts. She was the subject of comedy sketches, notably on *The Saturday Night Live* show and *The Cosby Show*. And then there was the musical *Bon Appetit!* based around her TV cooking programs. There was also a string of children's television programs in which she performed or was portrayed. Child relished this outbreak of publicity and even enjoyed the parodies but she did not approve of a popular cooking blog entitled

The Julie/Julia Project, which was transformed into a bestselling book *Julie and Julia: 365 Days, 524 Recipes, 1 Tiny Apartment Kitchen* by Julie Powell. This in turn was made into a hit film *Julie and Julia* with Meryl Streep portraying Julia Child with uncanny accuracy. Child's disciple Powell had set out to cook every recipe in *Mastering the Art of French Cooking* within a year and recorded the process. Child saw this as little more than a stunt and greatly disliked the project.

Child was delightfully blunt about this as she was of other things which met her disapproval. Speaking of the state of American cuisine she once said, "How can a nation be called great if its bread tastes like Kleenex?" And as for diets and health foods, Child was largely a skeptic. She believed that the "only time to eat diet food is while you're waiting for the steak to cook." Her view was that eating well and in moderation was far preferable to embarking on a faddish diet. Dismissing critics who complained of her rich food recipes she responded: "I would rather eat one tablespoon of Chocolate Russe Cake than three bowls of Jell-O." Vegetarians were also unlikely to warm towards her abrupt view: "I don't think pure vegetarianism is a healthy lifestyle. I've often wondered to myself: Does a vegetarian look forward to dinner, ever?"

However, she was not entirely inflexible in her championing of rich French cooking. In her later years, she tended to place less emphasis on fatty foods and red meat and experimented with dishes that could be prepared easily and quickly. By 2001, Julia Child moved to Montecito, California and helped establish the only restaurant in which she was directly involved, - Julia's Kitchen – situated in the famous wine-growing region of Napa Valley. Her husband Paul had died in 1994 after suffering a series of strokes and being confined to nursing homes. Her close friend and collaborator Simone Beck also died in 2002, and Child decided to move to a retirement home where she too died in 2004 at the age of 91, just days before her 92nd birthday. She was showered with awards before her death including a much cherished French Legion of Honor and the US Presidential Medal of Freedom.

A documentary television program about her life was shown in the year of her death, it was entitled *Julia Child! America's Favorite Chef.* This was no case of hyperbole. She was in many ways a very unlikely popular figure and a highly unconventional one, and an almost religiously conventional French chef. Perhaps it was this contradiction that explains how someone this quirky came to be so influential.

Child Recipes

Boeuf Bourguignon

Serves 6

Ingredients
6 ounces (175g.) bacon
1 tablespoon olive oil or cooking oil
3 pounds (1.35kg.) lean stewing beef, cut into
2-inch (5cm.) cubes
1 sliced carrot
1 sliced onion
1 teaspoon salt
¼ teaspoon pepper
2 tablespoons flour
3 cups (750ml.) full-bodied, young red wine, such as a Chianti
2 to 3 cups (500–750ml.) brown beef stock or
canned beef bouillon
1 tablespoon tomato paste
2 cloves mashed garlic
½ teaspoon thyme
crumbled bay leaf
blanched bacon rind
18–24 small white onions, brown-braised in stock
1 pound (450g.) quartered fresh mushrooms, sautéed in butter
parsley sprigs

Method
Remove rind from bacon, and cut bacon into *lardons* (sticks,
¼ inch (1cm.) thick and 1½ inches (4cm. long). Simmer rind and
bacon for 10 minutes in 1½ quarts (1500 ml.) of water.

Drain and dry.

Preheat oven to 450°F (230°C/Gas 8).

Sauté the bacon in the oil over moderate heat for 2 to 3 minutes to brown lightly. Remove to a side dish with a slotted spoon. Set casserole aside. Reheat until fat is almost smoking before you sauté the beef.

Dry the stewing beef in paper towels; it will not brown if it is damp. Sauté it, a few pieces at a time, in the hot oil and bacon fat until nicely browned on all sides. Add it to the bacon.

In the same fat, brown the sliced vegetables. Pour out the sautéing fat. Return the beef and bacon to the casserole and toss with the salt and pepper. Then sprinkle on the flour and toss again to coat the beef lightly with the flour. Set casserole uncovered in middle position of preheated oven for 4 minutes. Toss the meat and return to oven for 4 minutes more. (This browns the flour and covers the meat with a light crust.) Remove casserole, and turn oven down to 325°F (170°C/Gas 3).

Stir in the wine, and enough stock or bouillon so that the meat is barely covered. Add the tomato paste, garlic, herbs, and bacon rind. Bring to simmer on top of the stove. Then cover the casserole and set in lower third of preheated oven. Regulate heat so liquid simmers very slowly for 2½ to 3 hours. The meat is done when a fork pierces it easily.

While the beef is cooking, prepare the onions and mushrooms. Set them aside until needed.

When the meat is tender, pour the contents of the casserole into a sieve set over a saucepan. Wash out the casserole and return the beef and bacon to it. Distribute the cooked onions and mushrooms over the meat.

Skim fat off the sauce. Simmer sauce for a minute or two, skimming off additional fat as it rises. You should have about 2½ cups

(625ml.) of sauce thick enough to coat a spoon lightly. If too thin, boil it down rapidly. If too thick, mix in a few tablespoons of stock or canned bouillon. Taste carefully for seasoning. Pour the sauce over the meat and vegetables. Recipe may be completed in advance to this point.

For immediate serving: Cover the casserole and simmer for 2 to 3 minutes, basting the meat and vegetables with the sauce several times. Serve in its casserole, or arrange the stew on a platter surrounded with potatoes, noodles, or rice, and decorated with parsley.

For later serving: When cold, cover and refrigerate. About 15 to 20 minutes before serving, bring to the simmer, cover, and simmer very slowly for 10 minutes, occasionally basting the meat and vegetables with the sauce.

From: *Mastering the Art of French Cooking* by Julia Child, Knopf, 2001

Coq Au Vin

Another classic French dish from the same book.
Serves 6

Ingredients
3–4-ounce (80-110g.) chunk lean bacon
2 tablespoons unsalted butter
2½ to 3 pounds (1.1–1.3kg.) frying chicken, cut into pieces
½ teaspoon salt, plus additional for seasoning
⅛ teaspoon pepper, plus additional for seasoning
¼ cup (62ml.) cognac
3 cups (750ml.) young, full-bodied red wine, such as Burgundy, Beaujolais, Cotes du Rhone, or Chianti
1–2 cups (250–500ml.) brown chicken stock, brown stock or canned beef bouillon

½ tablespoon tomato paste
2 cloves mashed garlic
¼ teaspoon thyme leaves
1 bay leaf
12 to 24 brown-braised onions
½ pound (225g.) sautéed mushrooms
3 tablespoons all-purpose flour
2 tablespoons softened butter
fresh parsley leaves

Method

Remove the rind and cut the bacon into lardons (rectangles ¼-inch (1cm.) across and 1-inch (2.5cm. long). Simmer for 10 minutes in 2 quarts (1900ml.) of water. Rinse in cold water. Dry.

In a heavy large, heavy-bottomed casserole or Dutch oven, sauté the bacon slowly in hot butter until it is very lightly browned (temperature of 260°F/127°C for an electric skillet). Remove to a side dish.

Dry the chicken thoroughly. Brown it in the hot fat in the casserole.

Season the chicken with salt and pepper. Return the bacon to the casserole with the chicken. Cover and cook slowly (300°F/150°C) for 10 minutes, turning the chicken once.

Uncover, and pour in the cognac. Averting your face, ignite the cognac with a lighted match. Shake the casserole back and forth for several seconds until the flames subside.

Pour the wine into the casserole. Add just enough stock or bouillon to cover the chicken. Stir in the tomato paste, garlic and herbs. Bring to a simmer. Cover and simmer slowly for 20 to 25 minutes, or until the chicken is tender and its juices run a clear yellow when the meat is pricked with a fork. Remove the chicken to a side dish.

While the chicken is cooking, prepare the onions and mushrooms.

Simmer the chicken cooking liquid in the casserole for 1 to 2 minutes, skimming off fat. Then raise the heat and boil rapidly, reducing the liquid to about 2¼ cups (560ml.). Correct seasoning. Remove from heat, and discard bay leaf.

Blend the butter and flour together into a smooth paste *(beurre manié)*. Beat the paste into the hot liquid with a wire whip. Bring to the simmer, stirring and simmer for 1 to 2 minutes. The sauce should be thick enough to coat a spoon lightly.

Arrange the chicken in a casserole, place the mushrooms and onions around it and baste with the sauce. If the dish is not to be served immediately, film the top of the sauce with stock or dot with small pieces of butter. Set aside uncovered for no longer than 1 hour or cool, cover and refrigerate until needed.

Shortly before serving, bring the casserole to a simmer, basting the chicken with the sauce. Cover and simmer slowly for 4 to 5 minutes, until the chicken is heated through.

Serve from the casserole, or arrange on a hot platter. Decorate with sprigs of parsley

From: *Mastering the Art of French Cooking* by Julia Child, Knopf, 2001

Chocolate Mousse

Another classic recipe from the same source.
Serves 8

Ingredients
6 oz. (170g.) bittersweet or possibly semi-sweet
   baking chocolate, melted with:
¼ cup (22g.) strong coffee
3 ounces (85g.) unsalted butter
3 egg yolks
1 cup (250ml.) heavy cream
3 egg whites
¼ cup (33g.) finely ground sugar
whipped cream

Method
Beat the soft butter into the smoothly melted chocolate and coffee
mixture.. One by one, beat in the egg yolks. Beat the cream over ice
till it leaves light traces on the surface. Beat the egg whites till they
form soft peaks. While beating, sprinkle in the sugar by spoonfuls
and continue beating till stiff shining peaks are formed. Scrape the
chocolate mix down the side of the egg-white bowl, and delicately
mix in the whipped cream. Turn the mousse into attractive serving
bowls. Cover and refrigerate several hours. You may wish to
decorate the mousse with swirls of whipped cream, or possibly to
pass whipped cream separately.

Recipe can also be seen in *The Art of French Cooking by Julia Child
(with Bertholle and Beck)*, Knopf, 2009

The Writer Whose Subject was Food

Elizabeth David

$\mathcal{E}$lizabeth David (1913 –1992) remains a revered figure among professional chefs, food writers and many other people with an interest in food. She is widely credited with transforming British attitudes to food and cooking as the nation emerged from the austerity of the Second World War.

Her influence is such that it can be said without exaggeration that she revolutionized writing about food. In many ways, the impact she had on food in Britain is very similar to that of James Beard, her contemporary in America (Chapter 3), although he operated at a far more populist level than David and clearly did not share her aversion to publicity. Both David and Beard were self-taught and avid readers of culinary works. David never worked in a professional kitchen although Beard ran a small food business. Nevertheless, she clearly knew how to cook well, although her lack of professional experience sometimes shows up in her recipes. Nigel Slater, the chef and food writer, claims that "one of the things that very few people dare to mention about Elizabeth David is that some of her recipes don't work." However, many people still follow her recipes religiously.

David was a complex, contradictory and inspirational woman who, in today's world of celebrity and television chefs, would be distinctly out of place. As a person, she could be warm and engaging to those she regarded as equals but she was highly opinionated and dismissive of anyone who did not reach her high standards. In an age where appealing to the widest possible audience is considered highly desirable,

David stands out as someone whose prime interest lay in reaching a middle class audience and doing so in a manner that could be considered as snobbish. By all accounts, she could be far from pleasant, yet was surrounded by a small coterie of loyal friends although she also had a habit of falling out with those closest to her.

The contradictory side of David's character also revealed a woman who preached the virtues of complex dishes yet often relished simple food. She was impressed by "peasant" food from the Mediterranean, yet she initially despised the working-class food of her own country and seemed willing to pay quite a lot of money for simple, imported produce.

David had good reason to look down on the awful food which passed as the national cuisine in gloomy post-war Britain. Rationing was still in force until 1954, although food shortages continued for some time after. A rather more chipper attitude towards this situation was demonstrated by Marguerite Patten (Chapter 14) but David was not satisfied with "making do," she was in revolt against the food of the 1950s and early 60s. Food from this time was not only plain and often badly cooked but it was very often of inferior quality.

Cookbook writers who preceded David were either professional chefs or people like the very famous Isabella Beeton and Patten, both of whom were described as "home economists." She was neither and her books went a lot further than merely providing recipes. She supplied a carefully prepared portrait of the countries that gave birth to the food about which she was writing.

Indeed, David's writing is so exquisite that it evokes the smells, colors and the atmosphere of the food and the countries of the time. David never talked down to her readers, she expected them to be intelligent and engaged and to have a smattering of linguistic ability as she declined to supply English translations of some of the foreign language passages she quoted. Her biographer, Lisa Chaney, wrote: "She was first a writer, then one whose subject was food."

One thing that could unequivocally be said about David – she was never dull. Her writing is littered with telling anecdotes and marvelously pointed pieces of indignation. Writing in the *Tatler* magazine in 1986 she castigated one of the most popular kitchen gadgets: "I regard garlic presses as both ridiculous and pathetic, their effect being precisely the reverse of what people who buy them believe will be the case. Squeezing the juice out of garlic doesn't reduce its potency; it concentrates it and intensifies the smell. I have often wondered how it is that people who have once used one of these diabolical instruments don't notice this and forthwith throw the thing into the dustbin."

Nor was David hesitant in criticizing some of the biggest names in the industry. A collection of her books reveals this marginal note in a work regarded as a classic of modern French cookery, *Ma Gastronomie* by Fernand Point (Chapter 17) : "This is a really awful book," she proclaimed.

David introduced her readers not only to countries as a whole but to the specific regional areas from which the dishes are derived. This is based on the French notion of *la cuisine terroir,* the notion of *terroir* or territory also applies to wine and distinguishes the dishes and wines by the peculiar characteristics and history of the regions they come from. This notion of *terroir* has since spread from France and is now proudly proclaimed, for example, by artisan food makers in Britain.

When David's first book, *Mediterranean Food,* was published in 1950, it must have seemed like some exotic tale, mentioning places and ways of eating completely alien to the British public. Olive oil, hardly known outside pharmacies, was stated to be an integral cooking element and garlic also figured large, although it was practically impossible to obtain in most parts of Britain at the time.

Then there were vegetables such as *courgettes* (zucchini) and *aubergines* (eggplant) talked of as being commonplace, although they were as rare as gold dust in the Britain of the 1950s. Here she is writing about "the bright vegetables, the basil, the lemons, the apricots, the rice with lamb and currants and pine nuts, the ripe green figs, the white ewe's milk cheeses of Greece, the thick aromatic Turkish coffee, the herb-scented kebabs, the honey and yoghurt for breakfast, the rose-petal jam..." Not a single one of these foodstuffs, with the exception of lamb, was available or readily imaginable in Britain at the time she wrote about them.

David's books contained recipes but they were just part of a wider educational endeavor. She wanted readers to understand a great deal more about the context of the food and she was highly polemical in advancing strongly held opinions. Here is a marvelous example, drawn from *French Provincial Cooking*, first published in 1951. "Nobody has ever been able to find out why the English regard a glass of wine added to a soup or a stew as a reckless foreign extravagance and at the same time spend pounds on bottled sauces, gravy powders, soup cubes, ketchups and artificial flavorings. If every kitchen contained a bottle each of red wine, white wine, and inexpensive port for cooking, hundreds of store cupboards could be swept clean forever of the cluttering debris of commercial sauce bottles and synthetic aids to flavouring."

A number of obvious points need to be made here. First, wine was indeed a considerable extravagance for the average British cook at this time, whether it was a "reckless" extravagance is another question. Secondly, it is clear that David was only addressing a relatively small middle-class audience with this comment because the wider public was not even aware that wine could or should be used in cooking. Thirdly, comments on the use of wine for cooking have become irrelevant today because even in darkest Britain the influence of David and her followers has prevailed: practically everyone accepts that wine can go into food.

This book, which proved to be highly influential, also reminded readers that wonderful food did not have to be complicated. She enlists the support of the great chef Escoffier (Chapter 10) to remind readers to avoid "unnecessary complication and elaboration." She also reminds them that some of the most famous French dishes are hardly to be contemplated for commonplace eating but are reserved for feast days. And she brushes off one of the signature dishes of southern France, the bouillabaisse, saying "I would not myself think it a great deprivation if I were told that I could never again eat a bouillabaisse."

David not had only a seminal influence on the way that British people ate, an influence incidentally that extended to the United States, but she also persuaded a whole generation that their kitchens could become the center of the home, not some hidden away place designated for food production. She saw the large kitchen table as the centerpiece, surrounded by open shelves bearing decorated pots and pans, bowls of fruit and vegetables, wine racks, books and, a place to rest her endless supply of, oh yes, cigarettes, publicly frowned upon these days but still heavily consumed by professional chefs. In fact, as we shall see, her influence on kitchens was extended in 1965 when she started a kitchen shop in Chelsea that became a place of homage for her followers.

David's life, particularly her early life, was full of drama but she most certainly would not have been happy for it to be openly discussed. As far as she was concerned her books contained everything that anyone needed to know about her. However, there are two biographies and a TV drama called *A Life in Recipes* which would certainly have made her squirm. Nevertheless, one of the biographies, *Writing at the Kitchen Table,* by Artemis Cooper, was authorized by David.

Born in 1913, shortly before the First World War, David came from an upper middle-class family who lived in a manor house in the Sussex Downs. Her father, Rupert Gwynne was a Conservative Member of Parliament. She had three sisters, she was the second oldest, they had a governess and were sent to boarding school, following a well-trodden path for people of their class. Also, rather typically of the period, the family had little interest in food although they had the means to eat well.

So the young Elizabeth had no motivation to pay much attention to culinary matters. However, at the age of 17 she was sent to Paris to study French literature and painting. After two years, she went on to Munich to study German, she was also introduced to further travel by visiting her older sister who lived in Malta. This made her an unusually well-traveled and well-educated young woman in an age when most members of her sex, class and age were supposed to be focusing on the sole task of finding a husband.

It was in Paris that David discovered food when she lodged with the Robertot family. "Their food was lovely without being rich or grand," she later recalled. Her main memory, as she elegantly put it, was of "soups, delicately colored like summer dresses, coral, ivory or pale green, a salad of rice and tomatoes."

The young Elizabeth was particularly impressed by Denise, the daughter of the family. She described her as "the greediest girl I had ever seen. She worked as secretary to a world-famous Parisian surgeon and came home every day to the midday meal ... Munching through two helpings of everything, she would entertain us to gruesome details of the operations performed by her employer."

At the age of 19, she was given her first cookery book, *The Gentle Art of Cookery* by Hilda Leyel, a warm evocation of food in the eastern Mediterranean and Arab world. David said, "If I had been given a standard Mrs Beeton instead of Mrs Leyel's wonderful recipes, I would probably never have learned to cook." She was an unusually independent young woman. At first she thought she would like to be a painter but then turned to the theatre and found work at the Regent's Park Open Theatre. Here she started living on her own in an apartment where not only did she have to cook for herself but also started cooking for friends. Her trips to Malta provided an escape from drab London. "In those days," she wrote, "food was remarkably cheap in Malta, drink was untaxed and entertaining was easy, and immense fun."

Her life was punctuated by a number of love affairs that culminated, when she was 25, in a more serious affair with Charles Gibson Cowan, a married man with a dubious reputation. In 1939, with exquisite bad timing, they decided to buy a small boat and head for the Mediterranean via the French waterways. The Second World War was brewing but they had other things on their minds. All went well until they got to Italy where the boat was impounded as their arrival coincided with Italy's declaration of war on Britain. The hapless couple were suspected of being spies and deported to

Greece, ending up in the Greek island of Syros where they fell in with a bohemian expatriate community including luminaries such as the writers Lawrence Durrell and Norman Douglas.

The Nazis then invaded Greece and they were on the move again, this time to Crete, a temporary refuge before escaping to Cairo, the capital of Egypt. In Cairo, David joined the war effort by working for the Ministry of Information's reference library and quickly found herself comfortable in the midst of an eclectic and creative expatriate community where she was taken under the wing of Norman Douglas, wonderfully described as "a gamey old libertine who had decamped to Europe after allegedly molesting an under-age boy."

He too had an interest in food. In Cairo, the charms of her lover quickly faded and she dumped Cowan. Very quickly afterwards she entered into a marriage of convenience with Anthony (generally known as Tony) David, an Indian cavalry officer. A Lieutenant Colonel, he was posted to India eight months after they married. His new wife was pleased to see him go and that was the end of the marriage, although she kept his name.

When the war ended, David went back to Britain and was depressed by the drabness she found on her return. From London she hooked up with an old flame George Lassalle, and went to live in a hotel in Ross-on-Wye. It was sheer misery. There was an extreme winter in 1946–47, food was rationed, floods engulfed the land and she was becalmed in a hotel serving really dire food.

Writing about this David said, "I started to work out an agonized craving for the sun and a furious revolt against that terrible, cheerless, heartless food by writing down descriptions of Mediterranean and Middle Eastern cooking… words like apricot, olives and butter, rice and lemons, oil and almonds… Later I came to realize that in the England of 1947, those were dirty words."

David started to put her thoughts down on paper, encouraged by Lassalle. This became the basis for her first book, *Mediterranean Food*. Before the book was published she dipped her toe in the world of food writing by getting magazines to take some of her pieces. In 1949, the publisher John Lehmann gave her a one hundred pound advance for a work then titled *A Book of Mediterranean Food*. Jill Norman, her editor, wrote after her death that this book "was completely different to anything that had gone before. Not only did it describe little known ingredients and aromatic dishes, but its style was quite new. I, like so many others, was drawn to the grace of her writing and the ease with which she evoked markets and restaurants, or described the forms and textures of food." It was published the following year.

Although she had a minor stroke, the 1950s were an extremely productive time for David. She completed five books and wrote extensively about food and travel for *Vogue* magazine. David's book writing productivity slowed considerably in the following decades. Her first books were distinctive looking and carried memorable illustrations by John Minton. It later turned out, when her private papers were collected, that she hated these drawings. In a private letter she wrote: "I have to tell you that really I never did care very much for the John Minton illustrations for my books. They are so cluttered and messy. They embarrass me now as much as they did in 1950."

This is ungracious to say the least but she did not publicize her views. Later, she had what appears to be a happier relationship with the food photographer Anthony Denny, displaying the food as it was served in contrast to the highly stylized studio photographs, which were popular at the time.

French Provincial Cooking, published in 1960, is considered by many to be her finest work. It is a tour de force in a number of ways and confirmed David's depth of knowledge about the subject and a knack of making her enthusiasm contagious. There are also collections of her journalistic work such as *An Omelette and a Glass of Wine,* which give a better idea of her range of food interests, although these were largely confined to the food of the Mediterranean.

In later life, her interests were more scholarly and she started to study the food of her own country. One remarkable product of this interest was *Spices, Salt and Aromatics in the English Kitchen,* followed by *English Bread and Yeast Cookery,* first published in 1977. Her last book, published posthumously, was *Harvest of the Cold Months,* a work of considerable scholarship about food made with ice.

In 1963, when she was 49, David had a cerebral hemorrhage. This was a serious blow because although she recovered, her sense of taste and libido were irreparably damaged. Two years later, David opened the Elizabeth David Cookshop in London. It was an immediate success and she introduced French cookware to Britain where it has since become far more popular. However, David fell out with her partners and the shop was sold to another retailer in 1973 and then developed into a small chain.

By the end of the 1960s, David remained a revered figure in the British food world but her prominence declined with the rise of television food shows and the emergence of celebrity chefs. Nevertheless among serious food devotees, David's influence loomed large. In 1979, she was the a patron of Alan Davidson's publication *Petits Propos Culinaires,* which in turn launched the first Oxford Symposium on Food two years later.

Official recognition came first in the shape of the Order of the British Empire award in 1977, followed by her appointment as a Chevalier du Ordre Mérite Agricole from France and later, in 1986, she was made a Commander of the British Empire. Strangely, she only won a single food writers award but in 1982 was made a Fellow of the Royal Society of Literature, an honor that probably pleased her more than others.

Elizabeth David died in 1992. A *Daily Telegraph* obituary noted that "Mrs David's cookery books have earned their place on kitchen shelves from the Outer Hebrides to Tasmania. They had immediate universal appeal, both as kitchen manuals that became thumbed and sauce-spattered with use and for their incisive prose."'.

Across the Atlantic, the *New York Times* joined the fulsome tributes, quoting the American chef Alice Waters (Chapter 20), who said David "was her greatest inspiration." "When I go back and read her books now," Ms. Waters said, "I feel I plagiarized them. All of it seeped in so much, it's embarrassing to read them now."

David Recipes

The following recipes are selected to show, in the first example, how a dish prepared in many homes can be made more sophisticated. The second example, David's omelette recipes shows she was quite capable of also suggesting simple but satisfying dishes and the third example is included with the explanation she supplied. It demonstrates how David lifted the composition of recipes from the level of mere technicality into an area where context and understanding of how the recipe came about provides understanding as well as guidance.

Spaghetti Bolognese

Serves 6

Ingredients
225 grams (8oz.) lean minced beef
115 grams (4oz.) chicken livers
85 grams (3oz.) uncooked ham (both fat and lean)
1 carrot
1 onion
1 small piece of celery
3 teaspoons concentrated tomato puree
1 glass white wine
2 wine glasses stock or water
butter
salt and pepper
nutmeg

Cut the bacon or ham into very small pieces and brown them gently in a small saucepan in about 15 grams (½ oz.) of butter. Add the onion, the carrot, and the celery, all finely chopped. When they have browned, put in the raw minced beef, and then turn it over and over so that it all browns evenly. Add the chopped chicken livers, and after two or three minutes the tomato puree, and then the white wine. Season with salt (taking into account the relative saltiness of the ham or bacon), pepper, and a scraping of nutmeg, and add the meat stock or water.

Cover the pan and simmer the sauce very gently for 30–40 minutes. Some cooks in Bologna add a cupful of cream or milk to the sauce, which makes it smoother. Another traditional variation is the addition of the ovarine or unlaid eggs which are found inside the hen, especially in the spring when the hens are laying. They are added at the same time as the chicken livers and form small golden globules when the sauce is finished. When the ragu is to be served with spaghetti or tagliatelle, mix it with the hot pasta in a heated dish so that the pasta is thoroughly impregnated with the sauce, and add a generous piece of butter before serving. Hand the grated cheese round separately.

From: *Italian Food, Penguin Classics, 1999* – with an introduction by Julia Child

Omelettes

As everybody knows, there is only one infallible recipe for the perfect omelette: your own. But to anyone still in the experimental stage I submit the few following points, which I fancy are often responsible for failure when that ancient iron omelette pan, for 20 years untouched by water, is brought out of the cupboard.

First, the eggs are very often beaten too savagely. In fact, they should not really be beaten at all, but stirred, and a few firm turns with two forks do the trick. Secondly, the simplicity and freshness evoked by the delicious word "omelette" will be achieved only if it is remembered that it is the eggs which are the essential part of the dish; the filling, being of secondary importance, should be in very small proportion to the eggs. Lying lightly in the centre of the finished omelette, rather than bursting exuberantly out of the seams, it should supply the second of two different tastes and textures; the pure egg and cooked butter taste of the outside and ends of the omelette, then the soft, slightly runny interior, with its second flavoring of cheese or ham, mushrooms or fresh herbs.

As far as the pan is concerned, a 25-cm. (10-inch) omelette pan will make an omelette of three or four eggs. Beat them only immediately before you make the omelette, lightly as described above, with two forks, adding a light mild seasoning of salt and pepper. Allow about 15 grams (½ oz.) of butter. Warm your pan, don't make it red hot. Then turn the burner as high as it will go. Put in the butter and when it has melted and is on the point of turning color, pour in the eggs.

Add the filling, and see that it is well embedded in the eggs. Tip the pan towards you and with a fork or spatula gather up a little of the mixture from the far side. Now tip the pan away from you so that the unset eggs run into the space you have made for them.

When a little of the unset part remains on the surface, the omelette is done. Fold it in three with your fork or palette knife, hold the pan at an angle and slip the omelette out on to the waiting dish. This should be warmed, but only a little, or the omelette will go on cooking.

An omelette is nothing to make a fuss about. The chief mistakes are putting in too much of the filling and making this too elaborate. Such rich things as foie gras or lobster in cream sauce are inappropriate. In fact, moderation in every aspect is the best advice where omelettes are concerned. Sauces and other trimmings are superfluous, a little extra butter melted in the warm omelette dish or placed on top of the omelette as you serve it being the only addition which is not out of place.

Omelette with herbs
Prepare one tablespoon of mixed finely chopped parsley, tarragon, chives and, if possible, chervil. Mix half of this, with salt and pepper, in the bowl with the eggs, and the other half when the eggs are in the pan. If you like, put a little knob of butter on top of the omelette as it is brought to the table.

Tomato omelette
One tomato, skinned and chopped small, cooked hardly more than a minute in butter, with salt and pepper, is added to the eggs already in the pan.

Bacon omelette
Add a tablespoon of finely chopped bacon softened a minute or so in its own fat, to the eggs already in the pan; take care not to salt the eggs too much. Enough for one person.

From *At Elizabeth David's Table* by Elizabeth David, Ecco, 2011

Chicken with Tarragon

The French housewife mixes chopped fresh pork or pure pork sausagemeat with eggs and herbs to stuff a big fat fowl. She poaches it with vegetables and a bouquet of herbs and the result is that poule au pot which good King Henry of Navarre wished that all his subjects might eat on every Sunday of the year. Or perhaps that same housewife will cook her chicken without a stuffing and serve it with a dish of rice and a cream sauce; or if it is a plump young bird, she will roast it simply in butter and serve it on the familiar long oval dish with a tuft of watercress at each end and the buttery juices in a separate sauce-boat. The farmer's wife, faced with an old hen no longer of use for laying, will (if she has inherited her grandmother's recipes and has a proper sense of the fitness of things) bone the bird, stuff it richly with pork and veal and even, perhaps, truffles if it is for a special occasion, and simmer the bird with wine and a calf's foot to make a clear and savory jelly, so that the old hen will be turned into a fine and handsome galantine fit for celebrations and feast days.

Serves 4

Ingredients
1 kilogram (2.2lb.) chicken
30 grams (1oz.) butter
1 tablespoon tarragon leaves
half a clove of garlic, chopped
brandy
thick cream (optional)

Method
For a plump roasting chicken, knead the butter with the tarragon leaves, half a clove of chopped garlic, salt and pepper. Put this inside the bird, which should be well coated with olive oil. Roast the bird lying on its side on a grid in a baking dish. Turn it over at half-time (45 minutes altogether in a pretty hot oven at 200°C/400°F/gas

mark 6 or an hour in a moderate oven at 180°C/350°F/gas mark 4 should be sufficient); those who have a roomy grill might try grilling it, which takes about 20 minutes, and gives much more the impression of a spit-roasted bird, but it must be constantly watched and turned over very carefully, so that the legs are as well done as the breast.

When the bird is cooked, heat a small glass of brandy in a soup ladle, set light to it, pour it flaming over the chicken and rotate the dish so that the flames spread and continue to burn as long as possible. Return the bird to a low oven at 150°C/300°F/gas mark 2 for five minutes, during which time the brandy sauce will mature and lose its raw flavor. At this moment you can, if you like, enrich the sauce with a few spoonfuls of thick cream and, from where the recipe originally came (at la Mère Michel's Paris restaurant), they add Madeira to the sauce. Good though this is, it seems to me a needless complication.

From *At Elizabeth David's Table* by Elizabeth David, Ecco, 2011

Chapter 9

The Master

Georges Auguste Escoffier

The diminutive George Auguste Escoffier, who generally eschewed his first name, was born in 1846. He was arguably the most influential chef of the late nineteenth century, reaching the zenith of his career in the early twentieth century when he was lauded by the seminal *Larousse Gastronomique* as the finest chef in history; the "king of chefs, chef of kings," titles that were earlier bestowed on Antonin Carême (Chapter 6) and with equal reason.

Escoffier did a great deal to build on Carême's pioneering work and is rightly regarded as one of the masters of haute cuisine, which is recognized as the complex and rich cuisine mainly seen in upmarket French restaurants. However, one of his great aims was to simplify these dishes and produce recipes which could be followed in home kitchens.

Escoffier is credited with creating a staggering 10,000 recipes in his lifetime. In true Gallic manner he was not modest about his recipes. In the introduction to the *Complete Guide To The Art of Modern Cookery* he wrote: "In the course of more than forty years' experience as a chef, I have been responsible for thousands of menus, some of which have since become classical and have ranked among the finest served in modern times; and I can safely say, that in spite of the familiarity such a period of time ought to give one with the work, the setting-up of a presentable menu is rarely accomplished without lengthy labor and much thought, and for all that the result is not always to my satisfaction."

Not only was he a perfectionist; he was also somewhat dismissive of demands for novelty, stressing that although the desire for the novel in food "is imperiously demanded by everyone," reality dictates that "the number of alimentary substances is comparatively small, the number of their combinations is not infinite, and the amount of raw material placed either by art or by nature at the disposal of a cook does not grow in proportion to the whims of the public." In other words: be realistic about the limitations of new creations.

Escoffier insisted on obeying and creating the basic rules of dish preparation, starting with his classification system for "mother sauces" or stocks from which work on the rest of the dish was based. In his book, *Fonds de Cuisine,* he wrote: "Notwithstanding the fact that it is the usual procedure, in culinary matters, to insist upon the importance of the part played by stock, I feel compelled to refer to it at the outset of this work, and to lay even further stress upon what has already been written on the subject. Indeed, stock is everything in cooking, at least in French cooking. Without it, nothing can be done. If one's stock is good, what remains of the work is easy; if, on the other hand, it is bad or merely mediocre, it is quite hopeless to expect anything approaching a satisfactory result."

Escoffier's best known books started with *Le Guide Culinaire,* published in 1903, which has become a bible in professional kitchens. Three decades later in 1934, he published *Ma Cuisine*, a work for amateur chefs that became equally influential. But Escoffier's achievements do not end there; he literally revolutionized the organization of professional kitchens and food service in a manner that is now taken for granted. The *a la carte* menu, for example, is an Escoffier creation and he was the chef who finally laid to rest the classic French style of serving dishes together in a kind of buffet style. He favored the *a la Russe* (or Russian) method of service which had in fact been introduced into Western Europe a century earlier but was slow to catch on. The Russian method imposed a system of serving dishes in order so that the table was not crowded with an assembly of dishes that could not possibly be eaten at their best temperature and did not necessarily match each other.

Moreover, Escoffier became known for his insistence on instituting more humane work conditions in his kitchens, greatly improving the lives of a class of employees who, in his time, had lowly status and were often abused. Central to this was organizing the kitchen into brigades, known as *chefs de parties.*

Before his time, kitchens were crowded with chefs preparing entire dishes on their own or in small teams. This involved considerable duplication of effort and slow delivery of food. Escoffier realized that this work could be streamlined if chefs specialized in various aspects of food production ensuring that the various components of a single dish were made by specialist chefs with a precise knowledge of their ingredients. This new form of teamwork produced better food at greater speed.

The process ended with a chef responsible for final assembly and presentation, a matter Escoffier considered being of the utmost importance. He was a micromanager of presentation, paying close attention not just to the outlook of the food but also the crockery, cutlery, glassware, and table settings. Back in the kitchen, he was also involved in the improved design of cooking utensils. As a by-product of this work, he introduced the common frying pan to British kitchens.

Having grown up in kitchens he was well aware of the low status of their employees and the harsh working conditions. These conditions took, and continue to take, a heavy toll on the health of chefs who often resort to large amounts of alcohol to relieve the strain. Escoffier enlisted the help of a doctor to devise a healthy barley-based drink that was provided for all the chefs working in his kitchens and was part of an attempt to encourage the staff not to consume alcohol. He never drank alcohol, nor, unlike many of his counterparts, did he smoke, fearing it would interfere with his taste buds.

Head chefs could be brutal with their underlings, more accustomed to shouting than talking to them. Swearing was commonplace and a culture of barely disguised bullying of junior staff was widely tolerated. However, Escoffier banned swearing from his kitchens, exercised steely self-control and rarely lost his temper while working. Along with the controls on the behavior of his chefs came an insistence on cleanliness and encouragement to be well-dressed and well-behaved citizens both inside and outside the kitchen. Younger staff were encouraged to acquire better food knowledge and embark on training and were given opportunities to do so.

Escoffier was an opportunist in the best sense of the word, using his fame and that of the big personalities of his day to promote dishes and restaurants which became intensely fashionable. Like many great chefs, he had a limited academic education but experienced rigorous training on the job.

Born in 1846 in the small village of Villeneuve-Loubet, near Nice, Provence, he was the son of a blacksmith. More important perhaps, was his grandmother who gave him an early introduction to cooking, passing on her considerable enthusiasm.

By the age of 12, he left school and at 13 began work in his uncle's Le Restaurant Françaises in Nice. At school he showed an aptitude for art but the pragmatic Escoffier family thought it better that he should learn a trade with firm prospects of employment. Working for his uncle was not a soft option, he started at the bottom and underwent a strenuous apprenticeship that had him scrubbing floors and scouring pots before being allowed to become a *commis saucier*, a junior sauce maker. He also attended night school; Escoffier later said that this somewhat harsh apprenticeship gave him the solid foundations for his career.

By the age of 19, he was showing considerable aptitude as a chef and was moving up in the kitchen of his uncle's restaurant. At this point, he was given the opportunity to move to Paris and work in one of the French capital's most prestigious restaurants, Le Petit Moulin Rouge. He started as a sous chef and in the space of three years rose to become the head chef.

In 1870, the Franco-Prussian war began and young men of Escoffier's age were called up for military service. He had already taken leave from the restaurant to undergo military training but the army, displaying commonsense not always seen in military circles, realized that he could make a greater contribution to the war effort in the kitchens and he was appointed as Chef de Cuisine.

Here was an opportunity not just to experience the demands of mass catering but to study and develop techniques for food preservation and canning. This would ensure that the food could be transported to the battlefront with minimal need for preparation in the field. There does not seem to be a record of the outcome of Escoffier's work on the flavor front but he is recognized as a pioneer of the canning process (others are discussed in the following chapter).

At the end of the war, he returned to Le Petit Moulin Rouge and moved on to other notable restaurants in Paris. By 1871, he opened his own restaurant in Cannes called Le Faisan d'Or (The Golden Pheasant). However it was at Maison Chevet, at the Palais Royal hotel where he made his name for the presentation of spectacular banquets, many of which were for government occasions.

He moved from there to the equally fashionable Maison Maire. But it was in Switzerland that he was to establish the relationship which transformed his professional life when the Swiss hotelier Cesar Ritz appointed him to run the kitchens at the Hotel National in Lucerne. Ritz, a Swiss national, was a master hotelier and Escoffier the master of the kitchens; together they formed a formidable team.

From Switzerland, the pair moved to London in 1890 where they breathed new life into the Savoy Hotel over an eight-year period. Ritz was the hotel's general manager and Escoffier the head of restaurant services. It was at the Savoy that Escoffier created one of his most famous recipes: Peach Melba, in honor of the Australian singer Nellie Melba who lived at the hotel. Escoffier was an opera enthusiast and wanted to surprise the singing star with a culinary tribute appropriate to her art. Having watched her perform the Majestic Swan in *Lohengrin,* he devised a dish of peaches served on a bed of ice cream encased in a block of ice shaped as a swan. The dish was then covered in icing sugar topped with raspberry sauce.

The great chef was to repeat this opportunist mixing of celebrity with cuisine on a number of occasions. His famous frog's leg dish, Cuisses de Nymphe Aurore, for example was named after the Prince of Wales. It can therefore be said that he was a very early pioneer of the kind of dishes that celebrity chefs are famous for today.

However, Escoffier's residence at the Savoy ended in disgrace when both he and Ritz were dismissed over accusations concerning the disappearance of over £3,400 worth of wine and spirits and suspicion that Escoffier had taken bribes from the hotel's suppliers. Escoffier was mortified by this experience but Ritz lost no time in bouncing back and in 1898, he launched what in its day was the cutting-edge Hotel Ritz in Paris. The designer Coco Chanel was to make this her home for three decades. Ritz brought Escoffier back from London to join him. The Ritz quickly became a success, not least for its food. It also became the fashionable place for afternoon tea, a development that left Escoffier nonplussed. "How can one eat jam, cakes and pastries, and enjoy a dinner – the king of meals – an hour or two later?" he asked, "How can one appreciate the food, the cooking or the wines?"

Escoffier's stay at the Ritz was short and he returned again to the British capital to join the luxurious Carlton Hotel where he stayed for thirty years. Cesar Ritz also appears to have had a delayed reaction to the Savoy debacle as he suffered a nervous breakdown in 1901 and retired shortly afterwards. It was then Escoffier's turn to bounce back, making the Carlton kitchens world famous and embarking on a writing career that took off with his second book, the *Guide Culinaire,* which was followed by eight other major works.

An interesting footnote to Escoffier's time at the Carlton was his engagement of the Vietnamese revolutionary Ho Chi Minh as a pastry chef. Ho was then in exile in London before returning to his country to lead the overthrow of the French colonialists and subsequently to become president of a small nation that humbled the mighty United States in a prolonged war.

The Carlton allowed Escoffier to engage in other work which enhanced both his and the hotel's reputation. The German owned Hamburg-Amerika Lines invited him to create a restaurant service for its passengers in 1904. It was known as the Ritz-Carlton Restaurants. This too became the subject of legend when shortly before the start of the First World War the Kaiser Emperor William II journeyed on the liner Imperator and sampled Escoffier's food. It is widely believe that the Kaiser told him, "I am the Emperor of Germany, but you are the Emperor of chefs."

Escoffier presided over the Carlton's kitchens until 1919 when he was 73 and planning to retire with his wife to Monte Carlo. However these plans evaporated when he was offered a stake in the Hotel de L'Ermitage by the widow of Jean Giroix, a colleague at the Petit Moulin Rouge restaurant in Paris where he worked in his youth. If this were not enough he also developed another hotel, the Riviera, in Monte Carlo.

In 1920, he became the first chef to receive the Chevalier of the Legion d'Honneur, and then in 1928 was made an Officer of the Legion d'Honneur, the first chef to receive this award. Escoffier died in 1935 at the age of 89, only days after the death of his wife. A museum honoring his life's work was created in his birthplace at Villeneuve-Loubet.

Escoffier's name is synonymous with the notion of good food. Escoffier societies, devoted to fine dining, dot the globe in recognition of this simple fact. He would certainly have appreciated this because he craved recognition for his work and worked like a demon during his lifetime. The most lasting tribute to Escoffier is one seen literally every day as diners enter restaurants and pick up menus whose formats derive from the great chef, where service emulates his system and where recipes are derived from his influence. In other words, practically all aspects of modern day restaurant service retain the influence of Georges Auguste Escoffier.

Escoffier Recipes

Escoffier starts his litany of 'mother sauces' with the classic roux, the base for many dishes and a sauce that comes in three types: brown, pale and white. The recipe for a brown roux, used for dishes such as stews, is given below.

Brown Roux

Yields 1 pound (454g.)

Ingredients
8 ounces (225g.) clarified butter
9 ounces (250g.) best quality flour

Method
Mix the flour and butter in a very thick stew-pan, and put it on the side of the fire or in a moderate oven. Stir the mixture repeatedly so that the heat may be evenly distributed throughout the whole of its volume.

The time allowed for the cooking of brown roux cannot be precisely determined, as it depends upon the degree of heat employed. The more intense the latter, the speedier will be the cooking, while the stirring will of necessity be more rapid. Brown roux is known to be cooked when it has acquired a fine, light brown colour, and when it exudes a scent resembling that of the hazel-nut, characteristic of baked flour.

It is very important that brown roux should not be cooked too rapidly. As a matter of fact, among the various constituent elements of flour, the starch alone acts as the cohering principle.

This starch is contained in little cells, which tightly constrain it, but which are sufficiently porous to permit the percolation of liquid and fatty substances. Under the influence of moderate heat and the in-filtered butter, the cells burst through the swelling of the starch, and the latter thereupon completely combines with the butter to form a mass capable of absorbing six times its own weight of liquid when cooked.

When the cooking takes place with a very high initial heat the starch gets burned within its shriveled cells, and swelling is then possible only in those parts which have been least burned.

The cohering principle is thus destroyed, and double or treble the quantity of roux becomes necessary in order to obtain the required consistency. But this excess of roux in the sauce chokes it up without binding it, and prevents it from despumating or becoming clear. At the same time, the cellulose and the burnt starch lend a bitterness to the sauce of which no subsequent treatment can rid it.

From the above it follows that, starch being the only one from among the different constituents of flour which really affects the coherence of sauces, there would be considerable advantage in preparing roux either from a pure form of it, or from substances with kindred properties, such as fecula, arrowroot, etc. It is only habit that causes flour to be still used as the cohering element of roux, and, indeed, the hour is not so far distant when the advantages of the changes I propose will be better understood—changes which have been already recommended by Favre in his dictionary.

With a roux well made from the purest starch—in which case the volume of starch and butter would equal about half that of the flour and butter of the old method—and with strong and succulent brown stock, a Spanish sauce or Espagnole may be made in one hour. And this sauce will be clearer, more brilliant, and better than that of the old processes, which needed three days at least to despumate.

From: *The Escoffier Cookbook and Guide to the Fine Art of Cookery: For Connoisseurs, Chefs, Epicures Complete With 2973* Recipes by Georges Auguste Escoffier, Crown Publishers, Inc., 2000

Poulets Sautes or Sautéed Chicken

Modern recipe books provide readers with precise details of quantity, cooking times and things like oven temperatures. Escoffier and his contemporaries assumed a higher degree of food preparation knowledge and therefore excluded some of these details, focusing instead on the preparation method. Escoffier began with a generic explanation of how certain types of food should be prepared then gave a number of recipes that applied the general principles to specific dishes. The example given here is for sautéed chicken for which he recommended that the chickens should be "a la Reine," meaning of medium size, very fleshy, and tender. The original recipe follows:

The fowl which is to be *sautéed* should be cut up thus: after having emptied, singed, and thoroughly cleaned it; cut off its legs—quite a simple matter, since all that is necessary is the disjunction of the thigh-bones, after having cut the skin. Cut off the claws just below the joint of the tibia, and pare the spurs. Now cut the tibia above the joint, and remove the thigh-bone.

Cut the pinions at the first joint; remove the wings, after having cut round a portion of the breast in such wise that each wing holds one half of it; finally detach the centerpiece or breast-bone, which should be left whole if the fowl be small and cut into two if it be otherwise.

The carcass thus remains. Cut it into two, and trim each piece on both sides.

Before setting them to cook, moderately season the pieces of fowl with salt and pepper. Whatever the demands of a particular recipe may be, the preparatory principle of *sautéed* chickens is always as follows:

Take a sauté pan just large enough to hold the pieces of fowl, and heat therein two oz. of clarified butter; or, according to circumstances, half butter and half good oil. When the selected fat is quite hot, insert the pieces of fowl; let them colour quickly, and turn them over from time to time, that they may do so evenly. Now cover the utensil, and put it in a sufficiently hot oven to ensure the complete cooking of the fowl. Some tender pieces, such as the wings and the breast, should be withdrawn after a few minutes have elapsed, and kept warm; but the legs, the meat of which is firmer and thicker, should cook seven to eight minutes more at least.

When all the pieces are cooked, withdraw them; drain away their butter, and swill the sauté pan with the prescribed liquor, which is either some kind of wine, mushroom cooking-liquor, or chicken stock. This swilling forms, as I have already pointed out, an essential part of the procedure, inasmuch as its object is to dissolve those portions of solidified gravy which adhere to the bottom of the sauté pan.

Reduce the swilling-liquor to half, and add thereto the sauce given in the recipe. Put the pieces of carcass, the claws, the pinions and the legs into this sauce, and simmer for a few minutes. The other-pieces, *i.e.*, the wings and breast, are then added, but when the sauce is sufficiently reduced, it must stop boiling. When the pieces are completely cooked, it is obviously unnecessary for the sauce to boil, since the former would only be hardened thereby.
A few minutes before serving, put the pieces into a deep entree dish (fitted with a cover) in the following order:—The pieces of carcass, the claws and the pinions on the bottom of the dish, upon these the legs and the breast, and, last of all, the wings.

The sauce is then finished according to the directions of the recipe, and is poured over the pieces of fowl.

Some chickens are prepared without colouration—that is to say, the pieces are merely stiffened in butter without browning, and their cooking is completed in the oven as above. In this case the swilling-liquor is invariably white, as also the supplementary sauces, and the latter are finished with cream.

This method is then applied to a number of sautéed chicken dishes such as the following:

Poulet Sauté Archiduc

Fry the pieces of fowl without colouration, *i.e.*, merely stiffen them. Add four oz. of onions, previously cooked in butter, and complete the cooking of the onions and the fowl together.

Withdraw the pieces; dish them; cover the dish, and keep it hot. Moisten the onions with a small glassful of liqueur brandy; reduce the latter; add thereto one-sixth pint of cream and one-sixth pint of veloute, and rub through.

Reduce this sauce to a stiff consistence; finish it, away from the fire, with one and one-half ounce of butter, the juice of the quarter of a lemon, and a tablespoonful of Madeira, and pour it over the fowl.

Set about ten slices of truffle on the latter, and serve.

Desserts

Escoffier had an extensive dessert recipe list; alongside the classic French dishes he produced recipes for all the English classics from rolly polly pudding to rice pudding and Christmas pudding. One of his recipes, which remained popular and was once regarded as a sophisticated but simple dessert is for Jubilee Cherries, which appears below in its original form:

Jubilee Cherries

Stone some fine cherries; poach them in syrup, and set them in small silver timbales. Reduce the syrup and thicken it with a little arrowroot, diluted with cold water; allowing one table-spoonful of arrowroot per half-pint of syrup. Cover the cherries with the thickened syrup; pour a coffee-spoonful of heated Kirsch into each timbale, and set a light to each when serving.

From: *The Escoffier Cookbook and Guide to the Fine Art of Cookery: For Connoisseurs, Chefs, Epicures Complete With 2973* Recipes by Georges Auguste Escoffier, Crown Publishers, Inc., 2000

Peach Melba

This is based on the original Escoffier recipe created in honor of the singer Dame Nellie Melba but is presented in modern recipe form and serves 4 people.

Ingredients
3 cups (710ml.) water
½ cup (96g.) sugar
peel of 1 lemon, removed in strips
1 vanilla bean (pod), split lengthwise
½ cup (125ml.) plus 2 tablespoons peach schnapps
4 medium peaches, just shy of being perfectly ripe
vanilla ice cream
fresh mint sprigs, as garnish

For raspberry sauce (makes 1 cup; 250ml.):
2½ pints (1175ml.) fresh raspberries
½ cup (100g.) sugar
1 tablespoon fresh lemon juice

Method
To poach the peaches, place the water, sugar, lemon peel, and vanilla bean in a saucepan that's just large enough to hold the peaches with the liquid barely covering them. Bring the mixture to the boil over high heat, stirring to dissolve the sugar. Reduce the heat to low and add ½ cup (125ml.) of peach schnapps and the peaches. Cover the

pan and cook at a very low simmer until the peaches are tender when pierced with a small knife, 10–15 minutes, depending on the size of the peaches.

Remove the peaches from the poaching liquid with a slotted spoon and place them on a plate to cool. The peaches can be stored, covered, in the refrigerator for up to three days. Before serving, cut the fruit in half through the stem end and remove the pit. Carefully pull or peel off the skin and discard.

Remove the lemon peels and vanilla bean from the poaching liquid, discarding the peel and the vanilla bean. Then place the pan over a high heat and reduce the liquid to about ¾ cup (180ml.) to concentrate the flavors. Cool to room temperature then add the remaining 2 tablespoons of peach schnapps. Store the syrup, covered, in the refrigerator for up to 1 week.

For the raspberry sauce, rinse the berries and place them in a small saucepan with the sugar. Place the pan over medium heat and cook until the berries soften and begin to break apart, about 10 minutes. Force the mixture through a fine mesh sieve, discarding the seeds. Add the lemon juice to the sauce and refrigerate, covered, up to 3 days.

To assemble the dessert, place a scoop of ice cream in a bowl or large goblet. Top with 2 poached peach halves. Spoon some of the poaching syrup over the ice cream then drizzle raspberry sauce over the peaches. Garnish with mint sprigs, if you like. Serve immediately.

From: *The Escoffier Cookbook and Guide to the Fine Art of Cookery: For Connoisseurs, Chefs, Epicures Complete With 2973 Recipes* by Georges Auguste Escoffier, Crown Publishers, Inc., 2000

Chapter 10

The Man With a Can

Henry Heinz

$\mathcal{H}$enry John Heinz (1844 –1919) occupies a seminal place in the development of the food industry as an innovator and producer of preserved foods and sauces, equally famous for his company's canned and bottled products.

Heinz created a food manufacturing empire that now spans the world, has sales in excess of US$10 billion and employs some 32,500 people. His genius lies not in the invention of food preservatives but in marketing and giving universal appeal to products that have become an essential part of twentieth-century food consumption.

Well before Heinz was born, the preservation of food was a concern for people who were not sure whether their food supplies were sufficient to last beyond unpredictable harvests. They were also faced with problems of seasonal food availability and the limitations of transportation. Before modern preservation techniques were adopted, preservatives such as salt and brine alongside methods of storage involving leather and stoneware containers had been known and used for centuries.

What happened in the nineteenth century was that these processes were taken to a new level, literally transforming the dietary choices for millions of people who, for the first time, could eat products out of season and go on long journeys with a variety of food. These options would have been unthinkable before bottling and canning were introduced.

The twentieth century ushered in further revolutionary developments in food packaging and preservation. With the development of convenience food, it became possible to prepare a meal by simply opening a can, defrosting a semi-cooked vegetable or microwaving a ready-prepared dish.

Henry Heinz was one of the pioneers in this field and among those who realized the immense potential of the convenience foods market. Heinz also turned out to be the most internationally minded of American food manufacturers and spread his company's production and distribution network more extensively outside the United States than any of his predecessors. Indeed, in some countries, Heinz products became such a prominent fixture that many people purchasing the Heinz brand assumed that they were buying from a local producer and not an American conglomerate.

Henry Heinz first came into the food business in 1875 and soon realized that what people really wanted was variety. He also recognized that additives could transform their regular dishes from being mundane to exciting. Like all marketing geniuses, he not only understood what people wanted but was able to anticipate their desires.

As a result, he managed to create demand for food stuffs that customers had not even known they wanted beforehand. Today, the most famous Heinz product is tomato ketchup, which has a ubiquitous presence in just about every fast food establishment. Ketchup has demonstrated its versatility as an additive and a condiment beyond anything that Heinz himself could have imagined.

When Heinz entered the food business at the end of the nineteenth century, he quickly appreciated that it was a time of change in the food and drink industry. Tasty convenience foods were developing at a pace and the American appetite for these products was poised to explode. There was a proliferation of new products such as Coca-Cola (1886), which followed the development of the first potato chips in 1853 and chewing gum in the 1870s. Then there were the breakfast cereals developed in 1863 by James Caleb and taken to a new level by John Harvey Kellogg.

In 1869, a small company founded by Joseph Campbell and Abraham Anderson was busy turning out canned tomatoes and soups, among other food products. In 1876, that company became the Joseph A. Campbell Preserve Company, which later became the biggest rival to Heinz in the soup sector but less so in other areas where the two food behemoths are in competition. Although Campbell had a head start, Heinz soon caught up.

Before exploring Henry Heinz's contribution to the development of processed foods, let us quickly look at the origins of packaged and processed food because without the pioneering work of others, Heinz might have spent most of his life digging up vegetables in his mother's garden and searching for ways of preserving them, or maybe he would have taken over his father's brickmaking business, a more likely prospect since this is where he began his working life.

Nicolas Appert, a French confectioner, is credited with having found a method of preventing food spoilage by bottling. He discovered that all manner of foods could be preserved by putting them in airtight jars. Before bottling, the food was cooked and as much air as possible had to be removed from the jars that were sealed with corks secured by wires in the way champagne bottles are sealed today; below the seal was a mixture of cheese and lime. The bottles were then submersed in boiling water. Appert published a book detailing this process in 1810 and established a factory to produce preserved foods.

Bryan Dorkin in England worked on the same lines as Appert but came up with the idea of placing the cooked food in metal cans. While he was developing this product, and ended up becoming a naval supplier, two other entrepreneurs, Auguste de Heine and Peter Durand, took out patents for the manufacture of iron and tin containers for food canning.

So it seems that British companies came up with a method of storage that improved on Appert's idea which restricted packaging to glass, carrying attendant risks of breakage. Durand then established a factory in London to make canned food and by 1813 he too was supplying the navy.

What was not known at the time was that food spoilage was caused by microorganisms and it was the heating process that destroyed the bacteria. These pioneers got the result but did not understand the science of how it was achieved. This discovery was made by, among others, Louis Pasteur, who gave his name to the process of pasteurization.

Food canning did not arrive in the United States until 1819 but it had little impact until the Civil War was underway and there was demand for canned military food supplies. The United States was to eventually become the biggest player in this market but it was relatively slow getting there. Food canning was not cheap and its application was therefore limited.

The navy, for example, generally used canned food only for emergency supplies. There were also other problems caused by inadequate preparation of the food before it went into the cans, causing spoilage. Another problem concerned the quality of the cans which were crudely handmade and prone to rust.

Things began to change with the introduction of machine-made cans, first in the United States, then in Europe in the late 1860s. Americans took over the pioneering work of the Europeans and introduced products, such as condensed milk, to the range of foods available in cans. At the end of the century, researchers at the Massachusetts Institute of Technology found ways of improving the quality of canned and bottled food. The invention of the can opener also greatly enhanced the attractiveness of cans for household consumers.

It was not however until the 1960s that aluminum cans were introduced, greatly reducing the weight of canned food. A decade later, rip-off lids and pop-top lids came into being thus completing the circle of user-friendliness for canned products.

It was not until the 1880s that canned foods figured as a mainstream product. Hitherto there had been concerns over the taste and safety of food in cans and bottles made by industrial processes. Moreover, these industrially-packaged foods did not look attractive. Companies tended to use opaque green-colored bottles and the cans were crude in appearance. When Henry Heinz first got into the business with bottled, grated horseradish, one of the first things he did was to place the produce in clear glass bottles which made the food look more appetizing. He soon found that presentation was the key to sales and helped to design a variety of attractive bottles that caught the eye of customers in grocery stores.

Heinz, as his name suggests, was born to German immigrant parents who emigrated from Karlstad. He was one of eight children in a family that settled in Pittsburgh, Pennsylvania. The young Henry showed an interest in business and food at a remarkably young age. By the time he was six, he was helping his mother grow vegetables in the family's garden. At the age of eight, he had begun selling vegetables to neighbors, carting them around in a small basket. And when he was nine, he was growing, grinding, and bottling his own horseradish sauce for sale. He turned out to have a particular talent for grinding horseradish. His parents recognized his initiative and capability and at the age of ten, he was given his own piece of land; three quarters of an acre to grow vegetables. He soon graduated from a handbasket to a wheelbarrow for deliveries.

Two years later, he was cultivating a three and a half acre plot and using a horse and cart to deliver the produce to local grocery stores. By the age of seventeen, Heinz earned US$2,400 a year from this business, a most impressive sum at the time.

It may have seemed obvious that the Heinz family had a budding entrepreneur in its midst but his staunchly Protestant parents thought he would be better suited to a life in the church and so, at 14 years of age, he was sent to the Allegheny Seminary.

The church may have occupied his thoughts during school hours but it did not stop young Henry (called Harry by his family) from pursuing his business sideline. Eventually his parents had to concede that Henry was not destined for the ministry and he enrolled in bookkeeping classes at Duff's Business College in Pittsburgh. From there, he went to work in his father's brick making business and, at the age of 21, had acquired enough money to buy himself in as a partner, while maintaining the vegetable business as a sideline.

Some four years after working with his father, Henry Heinz decided that what he really wanted was a business of his own and that it had to be horseradish bottling. The business quickly gathered steam and in 1869, Henry felt he had achieved a position of sufficient financial stability to start a family. He married Sarah Sloan Young, a daughter of Irish immigrants. They went on to have five children. One died shortly after birth and two of the other sons joined their father's business. Sarah Heinz, as she became, died in 1894 after suffering from pneumonia. Her death marked the end of a 25-year long marriage.

The year of his marriage was also the year in which the Heinz, Noble & Company was formed. Heinz was 25 years old and keen to expand his operations. He teamed up with L. Clarence Noble, son of a wealthy Pittsburg family, which provided much of the capital required to expand the business. Heinz added to his successful pickled horseradish by developing celery sauce and pickle and a variety of other products that were launched under the Anchor brand. The new company declared that its pickled foods and other bottled produce were "pure and superior". Heinz assumed the role of chief salesman in Pittsburgh and was the food processing manager. Noble and his brother focused on sales in Woodstock, Illinois and St Louis and dealt with the finances. The business grew rapidly and a vinegar plant was built in St Louis and a warehouse established in Chicago.

By 1875, the company was making 15,000 barrels of pickles a year. It devised its own equipment and seemed destined to go from strength to strength. However in the wider economy, storm clouds were gathering. A panic gripped the financial system after the 1873 failure of Cooke & Co, one of America's biggest banks. Heinz's company was not immediately affected but two years later the virus of failure spread to the Heinz, Noble & Company. The horseradish harvest of 1875 was overwhelming and consequently the price plummeted. Unfortunately, the company had made forward commitments to buy at prices that prevailed before the harvest. The business was therefore committed to paying far more for its raw materials than the selling price of the finished product. Other raw material prices also began to tumble and the company was forced into bankruptcy. By 1877, the game was over.

However, Heinz was not a man to accept defeat and he mobilized his family's financial resources to get back into business. Heinz is one of many highly successful entrepreneurs who have suffered setbacks of this kind, learned from them and sprung back. Roy Kroc (Chapter 11), for example, did not actually go bankrupt but before buying into McDonald's; he was looking at a failing business. Those who succeed learn from failure rather than succumbing to depression.

As an undischarged bankrupt, Heinz could not set up his own company but joined his cousin Frederick and brother John to found F & J Heinz. The company expanded and Heinz embarked on a program of overseas sales, contacting relatives in Germany and managing to get his goods accepted by Fortnum & Mason, London's premier food shop. A British representative office was opened in 1896, the first outside the United States, followed by a British factory in 1905. Before all this however, in 1888, Heinz managed to pay off his debts and transformed the company by buying out his relatives and re-establishing it under his own name: the H.J. Heinz Company.

The factory, which remains at the heart of the company, on the North Shore in Pittsburgh, began construction in 1890 and was completed by 1898. Many other convenience food factories were built around this time but Heinz's genius lay in marketing. He rapidly became known as the Pickle King with a reputation for making good pickles as well as ketchup, mustard and vinegar.

Heinz had a seemingly endless enthusiasm for promotional ideas. In 1900, he ordered the erection of the largest electric advertising hoarding in New York, consisting of 1,200 lights illuminating a 40-foot-long green pickle. He also made sure that delivery vehicles advertised his products and obtained 200 black matching horses to make deliveries.

In another publicity coup, he introduced the famous "pickle pin" at the Chicago World's Fair in 1893. A million pins were given away and they became collector's items in tribute to their enormous popularity. And it was Heinz who came up with the now widely adopted idea of a factory tour to promote the company, allowing as many people as possible to observe the production processes.

Heinz understood both packaging and branding. His goods were easily distinguishable on the shelves of grocery stores. In 1896, he came up with the branding slogan of "Heinz 57 Varieties." This strange but highly effective marketing tool is still employed today although it is even less accurate than it was when Heinz introduced it as his company was already producing more than 60 varieties of products. There are many explanations for this slogan but the most likely seems to be that he got the idea from visiting a New York City shoe store that was advertising "21 Styles" for sale and he liked the numerical way of presenting his goods. But why the number 57? He later explained that he liked the sound of 7 because of the "psychological influence of that figure and of its enduring significance to people of all ages." As for the number 5, no satisfactory explanation has been given as to why this was chosen but Heinz ascribed an almost mystical significance to the figure of 57 and the public also seemed to like it.

It would be wrong to ascribe the success of the company purely to marketing because Heinz also understood the manufacturing process and realized that processed foods did not need excessive or, in many cases, any coloring or preservatives. He appalled many of his counterparts in the food manufacturing industry by becoming an enthusiastic supporter of the 1906 Pure Food and Drug Act, which laid down production standards many believed to be unrealistic and unnecessarily costly. Heinz took a different view and practiced what he preached when it came to hygienic production, indeed his company's own food hygiene manual became a standard for the industry.

Heinz was also very much in the tradition of paternalistic employers. His factories were known for their good conditions and workers were provided with a variety of free services including medical care, sports facilities and educational classes. A leading trade unionist, Harry W. Sherman, grand secretary of the National Brotherhood of Electrical Workers of America, remarked after visiting a Heinz plant that it was "a utopia for working men."

Heinz also had a good reputation for relations with both his suppliers and customers. One of his favorite maxims was, "Deal with the seller so justly that he will want to sell to you again." In modern day management speak, all this made H.J. Heinz an "ethical company." And it worked. As the company grew, its founder became very wealthy indeed with all the trappings of wealth that included the big mansion and major donations to places of learning that bear his name. In her famous autobiography, Edith Warton was to describe Heinz as one of the "Lords of Pittsburgh," along with Henry Clay Frick and Andrew Carnegie.

The company's most successful product was its tomato ketchup, which, during Heinz's lifetime, secured over half of the world market for this sauce. It remains as the company's iconic product and notches up worldwide sales of 650 million bottles per year. Tomatoes figure large in other products and Heinz became the world's largest tomato processor. Heinz initiated the international expansion of the company, which is now located in every inhabited continent of the world and is a market leader in many of these locations.

Today it operates in 200 countries and territories and manufactures some 6,000 varieties, of which the company claims 150 brands that occupy either the number one or two sales slot in more than 50 countries. Heinz has expanded well beyond canned goods and by a process of acquisition and internal development moved into frozen foods, dry goods and baby foods. Heinz also has health food lines, including the Weight Watchers line, which was sold in 1999.

Henry Heinz died at the age of 74 in 1919. At the time of his death, the company employed 6,500 workers and had 25 factories. His successor was his son Howard who saw the company through the Great Depression of the 1930s, largely by diversifying into baby foods and ready-to-eat soups. Howard Heinz was succeeded by his son Jack who proved to be an adept businessman and took the company public in 1946.

It was not until 1969 that a non-family member took over the reins of the company when R. Burt Gookin was appointed as its chief executive officer, while Jack Heinz remained as chairman until his death in 1987. It was at this point that the company had its first non-American chairman, Anthony or Tony O'Reilly, an Irishman. There is no longer anyone called Heinz sitting on the company's board of directors.

H.J. Heinz is perhaps not quite as dominant in the food industry as it once was but it remains one of the world's most important food manufacturers and is distinctive in many ways. Henry Heinz died in Pittsburgh in 1919 but his shadow still looms and his influence on the development of food surpasses that of any other single food manufacturer.

Chapter 11

The World's Most
Successful Restaurateur

Raymond
'Ray' Kroc

$\mathcal{R}$ay or Raymond Arnold Kroc (1902 –1984), to give him his full name, transformed the McDonald's fast food chain into a world-beating behemoth so widely recognized that its golden arches logo is almost as well-known as the Christian cross. But does this make Kroc a food guru?

The answer lies in turning the question around and asking how it is possible to ignore the work of a man who has probably done more than anyone else to influence global eating habits and methods of restaurant food production. It is perfectly possible to criticize the product of his work and critics are not at all hard to find, including Carlo Petrini (Chapter 16) whose anger over the establishment of a McDonald's branch in Rome sparked the creation of the Slow Food Movement.

It has been frequently stated that Kroc's genius lay in applying to the food industry the kind of production techniques which Henry Ford used to transform the automotive industry. Kroc liked to proclaim that he "put the hamburger on the assembly line." This claim is open to question because the founders of America's fast food business were Walter Anderson and Edgar Waldo "Billy" Ingram, who created the White Castle hamburger business in 1921 and established a widely copied prototype that set the standard for the fast food industry. Although their business was highly successful, its growth was constrained by an unwillingness to take on debt or to expand through franchising.

Kroc was first and foremost a hard-selling businessman and secondly, a master of production techniques. It was this combination of skills that made McDonald's the world-beating company it is today, while White Castle remained a strictly domestic player in the US.

The simple facts of the matter are that Kroc was neither an innovator nor even the founder of the company with which his name is now indelibly linked. He was, in the best possible sense of the word, an inspired opportunist. Kroc saw opportunities that the pioneers of the fast food business failed to recognize and he had the determination to turn these opportunities into reality.

Although Kroc had no training in food science, he applied himself with vigor to the issues that needed to be tackled to create a business that would produce an entirely standard and consistent food product that could be made anywhere from Alaska to Ankara. "There is a science to making and serving a hamburger," said Kroc. The beef patties, the heart of the hamburger, were made to precise specifications which meant that the standard patty weighed 1.6 ounces, 3.875 inches in diameter, with a fat content below 19 percent.

Kroc went on to build a factory laboratory in suburban Chicago, which devised what he saw as the perfect fried potato, a spindly, mildly deep fried product shoveled into cone-shaped cardboard containers leaving remarkably little grease residue.

Aside from the food production techniques, there were also strict service standards which meant that any customer who did not receive their orders within five minutes had their money refunded. Kroc was also relentless in insisting on cleanliness, making unannounced visits to outlets where the first thing he did was to check the standards of hygiene from the washrooms to the kitchen floors to staff uniforms. He instructed staff that if they had "time to lean, you have time to clean."

Kroc was convinced that customers would not return to a dirty restaurant, an obvious point and one now widely emphasized in the manuals that govern most fast food operations. Kroc's own operation manual ran to 75 pages.

Today, as in his day, there is a standard product that looks, and many say tastes, as if it had emerged from a production line of the type that can output any standardized product. This is the focus of the repulsion many food lovers have for McDonald's. There is no need to dwell on the question of whether this is good food but it is worth asking what the millions of people who consume a McDonald's hamburger every day of the week would be eating if not a Big Mac or some other product from this outlet? It is safe to assume that the alternative would not be particularly nutritious either and may not be available at the astonishingly cheap prices offered in the McDonald's outlets.

Once a comprehensive system for running a standardized restaurant is in place, the obvious way to expand the business is through franchising. Again, this was not a Kroc idea but he became one of the world's leading experts on the subject. In fact, franchising in America began in the 1850s with the Singer Sewing Machine Company selling franchises for the sale of its machines. Franchising spread to the fast food industry following the Second World War, notably via Dunkin' Donuts, which in the 1950s, was the most successful fast food franchise.

Ray Kroc understood how this worked seemingly better than the innovators. He never claimed to have been a franchising innovator, nor to have invented the hamburger for that matter, but insisted that he "just took it more seriously than anyone else." In fact, Kroc did not even invent McDonald's, which as the name suggests, was created by the brothers Maurice and Richard McDonald. The brothers who left New Hampshire in 1930 was mesmerized by the lure of Hollywood. However, show business did not work for them but they were successful in establishing a simple drive-in restaurant in San Bernardino, 55 miles east of Los Angeles.

Their restaurant catered to the needs of suburban Americans who were looking forward to the prosperity and changed circumstances which emerged in the wake of the Second World War. This was a generation seeking instant gratification and convenience in all things, food most definitely included. Ray Kroc understood that Americans did not necessarily wish to eat at home and would willingly go out if they could afford to do so. They weren't looking for fancy and formal restaurants but simple eating places with low prices, fast service and a casual atmosphere.

What this generation wanted most was what their parents did not have. Yet their parents also wanted new experiences and new ways of doing things. Fast food was already established as a phenomenon. A&W, Dairy Queen, Tastee Freez and Big Boy were already in the market and Burger King (known then as InstaBurger King) was making its mark as the burger chain market leader.

It was Kroc's genius to appreciate that food alone was not the defining factor marking out successful restaurants from the others. A restaurant required marketing and he realized that the marketing needed to reflect the American dream of a better life. This all sounds rather vague but Kroc had it right when he said, "the definition of salesmanship is the gentle art of letting the customer have it your way." McDonald's projected an image of being the quintessential progressive American way of eating food.

Kroc had a kind of epiphany when he came across the McDonald's restaurant in 1954. "Something was definitely happening here, I told myself," he wrote in his co-authored autobiography *Grinding It Out.* "This had to be the most amazing merchandising operation I'd ever seen."

What he saw was a very busy restaurant with a very slim, nine-item menu, focusing on burgers, French fries, shakes and pies. There was no seating and no crockery or cutlery, everything was served and consumed in paper and plastic. Prices were remarkably low, fifteen cents for a burger and ten cents for fries. And the service was brisk with food being delivered in about a minute. Kroc recalled, "When I saw it working that day in 1954, I felt like some latter-day Newton who'd just had an Idaho potato caromed off his skull." He digested the information and, "that night in my motel room I did a lot of heavy thinking about what I'd seen during the day. Visions of McDonald's restaurants dotting crossroads all over the country paraded through my brain."

Kroc was no stranger to the food industry. He visited a great many restaurants selling paper cups made by the Lily-Tulip Cup Company. He was a natural salesman and did well at the job. At the age of 37, he became convinced he could do better by leaving his employers and striking out on his own. His decision to quit was prompted by an association with one of his clients, Earl Prince, who invented a five-spindle milkshake mixing machine called the Prince Castle Multi-Mixer. Prince sold him exclusive marketing rights and he spent the next seventeen years traveling the country selling these machines to restaurants and drug stores with soda fountains. As he moved around the nation, he observed what he saw in these operations. "I considered myself a connoisseur of kitchens," Kroc said, "I prided myself on being able to tell which operations would appeal to the public and which would fail." And he wasn't shy in giving advice about what he perceived as the management failures of his customers.

The McDonald's restaurant originally caught his attention because at a time when sales of his mixers were declining, it ordered eight mixers at one go. At the restaurant, he discovered that the owner's franchising agent, Bill Tansley, was leaving and he quickly suggested himself as a replacement, initially thinking that this would be a good way of selling mixers to franchisees.

There were eight restaurants at the time, including two franchises in Phoenix and Sacramento, which made very little money for the McDonalds. Kroc knew he could do better but the brothers seemed satisfied to coast along with their relatively small but profitable business.

Kroc felt sure the brothers' operation could succeed wildly if it expanded. So he offered them a proposition: "Why don't you open a series of units like this?" The brothers demurred. The franchises in Phoenix and Sacramento had proved to be unprofitable and had reaped no great benefits. Kroc admired their operation but felt they were lacking in ambition and were failing to exploit the potential of what they had created. "The McDonald brothers," he wrote, "were simply not on my wavelength at all. I was obsessed with the idea of making McDonald's the biggest and the best. They were content with what they had; they didn't want to be bothered with more risks and more demands."

He, on the other hand, had a clear vision of what McDonald's could become and was determined not to let this opportunity slip through his hands. He realized that to make a deal with the brothers it would have to be one with no downside and plenty of upside for them. So he proposed an arrangement which would give the McDonalds 0.5 percent of the franchisees total sales while he kept 1.4 percent but out of his share would come all the marketing and overhead costs while the McDonalds took their share without deductions. The franchises were to be offered for a very modest US$950 each. The McDonalds had nothing to lose and so they accepted.

It was a massive gamble for Kroc who made what was then a comfortable US$12,000 per year income by selling mixers but realized that this business could evaporate under competition from the Hamilton Breach brand which was gobbling up market share. Kroc was 52 years old and as he recalled, "I had diabetes and incipient arthritis. I had lost my gall bladder and most of my thyroid gland in earlier campaigns, but I was convinced that the best was ahead of me."

Kroc had the exuberance and optimism of the natural salesman. Like many Americans, he came from a self-motivated immigrant family, which came from Czechoslovakia and had relocated to Oak Park in Chicago where he grew up. Again, rather typically of great salesmen, he started early as a teenager selling lemonade from a stand outside his home. When he was just 15, he lied about his age so he could sign up as an ambulance driver in the First World War. One of his fellow trainees in the military was Walt Disney with whom he later tried to do business. When the war ended, he was torn between becoming a salesman and a jazz musician. He had some aptitude for the latter and plenty for the former but it was only with the paper cup selling business that he finally settled, joining the Lily Tulip Company in 1922.

The three decades he spent as a salesman could be regarded as his preparation for success at McDonald's. Kroc's first store was in the

Chicago suburb of Des Plaines. It opened on 15 April 1955 and made a respectable US$366.12 profit in its first year of business. Kroc was an extremely hands-on owner. One of his first employers was Fred Turner, initially employed as a burger flipper; he eventually became his right hand man and was regarded by Kroc as a son. Within a year, Kroc had sold 18 McDonald's franchises.

However, he was not making much money because his share of the profits after expenses was tiny. Nevertheless, the business was rapidly expanding; by 1958, 79 franchises had been sold. On the surface, it looked as though he was making a fortune but by 1960, with a great many more stores opening and total sales reaching US$75 million, Kroc was making a mere US$159,000.

The deal struck with the McDonald brothers forced him into a narrow corner. It seemed as though expansion would do little to improve Kroc's fortunes. However, he had managed to attract the services of Harry Sonneborn, a former Tastee Freez finance executive who agreed to work for the very modest salary of US$100 per week. The other member of his management team was June Martino, who had been his secretary during his Multi-Mixer days. Kroc simply could not afford to give them pay increases, although the workload was rising, so he gave them a 30 percent share in the company. Another 22 percent of the equity went to two insurance companies in return for a US$1.5 million loan made in 1961.

Over 200 McDonald's outlets had opened but by then relations with the McDonald brothers were deteriorating. Standards at their outlets were below those Kroc expected and he feared contamination of the brand. Furthermore, they sold a franchise in Cook County, Illinois to a direct competitor of one his outlets. Kroc also wanted to make changes to the original McDonald's formulas but the brothers would not agree. Kroc realized that he had to buy out the founders, and secure title to their name if his plans were to succeed. The price for the buyout was US$2.7 million. In retrospect, this seems like an incredible bargain for Kroc but this was a formidable sum for the struggling entrepreneur. Kroc was already in debt and forced to borrow on interest terms that would eat considerably into his profits.

The negotiations were not amicable because at the last minute, the McDonalds insisted that the deal did not include their original restaurant in San Bernardino. Kroc had to concede this restaurant but told one of his employees "I'm not normally a vindictive man, but this time I'm going to get those sons-of-bitches." As the McDonalds had sold rights to their name, they had to rename the restaurant as The Big M. Kroc retaliated by opening a new McDonald's one block away and quickly put his rivals out of business.

More importantly, Kroc now had full control of the company and was able to run it exactly the way he wanted. Fortunately, Sonneborn had shown him how to dig his way out of the financial malaise that was holding back the company's development. In 1956, a subsidiary company was established called the Franchise Reality Corporation whose purpose was to buy up potential store sites or lease them and in turn, lease them back to franchisees who would pay for their leases with an initial fee amounting to 20 percent of sales, rising to 40 percent or an outright rental payment if the nominal rent was lower than the target sales target. This was the foundation of McDonald's fortune, and for the first time, gave Kroc a considerable slice of the upside in his franchisees business. Kroc spent much of his time scouting mainly suburban neighborhoods for potential sites in a small plane he owned.

Ray Kroc was aiming to open 1,000 restaurants in the United States, a goal already reached by the Kentucky Fried Chicken chain. In 1965, just four years after closing the deal with the McDonalds, he had opened more than 700 restaurants in 44 states and the company became the first fast food chain to be listed on the New York Stock Exchange.

Kroc realized that the key to success was to work with his franchisees as partners. He said: "My belief was that I had to help the individual operator succeed in every way I could. His success would insure my success. But I couldn't do that and, at the same time, treat him as a customer." The franchisees returned the enthusiasm of the parent company and major innovations in the menu, including the Big Mac, Filet-O-fish and the Egg McMuffin, were developed as result of their initiatives.

It was also a franchise owner in Washington who came up with the Ronald McDonald idea. Kroc was shrewd enough to realize a good idea when he saw it. In addition, he was protective of McDonald's customers as was seen when, after taking over the company, he asked Walt Disney whether he would like to have the fast food restaurants in his theme park. Disney was keen on the idea but insisted that the price of fries inside the park had to rise from ten to fifteen cents so that he could make a greater profit. Kroc refused as he believed this would entail gouging loyal customers.

Driving the expansion of the company was an aggressive advertising campaign. The first national advertising campaign was launched in 1967, spending what was then an unprecedented figure of 1 percent of sales on the effort. By 1972, there were 2,200 McDonald's stores in America, racking up sales exceeding US$1 billion, making McDonald's the biggest fast food outlet in the country.

As early as 1967, Kroc realized that McDonald's faced the danger of market saturation in the United States and embarked on a cautious overseas expansion program, first across the border in Canada and then into Europe. Going overseas forced the company to walk a tightrope between meeting local market demands while maintaining its rigid operating system that allowed no deviation in the US.

The basic model remained in place but local variations were permitted. When, for example, McDonald's opened in Germany, the company's strict no alcohol policy was broken and beer was sold. In the Philippines, McSpaghetti noodles were put on the menu and in Norway, the local love of salmon was catered for with a salmon fillet sandwich named the MacLak. In Muslim countries, McDonald's transforms itself into a halal restaurant. And when it came to marketing, the salesmen for McDonald's took pains to ensure that this quintessentially American product would not be seen as alien in its new homes overseas. In Japan, for example, the company trades under the Japanese sounding name of *Makudonaldo*, the name has also been changed for the Chinese market where, once rendered in Chinese characters it comes out, in the Cantonese dialectic, as *Macdonlo*. Indeed,

China is now the fastest growing market for the company. The net result has been that two thirds of the company's earnings are now generated overseas.

Kroc continued to run the company until 1974, when he stepped down as CEO. However, he retained the role of Chairman and then Senior Chairman until he died of heart failure in 1984, at the age of 81. In his old age, he finally became what he always wanted to be – a very rich man, amassing an estimated fortune of some US$500 million and using some of it to buy the San Diego Padres baseball team.

In many ways, when Kroc retired from running the company, he did so at the peak of its success. Even though there was considerable expansion to come after his departure, the glitter on the McDonald's golden arches was beginning to fade. The company became synonymous with what is now widely described as "junk food," lacking in taste, nutritional value and damned for the very consistency which Kroc so highly valued. Its employment practices and ways of doing things have been widely criticized, indeed the term "McJob" is now often applied to low paid and rather hopeless forms of employment.

Some 1.7 million of these jobs are at McDonald's itself. There was also unrest among the company's franchise holders who criticized McDonald for an aggressive expansion policy that threatened their livelihoods.

The company has tried to reinvent itself in a number of ways, even offering salads as part of its product mix and opening a successful and more up-market McCafé operation. The interiors of its stores have been revamped time and again and more recently, McDonald's has even attempted to jump on the green bandwagon. In the United States, for example, one of the more recent innovations has been to offer a battery charging service for electric cars.

These efforts to change the company's image have failed to assuage McDonald's many critics. Yet much of the criticism of McDonald's comes from people who would never dream of even entering one of its stores. It most certainly does not emanate from the 47 million customers it serves every day in the 119 countries on six continents where it operates. In March 2011, the Subway sandwich chain claimed that it had finally managed to overtake McDonald's in terms of the numbers of branches worldwide. Subway claimed to be operating 33,749 stores, compared with McDonald's 32,737. This still does not make Subway as globally famous or successful as its hamburger rival and its revenues lag those of McDonald's by a considerable distance.

Fast food and internationally branded chains offering these products are now taken for granted and patronized by millions of people every day. Many of them owe their form of organization and practices to the influence of Ray Kroc. Like many entrepreneurs, he was not really an innovator and certainly not an inventor, but he had the nose for a good idea and he had the knack of application, meaning that he knew how to transform these ideas into a profitable business.

If Kroc were still alive, the hyperactive, sales obsessed head of the company would probably be tearing his hair out as rivals bite into McDonald's market share. Unlike most of the food gurus in this book his main focus was not directed towards producing better food, he wanted better sales. In his world the best food product came from a successful formula, the very essence of which lay in its ability to be reproduced by even the least skilled cook. Yet Kroc, like the chefs who populate these pages, was a demon for perfection. He said, "Perfection is very difficult to achieve, and perfection was what I wanted in McDonald's. Everything else was secondary for me."

Chapter 12

The Mother of French Cuisine?

Catherine de Medici

$\mathcal{C}$aterina Maria Romola di Lorenzo de' Medici (1519 – 1589), known in the English speaking world more simply as Catherine de Medici, is controversially credited with transforming French food by importing the superior cuisine of her native Italy and introducing a revolutionary change in French eating habits.

The claims for this scion of the famous Medici family were not really made in earnest until the eighteenth century when French writers intensified their efforts chronicling the progress of France's culinary development. By then, of course, they were confident that French cuisine had surpassed any other cuisine in Europe, and, in their eyes, Europe was pretty much all that mattered in the world. If it is true that Catherine laid the foundations for the dominance of French cuisine, which prevailed until at least the later part of the twentieth century, then she can be said to be the pioneer of one of the most significant culinary movements in history. It should be emphasized at this stage that this claim has been greeted with considerable skepticism. Alan Davidson, the compiler of the definitive *Oxford Companion to Food,* describes claims made on Catherine's behalf as one of the greatest "food myths."

However, there is a considerable body of opinion on the other side of the argument. In Denis Diderot's famous *Encyclopédie* published in 1754, Le Chevalier de Jaucourt provided this double-edged support for Catherine's contribution to the development of French cuisine: it was the Italians, he wrote, who "made the French acquainted with the art of dining well, the excesses of which so many of our kings tried to suppress... The Italians inherited the art of cookery from the Romans; it was they who introduced fine food to the French . . . During the reign of Henry II, cooks from beyond the Alps came and settled in France, and we are eternally indebted to this motley band that served at Catherine de Medici's court. . . The French, finely attuned to the flavors that should dominate in each dish, quickly surpassed their masters who were soon forgotten. From that moment on, as if they had successfully met the challenge of stressing what was important, they could pride themselves in the knowledge that the taste of their cuisine had surpassed that of all others and reigned supreme in opulent kingdoms from North to South."

So here we have an encapsulation of a common eighteenth-century view, namely that the Italians, in the shape of Catherine de Medici, should be credited with some of the pioneering work in getting French cuisine off the ground but it was the French themselves who perfected the exercise. It is interesting to note that the most prominent claims of Catherine de Medici's contribution to French cuisine came from French sources, not Italian ones, and they have been taken up with glee, particularly in Britain where rivalry and animosity to the French is a harmless national pastime.

Much of the controversy over Catherine's role is derived from the paucity of contemporary written records specifying how she might have transformed French cuisine. Besides this, there is also evidence that before her arrival the French (meaning the French aristocracy) were already enjoying sophisticated cooking.

However, it seems incredible to believe that French gastronomic writers conspired, for reasons entirely unclear, to produce a fantasy about how a foreigner molded their national cuisine. On the contrary, the French culinary authorities making the claims on Catherine's behalf tended to do so in a manner which expresses grudging admiration rather than starry-eyed praise for the young Italian who arrived in France in 1533, at the age of 14, to marry Henry of Orleans, the second son of King Francis I.

In the five decades that Catherine lived in France, she arguably became one of the nation's most famous queens. It is her contribution to

French cuisine that concerns us here but she was better known for her involvement in France's bitter religious wars and for introducing her adopted country to many aspects of science and the arts, particularly ballet. Her role in all these things remains controversial and when it comes to the claim that ""she taught the French to eat," there is no doubt a large degree of exaggeration.

Before the arrival of Catherine in France, there was a body of French culinary literature with many chefs producing sophisticated food. However, French chefs were not recognized among Europe's leaders in the culinary field. Italy, on the other hand, had a firm reputation for its food at this time. Although not yet the unified nation it became, what we think of as Italy had been seized by the Renaissance, which began in Florence in the fourteenth century under the patronage of Catherine's family, the Medicis. The Renaissance had a primary impact on the arts but the new movement also influenced all manner of social activities. Italians pioneered many of the things we would now describe as gracious living. This was reflected in the architecture and fabulous garden landscapes of the day as well as in the food. It also included a search for new foodstuffs and the birth of intricate methods of food presentation which stunned foreigners when they visited Italy.

Cookbooks were commonplace in Italy and the first modern cooking academy was founded in Florence during the early 1500s. Catherine came from the very heart of this Renaissance movement, which arrived in France at the same time as she arrived in the French court.

There is some evidence, mainly through books published at the time, that the French were, if anything, mainly influenced by German cuisine, not Italian; but in terms of food presentation and eating methods, the Italian influence is most evident. Maybe Catherine can therefore only be credited with influencing food presentation but as Antonin Carême (Chapter 6) was to demonstrate two centuries later, presentation is a key to fine cuisine. Carême, incidentally, was among those who credit Catherine for introducing fine Italian food to the French court.

Catherine was born in Florence to Lorenzo II de Medici and a French mother, Madeleine de la Tour d'Auvergne. Her grandfather was Lorenzo the Magnificent. Although she came from this grand family, she was orphaned shortly after her birth, which left her in a somewhat poor situation. Despite this setback, she grew up surrounded by luxury in a city where refinement and culture were highly valued and she was in the embrace of a family that epitomized the wealth and arrogance of Italy's dominant position in Europe's social affairs.

There was nothing unusual about sending a scion of this family to marry into a princely household at a young age, although it was not expected that Catherine would end up marrying a king. Henry, like his wife-to-be, was only 14 when they married in 1533. He was the second son of Francis I and inherited the throne in 1547 after his older brother mysteriously died while playing tennis.

When Catherine arrived in France, her husband took an instant dislike to her as she was not beautiful, and she had little money. The union was made for political reasons and nothing else. Henry's father had arranged the match to please Pope Clement VII, Catherine's uncle, but even this plan went array as the pope died shortly after the marriage.

So Henry largely ignored her and flaunted his relationship with his much older concubine Diana de Poitiers, who acted as queen in all but name. Perhaps reflecting the confidence she felt in her position, de Poitiers insisted that her lover occasionally slept with his wife for the purpose of producing heirs. The French court also looked down on Catherine and for a long time she failed to produce an heir. Nor was she popular with the wider French public who called her "the Italian grocer." Her position appeared tenuous but all that changed once she started to produce children. She ended up bearing ten children for her husband, three of whom became kings of France and one a queen.

During her husband's lifetime she remained isolated at court and largely friendless in her adopted country. Catherine leant heavily on the Italian entourage of servants and friends who accompanied her on the journey to France. Among the servants were Florentine cooks who had been employed in the grand Medici kitchens and apparently found conditions in France rather primitive. Food seemed to be an area where Catherine, something of glutton, could make an impression. She staged magnificent banquets, which may have helped persuade her husband that she was not quite as useless as he thought she was. There is a record of a banquet she organized in 1549, where she served 30 peacocks, 33 pheasants, 21 swans, 20 cranes, 66 guinea hens, 30 capons, 99 quail and a selection of hares, rabbits and pigs. Not forgetting 60 salads and 26 sweet courses. This feast was provided for a mere 50 guests.

Catherine dazzled with scale. It was not that French food was primitive, far from it, but it still followed medieval traditions and there was a lack of discipline in the way kitchens were organized. Jean Orieux, a biographer of Catherine, wrote: "It was exactly a Florentine who reformed the antique French cooking of medieval tradition; and was reborn as the modern French cooking." The Italians also brought over vegetables that were popular at home such as artichokes, beans, broccoli, peas and maybe tomatoes which had just begun to make an impression on Italian cuisine.

The Florentines are also credited with introducing the French to dishes that are now thought of as classics such as onion soup and duck in orange, alongside the classic French sauces, the sauce *béarnaise* and sauce *mornay*. But it seems that the deepest impression was made by Italian confections. Florence was famous for its sorbets and ice creams but there were also pastries, and preserved fruits and tarts, which deeply impressed all those who had never seen food of this kind before.

Again, it should be stressed that there is controversy over whether it was Catherine and her retinue that introduced these foods to France or whether they were adopted over a period of time. It is also entirely possible that it was not Catherine but some of her other countrymen in France who introduced the French to Italian food. For example, she is said to have introduced ice cream and sorbets to the court but Francisco Procopio, a Sicilian living in Paris, opened the first ice cream shop in France. What is certain is that food that was popular in Italy became popular in France and that even if these dishes and foodstuffs were not adopted wholesale as a result of Catherine's influence there is certainly a coincidence of timing here.

Less controversy surrounds the way that Catherine influenced the eating habits of the French aristocracy in ways that trickled down to the rest of the population. Although she cannot be said to have been a feminist, it was Catherine who insisted that women be allowed to attend the grand banquets at court. No longer were they to be confined to their own quarters while these feasts were underway.

She dazzled the French court with the elegance of her banquets and replaced plain table settings with elaborate designs that included silverware and fine glassware, commonplace in the Italian courts but not in France. She also appears to have introduced the practice of eating with a fork, adding to the spoons and knives that had been used hitherto. Moreover, she introduced the concept of separating sweet from savory dishes. The old practice of placing all the food together on the table was commonplace and dated back to medieval times. In Italy, the distinction between what became known as courses was starting to take hold. Extraordinary as it may seem today it was not until the late nineteenth century, under the influence of the great chef Escoffier (Chapter 9), that a new system of fully separating courses came into being.

Catherine's husband Henry II died in 1559 and she became Queen Regent for three decades, wielding considerable power during the reigns of her three, largely ineffectual sons. By then, she was 40 years old and had led a frustrated life. Now she was able to do many of the things she could not have even have thought of while her husband reigned. Among the first of these things was banishing her husband's mistress Diana. Most controversially, she played a major role in the seemingly never-ending war between Huguenots and Catholics. But on the lighter side, she also became known for the balls and theatrical events she staged at court that were accompanied by lavish banquets, setting an example of opulence which reached its height in the court of Louis XIV.

Catherine died on 5 January 1589 of natural causes in her sleep. She was widely vilified for her role in massacring Huguenots at the St. Bartholomew's Day Massacre in 1572; however history has been somewhat kinder to her. As for her contribution to French cuisine, this remains controversial. There is a growing trend to dismiss her work but there is a convincing body of evidence that suggests she did much to influence the evolution of French cuisine.

de Medici Recipes

A number of dishes bearing Catherine's name remain to this day. The first is said to be her own invention but has been updated here in modern form.

Pears Catherine

Ingredients
4½ cups (1kg.) sugar
1 teaspoon vanilla extract
6–8 pears
4 cups (950ml.) raspberries or blackberries
2 tablespoons. kirsch liqueur
3 tablespoons almonds, chopped finely

Method
Prepare the syrup by dissolving 4 cups (900ml.) of the sugar in 4½ cups (1065ml.) of water and bringing to a boil. Strain, add the vanilla and filter through several layers of muslin. Pour the syrup into a clean saucepan and in this poach the pears until they are soft, but taking care not to cook so long that they become mushy.

In a mixing bowl, crush the berries. Add the remaining sugar, mix well put through a sieve. Stir in the kirsch. To serve, spoon the berry puree over the pears and sprinkle with the almonds.

Bombe Medicis

This dish is said to have been prepared in honor of Catherine's 70th birthday, very shortly before she died. She reportedly said: "after having tasted something so wondrous, one may be comfortably assured that there is indeed a Paradise that awaits us."

Serves 8 to 12

Ingredients
4 cups (950ml.) pear or orange slices
2 cups (425ml.) peaches, peeled and diced
½ cup (125ml.) kirsch liqueur
8½ cups (1.8kg.) sugar
6 large peaches, halved and peeled
32 egg yolks
1 teaspoon vanilla extract
3 cups (750ml.) sweet cream, whipped stiff

Method
Line a bombe mold or earthenware bowl with the ices and place in the freezer until solidified. In a small bowl, steep the diced peaches in the kirsch for 1–2 hours. In a small saucepan, dissolve 1½ cups (340g.) of the sugar in 2 cups (475ml.) of water and bring to the boil. In this syrup, simmer the peach halves until soft. Drain and puree the peaches.

In a saucepan, dissolve the remaining sugar in 4 cups (1ltr.) of water. Bring to a rolling boil, strain and filter. In the top of a large double boiler over, but not in hot water, combine the syrup and egg yolks, stirring regularly with a whisk and when the mixture attains the consistency of thick cream and rub it through a fine sieve into a bowl. Add the vanilla extract and continue to stir until the mixture is fully cool. Add to the mixture the peach puree and diced peaches and then add an equal volume of the whipped cream. Place the mixture in a stone or porcelain container, cover and refrigerate until completely cold (4–5 hours).

When the mixture is cold, fill the center of the bombe. Seal the mold and let it stand in the freezer until solid throughout (2–3 hours) before unmolding and serving.

Insalata de Caterina

This is reported to have been one of her favorite salads.
Serves 4 to 6

Ingredients
mixed salad greens
soft Tuscan Pecorino cheese (sheep's milk cheese)
hardboiled egg (½ per person)
anchovy packed in oil
capers
vinegar
olive oil
salt and pepper

Method
Wash the different varieties of salad greens (at least 3), dry well and place in a large salad bowl (a wooden bowl is ideal and typical for this dish).

Add the pecorino cut into small cubes, little pieces of anchovy fillet and a few capers. Sprinkle salt and pepper lightly and dress with oil and vinegar, toss well and serve immediately, decorated with wedges of hardboiled eggs.

Chapter 13

The Food Campaigner

Jamie Oliver

*J*amie Oliver, the cheeky chap with a tuft of hair flying upwards, has reached the stage where his first name is probably more recognizable than his proper name which is James Trevor Oliver. He seems so familiar and accessible that it is hard to remember that he is almost certainly not what he primarily claims to be, namely, a chef. The reality is that his cooking does not explain his extraordinary contribution to the ranks of food gurus.

There is nothing that can be described as a Jamie Oliver-style of cooking and he is certainly not an inventor of a type of cuisine like some of the other food gurus in this book. These other chefs have spent most of their time cooking in a restaurant but there has never been a restaurant with Jamie as a full-time head chef. This is not to make the nonsensical claim that Jamie Oliver is not a good cook but it is equally hard to assert that he has earned his spurs in a kitchen where he developed a distinctive style of cooking with which he can be instantly identified. His genius lies elsewhere.

Genius is not an exaggeration because it is hard to find another individual who has had such a profound impact on the eating and cooking habits of his generation and who has almost single-handedly made the question of healthy eating a part of the national agenda in ways that have had an immediate impact. The hype that surrounds his achievements and the hyperbole of his own language, which lamentably includes excessive use of exclamation marks, tends to detract from his real achievements.

He has a consistent belief in food made from scratch using good quality ingredients. This seemingly obvious formula for good eating has been almost abandoned by a generation wedded to microwave ovens and pre-cooked and packaged foods. Many people are simply not confident in using fresh produce because turning raw food into meals seems too difficult and too time-consuming.

Here lies Jamie's genius. He understands this lack of confidence and reluctance to prepare meals when easy alternatives proliferate and he tackles this dilemma with wit, an easygoing manner and the master salesman's ability to convince a reluctant buyer that they should purchase something they had never thought of buying previously.

Maybe only his fellow countrymen can fully appreciate how his personality has helped to crash through the barriers which separated the British from good eating, leaving home cooking in a largely dire state especially for the less well-off. Speaking of his well-publicized efforts to change eating habits in the working class northern English city of Rotherham, Jamie said "They thought that cooking a meal and feeding it to your family was for posh people."

Famous British chefs used to have upper-class accents and were associated with a lifestyle quite removed from the bulk of the population. Even the famous TV chefs often appeared to have descended from the Planet Posh but Jamie works hard at being the common man. He has what seems suspiciously like a not quite real "mockney" – a sort of London working-class accent, liberally sprinkled with cozy alliterations such as "lovely jubbly" and has a way of connecting with people who were quite convinced that cooking and being interested in food was not for them.

Once established as a television personality, he used his fame to improve eating habits in Britain and then the United States, especially among the young. He is actively engaged in training new recruits to the restaurant business and drawing them from the ranks of those who never thought they would head in this direction. Behind his matey, carefree exterior is a skillful business operator who has earned a small fortune.

Learning to become a chef is a laborious business, involving a long apprenticeship usually accompanied by a high level of exploitation by restaurant owners and head chefs, jealous of their own position and always on the lookout for ways of getting more out of their staff at minimal cost.

However, Jamie Oliver was not only very lucky to have had a mentor in the shape of Gennaro Contaldo, with whom he still works, but he also benefited from a piece of serendipity which catapulted him from being a lowly sous chef in London's well-regarded River Café (run by two very well-known chefs: the late Rose Grey and Ruth Rogers) into becoming a television star. It happened when the producers of the show being recorded in the restaurant spotted Oliver and, as television people do, quickly recognized a formidable on-screen personality.

It took very little time for him to be whisked out of the kitchen and into the recording studios where Jamie's television career was launched with the *Naked Chef* series. He has spent many years trying to explain that a) the title was not his own and b) it was not the chef who was naked but the food – simple and stripped down for everyone to make.

It says a lot about the cult of celebrity in the age of instant communication that a relatively inexperienced chef could have been catapulted into this kind of fame but Jamie Oliver has a personality and the instinctive skills that make him attractive on screen. Some people suspect that this persona has been carefully cultivated purely for the purposes of television but it's a belief founded on a thin basis.

In class-obsessed Britain, there is understandable interest in Jamie's origins and accent, which suggests a working-class background. The reality is that Jamie Oliver, born in 1975, is the son of a middle-class family (okay, maybe lower middle-class for those obsessing with the minutiae of these matters) who run a successful gastro pub restaurant called "The Cricketers," located in Essex on the outskirts of London. It was here that he was introduced to the world of kitchens and, by his own account, started helping out at the age of seven or eight and by 11, "wasn't half bad at vegetable prep," which means chopping and cleaning vegetables before cooking.

Under the watchful eye of his father, who had a harsh work ethic, Jamie spent more and more time in the kitchen. By the age of 13, he was doing real cooking alongside the head chef. Things were not going well for him at school where his dyslexia and hyperactivity made him into a "special needs" child who was going nowhere academically. At the age of 16, he failed all his "O" level exams except for art, where he got an "A" and geology where he obtained a "C."

Clearly an academic future did not beckon but Jamie had already discovered that his real interest lay in cooking. Off he went to the Westminster Catering College, one of the workaday London schools that have a reasonable reputation for turning out future chefs. He then had a mini-apprenticeship in France and really landed on his feet by becoming the pastry chef at Antonio Carluccio's Neal Street Restaurant, a chic and highly popular Italian restaurant in the center of London where he came under the wing of Chef Contaldo. From there, he moved to the River Café, which also specializes in Italian food. Jamie stayed with the formidable Grey and Roger's kitchen for three and a half years before moving into television.

In other words, Jamie Oliver spent less than a decade in these two kitchens as a professional before appearing on the small screen and telling the British public how to cook. The former sous chef soon found himself preparing a dinner for Prime Minister Tony Blair in 1999 and secured a million-pound deal as the public face of the Sainsbury's food supermarket chain.

Little wonder that other chefs who had served longer apprenticeships, which are considered the norm, were distinctly sniffy about Jamie Oliver's success and quick to dismiss him as all showmanship and little depth. But they miss the point because it is precisely showmanship which is his strength. The *Naked Chef* series had immediate impact because of Jamie's chatty style: where other chefs emphasized precision, he favored terms such as "bung in" or "get a handful" of herbs. He said, "all I ever wanted to do was to make food accessible to everyone; to show that you can make mistakes - I do all the time - but it doesn't matter."

The idea was to make recipes less formidable and reassuringly easy. In reading these recipes in the books accompanying the shows, it becomes clear that there is quite enough precision for the novice cook to know what to do, albeit with some annoying gaps. Readers of the *Naked Chef* book learn not to be nervous about seasoning – Jamie is basically of the more is better school. It is clear that Italian cuisine remains his major influence, although he has developed a strong, even a campaigning, interest in British food.

Jamie edges his followers towards spending more money to obtain fresh or organic produce, to use virgin olive oil and to buy cuts of meat that they might not have considered before. "As a general rule," Jamie writes in his introduction to *Jamie's Dinners,* "when the food is cheap it is not going to be so good...it all comes down to your perception of value – is it about buying the cheapest thing you can get, or is about spending a little more and getting something that tastes nicer, smells better and makes you feel good in return?"

If the criticism is that Jamie's recipes are not particularly original, he should plead guilty but in so doing he could add that all chefs devour other chef's recipes and modify them. This is how cuisine develops; it is a simple fact of life. The genius lies in the adaptation and, when addressing a non-professional audience, it lies in the methods employed. Jamie is a master of the short-cut and regularly offers ways of eliminating unnecessarily complicated steps. He often suggests, for example, not to make a béchamel sauce, which is slightly laborious but substitute it with crème fraîche – it's not the same but it certainly works.

Most importantly, however, Jamie Oliver has become a food campaigner; he is quick to absolve himself from being "preachy" on the subject and is worried that some people will think he is "ranting." However he insists that "we've reached a crucial stage in history now – the way we produce and cook our food is going to radically affect what the next generation grows up on. Either we change back to the natural methods of food production or things will get more 'sci-fi' and mass-produced."

The first major manifestation of Jamie Oliver's campaigning efforts was the launch of the Fifteen Foundation in 2002. The idea was to help young people from disadvantaged backgrounds get into the catering industry by establishing a restaurant with 15 entirely novice chefs. It didn't hurt that this was also ideal material for a reality TV show, called *Jamie's Kitchen*.

Of course, the idea is hardly novel. Restaurant kitchens have a long history of attracting disadvantaged kids, lacking in formal qualifications. Training as a chef is a classic form of apprenticeship, and even the added human interest of attracting kids with criminal backgrounds is not unusual. Anyone familiar with professional kitchens will tell you that they are no strangers to drug dealing, excessive drinking and gambling. The Oliver campaign, however, had a purpose, which it arguably fulfilled. It inspired many young people to think of catering as a desirable career and showed them that it was neither a soft or dowdy option. The first Fifteen restaurant in London has spawned similar projects in Amsterdam, Cornwall and Melbourne. It should also be said that they are not just worthy do-gooder projects, they serve excellent food.

The Fifteen Foundation proved to be a mere shadow compared with a far more ambitious campaign, launched in 2004, to change the food served at schools to British children. Providing meals in schools has a long history in Britain, dating back to the 1870s when initiatives were taken to fight malnutrition among poor children.

By 1944, the government made it compulsory for schools to supply meals at nominal cost to improve children's diets. Over time, these meals attracted a terrible reputation for taste, quality, and then for poor nutritional value. Jamie Oliver thought he could do something about this and set out to prove that it would not cost that much more to supply better quality and more nutritious food. Again, with the cameras in tow, he volunteered to take over the kitchen of a school in Greenwich, southeast London, to show how this could be done. From there, he went on to take over the school meal system in the entire area. When the project reached the television screens in 2005 there was a massive response. A total of 271,677 people signed an online petition demanding better school food. The government was forced into a rapid response, promising more cash and training for kitchen staff. A follow-up television show, 18 months later, kept up the momentum for improvements to school meals and brought the total additional public investment in the project up to £650 million.

The makers of the notorious Turkey Twizzlers, a very popular frozen dish, were shamed into withdrawing it from the market and awareness increased over the reliance on other deep fried and unhealthy foods, many of which contained misleading names. Studies in Greenwich showed that unauthorized absences (mainly due to illness), fell by 15 percent in the wake of the campaign. There was additional evidence of improved academic performance.

However, there was also an avalanche of complaints about the new food regime. Children brought up on a solid diet of McDonald's-type fast food found it very hard to adjust to the new, more subtle tastes and significant numbers of pupils withdrew from the school's food program. Staff in school kitchens, who had previously done no real cooking, merely just defrosting and deep-frying, also found it hard to adjust. The real kicker came with a study showing that the main beneficiaries of the better eating campaign were not the children from poorer homes who qualified for free meals but the children of wealthier parents. The less well-off were more likely to drop out of the program.

In 2010, Britain's new coalition government suddenly dropped the minimum nutritional standards for school meals that had been introduced as a result of the campaign. The *Daily Mirror* newspaper, a big backer of the original campaign, said "it gave the green light for schools to start serving up junk food again."

Jamie Oliver soon realized that if school meals were not up to scratch it was unlikely that home meals were any better. So he launched the Ministry of Food, this time taking the cameras up to the northern English city of Rotherham where he embarked on a weekly cooking class, which morphed into a bestselling book of very simple recipes: *Jamie's Ministry of Food.*

This in turn has spawned a similar project in the United States with Jamie heading for Huntingdon, Virginia, billed as the "fattest city in America," to establish a new school meals program. (Alice Waters, Chapter 20, is engaged in similar projects but without the television cameras in tow.) The challenges here were every bit as daunting as in Britain and the results distinctly mixed. When in 2011, a similar project was proposed for schoolchildren in Los Angeles, it was blocked by the local authorities who cited concerns over the controversy it was likely to produce. They were not alone in their skepticism; even before the school projects began, the TV chat show host David Letterman told Jamie on air that he would fail and that in America, only diet pills would bring down weight.

The ultimate verdict is still out on the American projects and arguably the same is true for the project in Rotherham but the attention both programs have raised and the discussions they have stimulated are, in themselves, indications of success. Just because these projects make for compelling television does not mean that they do not have other beneficial results. Not everything on television is bad for you. Nevertheless, quite a strong case could be made for a quick squirm at the memory of Jamie's *Happy Days Live* tour which began in 2001 and appeared on television, showing the great chef leaping from the kitchen stove to a drum set and unconvincingly mixing pop music with cooking.

The overwhelming nature of Jamie's showmanship sometimes makes it hard to remember that he is a serious chef and has a serious business empire employing over 2,000 people. He has become a multi-millionaire from the proceeds of the TV shows, cookbooks, shops, celebrity endorsements, a magazine and the 14 Italian restaurants he owns with more in the pipeline (the Fifteen restaurants are not for profit).

Jamie Oliver has earned a number of honors, including royal recognition for his work. In 2010, he received the prestigious TED prize given to people who have significantly changed society. "Jamie Oliver is transforming the way we feed our children, and ourselves," said the organizers, encapsulating what he has achieved. This is a simple statement of fact despite the carping of critics. Indeed precisely because he attracts criticism he stimulates debate, and the debate itself generates the discussion required to, at the very least, examine whether there is a better way of feeding prosperous nations who have long abandoned subsistence diets but by tragic irony are returning themselves to the poor nutritional levels found in nations where food is hard to come by. Jamie actively engages in this debate with wit and style and some rather nice food.

Oliver Recipes

Here are three recipes which classically illustrate the Oliver approach; they are reproduced in their full chatty form. The Cannelloni recipe shows how a more complicated process can be adjusted without any compromise on flavor; indeed it may be argued that this method produces something far more interesting. A novice cook could make the Beef and Ale Stew without the slightest difficulty, it is precisely the sort of dish Jamie Oliver suggests to people who are not used to cooking from scratch. As for the Bun and Butter Pudding, this is a very clever adaptation of the classic Bread and Butter Pudding but infinitely richer and as easy to make as the original but with more rewarding results.

All these recipes can also be found at the website, *www.jamieoliver.com*

Awesome Spinach and Ricotta Cannelloni

Jamie Oliver writes: "This is such a wonderfully light and super-tasty cannelloni, and again I've avoided making the frustrating, painstaking béchamel sauce and given you a much tastier and simpler version. All you need to make sure of is that you fill the cannelloni well with the ricotta and spinach mix, so it's not all full of air. And the lovely thing about it is that it goes crispy and golden on top, but remains soft and moist at the bottom. You'll love it!"
Serves 4

Ingredients

2 knobs of butter
olive oil
2 cloves of garlic, peeled and finely sliced
large handful of fresh marjoram or oregano, roughly chopped
¼ of a nutmeg, grated
8 large handfuls of spinach, thoroughly washed
handful of fresh basil, stalks chopped, leaves ripped
2 cans of 400 grams (14oz.) good-quality plum tomatoes, chopped
sea salt and freshly ground black pepper
pinch of sugar
400 grams (14oz.) crumbly ricotta cheese
2 handfuls of freshly grated Parmesan cheese
16 cannelloni tubes
200 grams (7oz.) mozzarella, broken up

For the white sauce:
500 milliliters (2 cups) tub of *crème fraîche*
3 anchovies, finely chopped
2 handfuls of freshly grated Parmesan cheese

Method

Preheat the oven to 180ºC/350ºF/gas 4. Then find a metal baking tray or ovenproof dish that will fit the cannelloni in one layer so it's nice and snug. This way you'll get the right cover of sauce and the right amount of crispiness on top. When I cook this at home I just use one pan to cut down on lots of washing up! Take your metal tray or a saucepan, put it on a high heat and add your butter, a drizzle of olive oil, one of the sliced garlic cloves, a handful of marjoram or oregano and the grated nutmeg. By the time the pan is hot the garlic should be soft. Put as much spinach as will fit into the pan. Keep turning it over; it will wilt quickly so you will be able to keep adding more spinach until it's all in. Moisture will cook out of the spinach, which is fine. By cooking it this way, you don't lose any of the nutrients that you would if boiling it in water.

After 5 minutes, put the spinach into a large bowl and leave to cool. Place the pan back on the heat, add a little olive oil, the other clove of sliced garlic, your basil stalks and the tomatoes, then fill one of the empty tomato tins with cold water and add this, too. Bring to the boil, then turn the heat down, add a pinch of salt and pepper and the sugar, and simmer for about 10 minutes, until you get a loose tomato sauce consistency. Then take the pan off the heat and add the basil leaves.

By now the spinach will have cooled down, so squeeze any excess liquid out of it and pour this back into the bowl. Finely chop the spinach and put it back into the bowl. Mix it with the liquid, add the ricotta and a handful of the Parmesan, and then use a piping bag to squeeze the mixture into the cannelloni. You can make your own piping bag by getting a sandwich bag and putting the spinach mix into the corner of it. Then twist the bag up and cut the corner off. Carefully squeeze the filling into the cannelloni tubes so each one is filled right up – really easy.

Lay the cannelloni over the tomato sauce in the pan. Or you can pour the tomato sauce into your ovenproof dish and lay the cannelloni on top. To make the white sauce, mix together the crème fraîche, anchovies and the 2 handfuls of parmesan with a little salt and pepper, then loosen with a little water until you can spoon it over the cannelloni. Drizzle with olive oil, sprinkle with the remaining Parmesan and the mozzarella pieces, and bake for about 20 to 25 minutes until golden and bubbling.

From: *Jamie's Dinners* by Jamie Oliver, Penguin Books, 2004

Beef and Ale Stew

Jaime Oliver writes: "You are going to love this slow-cooked stew recipe, because it's so simple and gives consistently good results. The meat should be cut into approximately 2cm cubes. Packs from most supermarkets are normally about that size. In stew recipes you're often told to brown off the meat first. But I've done loads of tests and found the meat is just as delicious and tender without browning it first, so I've removed this usual stage from the recipe."
Serves 4 to 6

Ingredients
3 fresh or dried bay leaves
500 grams (20oz.) diced stewing beef
500 ml. (1 pint) ale, Guinness or stout
2 sticks of celery
2 medium onions
2 carrots
olive oil
1 heaped tablespoon plain flour
400 grams (14oz.) of canned chopped tomatoes
sea salt and freshly ground black pepper

Method
If using the oven to cook your stew, preheat it to 180ºC/350ºF/gas 4. Trim the ends off your celery and roughly chop the sticks. Peel and roughly chop the onions. Peel the carrots, slice lengthways and roughly chop. Put a casserole pan on a medium heat. Put all the vegetables and the bay leaves into the pan with 2 lugs of olive oil and fry for 10 minutes.

Add your meat and flour. Pour in the booze and tinned tomatoes. Give it a good stir, then season with a teaspoon of sea salt (less if using table salt) and a few grinds of pepper. Bring to the boil, put the lid on and either simmer slowly on your hob or cook in an oven for 3 hours. Remove the lid for the final half hour of simmering or cooking. When done, your meat should be tender and delicious. Remember to remove the bay leaves before serving, and taste it to see if it needs a bit more salt and pepper. You can eat your stew as it is, or you can add some lovely dumplings to it.

From: *Jamie's Ministry of Food: Anyone Can Learn to Cook in 24 Hours* by Jamie Oliver, Michael Joseph, 2008

Bun and Butter Pudding

Serves 6

Ingredients
600 milliliters (2.5 cups) semi-skimmed milk
600 milliliters (2.5 cups) double cream
1 vanilla pod
4 medium eggs, preferably free-range or organic
170 grams (6oz.) caster sugar
6 Taste the Difference hot cross buns, sliced in half and
    spread with a knob of butter
3 tablespoons cognac
a handful of dried apricots, chopped
zest of 1 orange
a little icing sugar

Method
Preheat the oven to 170°C/325°F/gas 3. For the custard base, bring the milk and cream just to the boil in a saucepan. Cut the vanilla pod in half, scrape out the seeds and add to the pan. Whisk the eggs with the sugar until pale, then whisk in the milk and cream mixture, removing the vanilla pod shell.

Dip the hot cross bun halves in the mixture, then place in an ovenproof dish. Drizzle over the cognac and sprinkle over the apricots and the orange zest. Sieve the custard over, and leave it all to soak for at least 15 minutes.

Place the dish in a roasting tin, half-fill the tin with hot water, then bake the pudding for about 45 minutes. When cooked it will have a slight crust on top but will still be slightly wobbly inside. Dust with the icing sugar and serve.

Chapter 14

Doing Her Bit

Marguerite
Patten

$\mathcal{H}$ilda Elsie Marguerite Patten (née Brown), born in 1915, and still going strong in her nineties, is better known as Marguerite Patten. This grande dame of British cookery often insists that she is nothing more than a home economist but having written a greater number of cookery books than practically anyone in Britain, she can hardly be described as less than a culinary genius. There are 165 cookbooks written by Patten, with sales exceeding 17 million as well as recipe cards with sales of more than 500 million.

Patten has also undertaken the ambitious task of becoming a food historian with the publication in 2001 of her book, *A Century of British Cooking*, which charts the development of eating habits through the recipes of the last century.

Ever practical and aware of developments in kitchen equipment, Patten also wrote the first cookbooks specifically for foods made using pressure cookers and food mixers. She has since written about the use of food processors, microwaves and, in the spirit of her role as a home economist, given advice on the best use of washing machines.

Patten was one of the earliest television cooks, though not the first, as some people believe. Patten herself has claimed, "I was the first to cook on television, but I don't think I'm a chef and I'm definitely not a celebrity." In fact, even the BBC is not sure who can rightly claim to be the first British television chef. Its press office has tentatively suggested that Moira Meighn was the first cook to appear on television, and Marcel Boulestin was the first to host a series. However Philip Harben, who later co-hosted a program with Patten, made a somewhat greater impact. Patten went on to enjoy a long television career and was resolutely practical in her approach leaving it to the ebullient Fanny Cradock to begin the cult of the television celebrity chef.

Patten frequently disclaims any interest in being a celebrity. She saw her role on television as "giving advice to people" and said, "The food was always more important than we were. The problem with celebrity chefs these days is that the personality overrides the food".

Patten's television style seems almost inconceivable to a modern audience because it is completely devoid of the showmanship expected from current celebrity chefs. Then there's her deeply unfashionable cut-glass accent that is only allowed on television as parody these days. Nonetheless, her television shows worked well and attracted very large audiences for a medium that was then relatively undeveloped.

In her early days, she was better known for appearances on BBC radio, first during the war in the early morning series, *Home Front* and then on the *Woman's Hour* program, starting in 1946 and continuing into the second decade of the twenty first century.

However, what really launched her culinary career was the work she undertook in improving the nation's diet both during and after the Second World War. In many ways, Patten personifies the evolution of British eating in the second half of the twentieth century. She is a no-nonsense pragmatist who recognized the limitations and the possibilities of what could be achieved in ordinary household kitchens. Delia Smith, whose career is examined in Chapter 19, is very much in the Patten mold but has yet to develop the kind of track record of her predecessor.

What ties these two remarkable women together is their level of popularity and the way they have been treated with condescension by some food writers and chefs who see themselves operating at a more sophisticated level, while these two women muddle along in their vaguely distasteful, populist way. Patten and Smith are resolutely down to earth and would never be insulted by the idea that they are populists, remote from the elite of the culinary world. Their skill lies in making this complex world accessible to domestic cooks struggling to put something interesting and possibly delicious on the table.

Patten has said that her favorite decade in food was the 1960s when food scarcity was finally put to bed and people started to travel overseas. This appetite for travel led to an enthusiasm for new kinds of food. She is philosophical about what's happening nowadays where there is even more choice, certainly more exposure to foreign influences and an explosion of interest in cooking as reflected by the proliferation of cooking shows on television.

Yet in many homes there is less cooking going on than ever before simply because of the hectic modern lifestyle. In an interview Patten said, "I am sympathetic about the lack of time, and I don't want to start castigating the British public for being lazy – I'd rather they buy a ready meal than have a breakdown… but I'm saying if you can find a little bit more time, you can eat more cheaply and better, even if it's just cooking a few vegetables in the microwave."

She told the *Financial Times*, "If people today don't cook and eat well, they are being very unforgivable. There is so much good food about." She also pointed out that, with the availability of better methods for food storage and defrosting today, it is ironic that households use these devices not for preserving a wide variety of fresh food but in order to have processed food readily at hand.

Other food gurus in this book, notably Jamie Oliver and Delia Smith, have taken up this theme of wasted opportunities in food. They too are on a mission to urge the British public to cook and to persuade them that good nourishing food is easy to prepare and an excellent and healthier alternative to processed foods. When Patten started writing cookery books, she saw them as instruction manuals designed to give confidence to nervous beginners who may well have been deterred by the perplexity of other books available at the time. Even Mrs Beeton's famous work (Chapter 4) must have discouraged those timorously venturing into the kitchen. Beeton's book sits alongside the works of the great French chefs and others that might just as well have labeled them "not for amateurs" because not only did they contain lists of ingredients that were hard to find but also the recipes were often somewhat imprecise when it came to detailing preparation methods. Whereas Marguerite Patten was not trying to impress, she was attempting to teach and to do so with a deft touch. "I considered myself an informer, giving advice to people," she said.

Patten sometimes gives the impression of coming from a rather grand family but she was actually born in relatively modest circumstances in Bath and grew up on the outskirts of London in Barnet. The young Marguerite learned about loss at the early age of twelve when her father died of injuries he had sustained in the First World War. His demise forced her mother to go back to work as an English teacher assuming responsibility of earning the family income and raising three young children. Since Marguerite was the oldest, it fell to her to help her mother in the kitchen. She says that both her mother and her paternal grandmother were good cooks proving that her culinary talent run in the blood. Although she never knew her grandmother as she died when she was just a baby, her mother seemed to believe that she had inherited her talents and congratulated the young Marguerite on being like her when she produced something good in the kitchen.

Theirs was a traditional household where basic British food was served, using the fruits and vegetables that came from the family garden. In later life, Patten has frequently lamented the failure of families to sit down and eat together comparing it to the time when she was a child and her hard-working mother cooked every day and ate with her children, making them appreciate the food and the social graces that came along with it.

"Mealtimes don't consist of just eating," Patten said in an interview, "they consist of conversation, exchanging views, listening, not only mums and dads but the children too. That's how they learn to communicate." And she worries, "If children and young adults eat separately, how do you know they're eating well?"

Patten's mother wanted her daughter to follow her in the teaching profession, but she had her heart set on being an actress, preferably a Shakespearian one, and she gained admission to the Royal Academy of Dramatic Art, although she lacked the funds required to take up the offer. Teaching did not appeal but she eventually followed her mother's advice and took a culinary training course, which led to her first job as a junior home economist with the Eastern Electricity Board.

The dream of acting lingered and Marguerite must have had some talent because she did eventually find a job as an actress, using the stage name of Marguerite Eve, first in the Everyman Theatre in slightly bohemian Hampstead and then with Oldham Repertory, in the North of England. This lasted nine months and then the season came to an end and there were no other acting offers. "I knew without a doubt that I wanted to go back to being a home economist," she claimed in an interview, "I loved meeting people, you see."

What is equally possible is that the practical young Miss Brown decided she had better find a more stable means of employment and applied to the Frigidaire company for a job as a home economist. She later recalled her job interview,   "They did a terrible thing for most people, they made us give a demonstration, but without a refrigerator, or a cooker or a table. After rehearsing in rep[ertory], I was used to performing with non-existent props so I launched forth pretending I'd got the refrigerator. I really shouldn't have had that job, I wasn't experienced enough, but it's like everything in life, if you get something you very speedily get the experience to meet the challenge."

It proved to be a real challenge to persuade British consumers that they needed one of these fancy American fridges when they were managing perfectly well storing food in chilly pantries. Fridge sales may have been slow, but Patten relished traveling around, staying in first class hotels and giving demonstrations, many of which involved food made in aspic, "We were aspic mad," she recalled in a 2010 interview.

With the outbreak of the Second World War, Frigidaire ceased icebox production and Patten was out of a job. But the war provided her two major opportunities. For a start, she moved to Lincoln where, in 1942, the food ministry employed her as a home economist. It was there that she met her husband to be, known as Bob Patten, although his actual name was Charles. He was an airforce Lancaster bomber gunner who notched up a remarkable record of surviving 84 operations, including three crashes. They remained married for 54 years until 'Bob' Patten's death in 1997.

Meanwhile, Britain, unlike Germany, was fully mobilizing its civilian population and putting them on stringent food rations. Rationing began in 1940 and the following year, Britain narrowly avoided major food shortages thanks to emergency deliveries from the United States. By now it was clear that the war would not end anytime soon and the Ministry of Food focused its attention on controlling supplies but also on the massive task of persuading the British public to think differently about how they ate and how to make the best of what was available. Patten joined the ranks of the Food Ministry, touring the country and giving talks about the best way to use food and to extract the highest level of nutrition from it. The task of Patten and her colleagues was nothing less than to teach British people to revolutionize their diet. Every demonstration started with the preparation of a large bowl of raw vegetables made into a salad. Participants were coaxed into eating raw carrots, cabbage and other root vegetables to extract as much vitamins out of the food as possible. Eating raw vegetables was hardly commonplace at the time but it was certainly healthy. Patten looks at the way officials are trying to transform eating habits today and compares it with her wartime experience, "The government now has a finger-wagging approach to what food we should be eating, which isn't right at all. At the Ministry of Food, we were taught never to lecture, but to tempt people, to lure people. That's the single best bit of advice I've ever had. We used to stand in factory canteens and say 'Ooh, what a lovely pudding this is! Isn't it a blessing that it wasn't made with an egg?' "

In some ways, the war helped people appreciate better ways of cooking. Britain's dismal method of boiling vegetables to death was swept away in a campaign to persuade the public that less cooking produced better nutritional value and better taste.

In late 1943, Patten was deployed to the fashionable Harrods department store in Knightsbridge to establish a food advice bureau and a year later her acting skills were utilized for the food ministry's five minute radio program called *Kitchen Front.*

Patten still regards her wartime work as the most important work she has ever undertaken, "we did a jolly good job," she said. Rationing continued in Britain until the 1950s and there was a considerable backlash against government meddling with food supplies. The ministry closed its food bureau but Patten remained at Harrods where the ministry's food advice bureau was transformed into the Harrods Food Advice Bureau. This in turn became the store's focal point for demonstrating new cooking appliances.

Patten was becoming well known through her appearances on television in 1947. But there was a bigger audience gained from a number of radio shows, mainly the BBC's flagship program *Woman's Hour.*

Her first book also came out in 1947, *Harrods First Book of Recipes,* which was rapidly followed by a second book and then a book on cooking with pressure cookers. In 1951, she decided to leave Harrods and embark on a freelance career as a cookery writer and food presenter.

A senior editor at the publishing company Hamlyn approached her and offered her a chance to write her own works without the Harrods mantle. This marked the start of a four decades long relationship with the publisher, beginning with the immensely successful *Cookery in Colour,* which sold an initial 30,000 copies in hardback and broke new ground with the use of different colored paper, foreshadowing the lavishly illustrated cookbooks of today. Her productivity in book writing was prodigious, at one point she was turning out three books per year alongside her many other activities, which included cookery demonstrations, radio and TV shows, newspaper and magazine articles and advisory work for food companies. These food demonstrations in the 1950s filled the seats of the London Palladium, a venue better known for top-of-the-bill variety shows.

The enduring influence of Marguerite Patten is demonstrated by a new generation discovering her books and their re-publication. Some of these books, such as *The Spam Cookbook*, seem to be less than serious but the sum total of her work is an encyclopedia of cookery in Britain, some of it of historic interest, while other aspects are contemporary and reflect newer concerns with healthy eating and food for children. Patten has collaborated with a physician, Jeannette Ewin, on a book about food that that is aimed at combating athritis and designed for the elderly, a description she shuns for herself, but pointers on how to achieve her robust health and longevity can be found in *Eat Well – Stay Well*.

Patten is also laying claim to the title of the "world's oldest podcaster," where she is to be found giving tips and offering recipes. In addition, a stream of well-known chefs and journalists are still making their way down to her home in Brighton, Sussex where she holds court and offers sumptuous teas to visitors. She has also been showered with honors, which seem appropriate for someone who has the status of being a national treasure. Official recognition has come in the form of two honors from the Queen. In 1991, she was granted the Order of the British Empire (OBE) and in 2010, she became a Commander of the Order of the British Empire (CBE). Over time, she has received many lifetime achievement awards from her peers in the food industry, and in 2007 received the British Woman of the Year Award.

As we have seen in the previous chapter about Jamie Oliver, and will see in the chapter on Alice Waters, there is a great deal of attention paid to the eating habits and the education of the youth. Patten was onto this well before them. She was involved in the Schools Food Trust, an ambitious government-backed scheme to create 4,000 after-school clubs for pupils and their parents and she is proud to recall an experiment she led in 2003: "I did two weeks of wartime school dinners for a class of 30 eight-year-olds. It was wintertime so we had to use root vegetables, and not one of those children had ever seen a parsnip before – or a turnip or a swede – let alone eaten one. They had seen cabbage and were determined they weren't going to eat it. By the end of the fortnight, because they weren't given any choice, they were all eating dishes like Irish stew, shepherd's pie – with all the vegetables – and enjoying it.

I think it's a question of re-educating children's palates when they're not used to healthy food."

Patten believes that official initiatives to get children to eat better are misguided. She said, "There's no home economics in schools any more, which is all the government's fault." Adding, "In their wisdom they've introduced this ridiculous subject of 'Food Technology'. And all you learn there is how to design a perfect teapot or how to make a packet of flour, never mind about actually using the flour to cook something. It's madness."

Marguerite Patten is indefatigable, even though she suffers from arthritis and is far less mobile than she used to be but she wants to carry on 'doing her bit,' a refrain from the war and a generation accustomed to hard work.

Patten Recipes

Here are three recipes that illustrate Patten's down-to-earth practicality and highlight dishes. In the first instance, there is a recipe that is still produced but considered something of a joke. In the second recipe, we see a wartime dish, reproduced here for historical interest although it is unlikely to be cooked today. Thirdly, there is a hearty dish which is quite likely to be cooked by anyone with a modicum of competence in the kitchen.

Spam Fritters

Ingredients
40 grams/12 ounces Spam - chopped pork and ham
oil for frying or deep frying

For the batter:
125 grams/4 ounces (1 cup) plain flour
pinch of salt
1 large egg
125ml./4 fl. oz. (half cup) milk, or milk and water,
   or water, or beer.

Method
Mix together all the batter ingredients in a bowl. The mixture should be thick, in the proportions given above, in order to coat the Spam well. Cut the Spam into eight slices.

Meanwhile, heat 2–3 tablespoons oil in a frying pan or wok, or heat a depth of oil in a deep-fryer to 170°C/340°F or until a cube of day-old bread turns golden in 1 minute.

Coat the Spam slices once or twice with the batter then drop them into the hot oil. If shallow frying, allow 2 –3 minutes on each side; if deep frying allow a total cooking time of 3–4 minutes, turning over the fritters as required. Drain on kitchen paper. Serve with mash.

From the *Spam Cookbook* by Marguerite Patten, Hamlyn, 2011

Eggless Sponge Cake

This is one the famous wartime recipes, designed for a time when eggs were scarce.

Ingredients
6 ounces (170g.) self-raising flour with one level teaspoon
   of baking powder, or 6 ounces plain flour with three level
   teaspoons of baking powder
2.5 ounces (70g.) margarine
2 ounces (56g.) sugar
1 level tablespoon golden syrup
a quarter of a pint (118ml.) of milk, or milk and water
jam for filling

Method
Sift the flour and baking powder. Cream the margarine, sugar and golden syrup until soft and light, add a little flour, then a little liquid. Continue like this until it is a smooth mixture. Grease and flour two 7-inch (18cm.) sandwich tins and divide the mixture between the two. Bake for approximately 20 minutes or until firm to touch, just above the center of a moderately hot oven. Turn out and sandwich with jam.

From *Feeding the Nation: Nostalgic Recipes and Facts from 1940-1954* by Marguerite Patten, Hamlyn, 2005

Navarin of Lamb

A more conventional recipe for a delicious dish of the type that more typically fills Patten's recipe books
Serves 4

Ingredients
750 grams (25oz.) lamb, diced
2 teaspoons sugar
50 grams (1.8oz) butter
25 grams (1oz.) flour
1 bouquet garni
1 clove garlic, crushed
3 tomatoes, skinned and chopped
750 grams (25oz.) young vegetables

Method
Sprinkle the meat with salt, pepper and the sugar.

Heat the butter in a large saucepan, add the lamb and cook gently, stirring once or twice, until it is delicately browned; the sugar gives it a faint caramel taste. Blend in the flour, then add the water and stir as the liquid comes to the boil and thickens very slightly. Add the bouquet garni, garlic, tomatoes and any extra seasoning required.

Simmer gently for about 45 minutes then add the selection of young vegetables, such as new potatoes, baby carrots, young broad beans, diced young turnips, fresh peas when available. Check there is sufficient liquid when adding and cooking the vegetables. Cover the pan and cook until the meat and vegetables are tender.

From *ocado.com,* Patten is a consultant to this online grocery company.

Chapter 15

Savoring the Snail's Pace

Carlo
Petrini

*U*nlike other food gurus in this book Carlo Petrini, the President of the Slow Food Movement, is neither a cook, nor in the restaurant business, nor a food producer nor even, primarily, a food writer but a dedicated food campaigner. However, he is the charismatic figure behind the founding of a movement, which offers an explicit counterpoint to the culture of mass-produced fast food. Fittingly, the movement has a snail as its emblem, a creature that is both slow moving and edible.

Petrini's contribution to the development of food and eating habits is at least on a par with those who have a history of producing food. While he is "merely" a consumer, he hates the idea of the public being viewed as consumers and most certainly does not accept that consumers should be passive. In many ways, he personifies a profound change in the way that contemporary society is starting to approach questions of food production and consumption.

Petrini's influence is felt at a time when a significant proportion of the world's people are confronting the consequences of excess rather than scarcity. This is a well-known fact but nevertheless remarkable because, as we have seen in previous chapters, it is only since the latter half of the twentieth century that people have moved away from the slog of acquiring sufficient food for sustenance to dealing with the complex problems of choice.

For many of the world's people, this new type of complexity remains unknown but in the developed world the plentiful supply of food has been taken for granted by post-Second World War generations in the West. So it is only economically advanced societies that have an opportunity to elevate food to a level where pleasure and sophistication supersedes questions of food for sustenance.

There were, it should be stressed, concerns with healthy eating well before the current period but they were almost entirely confined to a tiny strata of wealthy people. This is clearly no longer the case. Healthy eating has become a major issue and is often fused with a wider environmental awareness which is manifested by social and political activism.

Even those not inclined towards activism are nevertheless concerned about their personal consumption of food and the affect it has on their health. The widespread adoption of dieting is the most obvious manifestation of these personal concerns and, as have seen in Chapter 2, which looks at the work of Robert Atkins, this too, is the subject of enormous debate.

Carlos Petrini, however, is mainly focused on the social and political aspects of food. He and his colleagues are concerned about the entire universe of food consumption, production and attitudes to what we eat. No one can fault Petrini for lack of ambition – indeed he is often hailed as a visionary – but his views have also attracted sharp criticism, stimulating a widespread debate about food in all its aspects. It is important to add a vital caveat at this stage, contradicting the notion that advocates of slow food are puritans, likely to dismiss the pleasurable aspects of eating. On the contrary, members of the Slow Food Movement pride themselves on being food lovers with a deep appreciation of fine cuisine. Petrini goes to some lengths to stress this point.

The original *Slow Food Manifesto*, released in Paris on 9 December 1989, also made this clear. It declared that it was a call "against the universal madness of the Fast Life, we need to choose the defense of tranquil material pleasure. Against those, and there are many of them, who confuse efficiency with frenzy, we propose the vaccine of a sufficient portion of assured sensual pleasure, to be practiced in slow and prolonged enjoyment."

The Slow Food Movement has matured and greatly expanded since its founding conference and has widened its scope of interest. The Movement now states: "that everyone has a fundamental right to pleasure and consequently the responsibility to protect the heritage of food, tradition and culture that make this pleasure possible. Our movement is founded upon this concept of eco-gastronomy – a recognition of the strong connections between plate and planet."

Eco-gastronomy, a concept developed by Petrini, remains to the fore of the Movement's thinking as it continues to stress its commitment to quality in a number of forms: "Slow Food is good, clean and fair food. We believe that the food we eat should taste good; that it should be produced in a clean way that does not harm the environment, animal welfare or our health; and that food producers should receive fair compensation for their work."

The Movement talks of ensuring that the "enjoyment of excellent food and drink should be combined with efforts to save the countless traditional grains, vegetables, fruits, animal breeds and food products that are disappearing due to the prevalence of convenience food and industrial agribusiness."

Very conscious of accusations that supporters of Slow Food are essentially a body of fussy consumers, the Movement insists that it considers itself as "co-producers, not consumers, because by being informed about how our food is produced and actively supporting those who produce it, we become a part of and a partner in the production process." The extent of this partnership is distinctly limited, but as we shall see in Chapter 20, Alice Waters demonstrates how it can be done.

Petrini was brought up as a teenager in the heady days of the 1960s, when Italy was bitterly divided along the broad trajectory of left and right wing politics. On the left, where Petrini was located, there was a clash between the well-established and powerful Italian Communist Party and the new left which shunned the statism and pro-Soviet stance of the Communists. While on the right, the remnants of the fascist movement re-emerged with new names and found itself in conflict with the established Christian Democrats who were conservatives, rather than radicals. This ideological turmoil was the breeding ground for many activists who later turned away from politics in a party political sense. Petrini was among them. He had been an eager participant in the ideological debates of the 1960s and '70s, positioning himself among the non-Communist left. Along the way, he acquired a useful experience of campaigning and dealing with opposition. He was the founder of Italy's first independent radical radio station and this combined with other experience as a political activist, armed him with the weapons to wage a food campaign.

Petrini's interest in environmental issues, which many of the left were slow to embrace, gradually evolved into a focus on food in the late 1970s. Other left-wing activists also ended up realizing that this focus on food issues was compatible with their general anti-capitalist stance. Petrini says he can pinpoint the moment he became convinced that he had to get involved in food campaigns. "I went to eat in a small restaurant in my own native territory near Turin," he said, "I had grilled sweet red peppers with olive oil and garlic, a specialty of the Piedmont region. I tasted it, and there was something wrong with it. They just weren't that good. I asked, 'Where do these peppers come from?' They said 'Oh, they're from Holland.' They were grown hydroponically. They were all identical. There were 32 to a box, not 31, not 33. 'And they cost less than ours,' the cook was proud to say. 'And they last longer than ours.' But, of course, there was no pleasure of taste. And so I asked the farmers around this restaurant, 'Hey, where are those local peppers you used to have around here?' And they said, 'Well we just don't grow them anymore because we can't make money on them.' And I said, 'Well, inside those hot houses where you used to have red peppers, what do you have now?' And they said, 'Tulip bulbs!' "

Petrini, born in 1949, is proud to be an Italian who, since childhood, has lived outside the main metropolitan areas. His hometown of Bra is in the Piedmont region where he still lives. Petrini describes his family as being "somewhere between the working class and the middle class." He has vivid recollections of the food culture that prevailed in his home. "I remember after school snacks of *soma d'aj*, a slice of bread toasted on the stove, rubbed with a clove of garlic and sprinkled with a little salt and oil sprinkled on top. Few would probably dream of preparing such a thing for their children these days, but for me, it was a sort of 'education in garlic,' and I certainly don't regret it. Two other dishes that were important to my childhood are meat ravioli, made to last the week and totally sublime in the delicateness of the pasta sheets, and *rolatine*, strips of meat rolled up around a filling of egg, vegetables, cheese, and breadcrumbs, served with Piedmontese salsa verde. This last dish is hardly to be found any more, but when I'm able to find it, it never ceases to bring back a rush of memories."

Petrini obtained a degree in sociology at Trento University and worked as a journalist, mainly for left-wing newspapers. He specifies 1977 as the year in which his journalistic interests turned to food. Petrini's writing about wine and food grabbed attention because he went beyond the traditional sphere of food criticism that focused on restaurants. He was interested in questions of how tastes were changing and were influenced by artificiality in food production; he was worried by the rise of agri-business, the destruction of food traditions, especially the erosion of regional specialization and the way that food production was impacting on eco-systems. His earlier work appeared mainly in the left-wing daily *Il Manifesto* but gained a wider audience in the more mainstream *La Stampa* newspaper. He remains a prolific writer of books and journalistic pieces that now mainly appear in *L'Espresso* and *La Republica*.

Petrini became an active participant in ARCI (Associazione Ricreativa Culturale Italiana), a loose coalition of leftists. In 1986, this association morphed into a new organization called Arcigola which launched a magazine, *La Gola*, a name that in English can be understood as *Arch Appetite*.

Arcigola initially had little impact but it dramatically burst into public consciousness in 1986 with a protest against the opening of a McDonald's fast food outlet near the Spanish Steps or Piazza di Spagna in Rome. This was the second McDonald's store in Italy but the first in such a historic location.

Petrini later recalled that "the strategy of penetration of McDonald's in Italy brought its own antidote." He pointed out that in other countries the American fast food chain began its penetration of the market by spreading from the provinces to the metropolitan centers but in Italy it chose to appeal to "a public that was already Americanized." He said that this gave those outside the cities time to realize that the expansion of McDonald's posed a risk to traditional Italian eating houses.

Petrini later explained the thinking behind the McDonald's protest in his co-authored book *Slow Food: The Case for Taste.* He wrote: "Slow Food is not against McDonald's just because it hates hamburgers and French fries and regards spending a long time around the dinner table as compulsory . . . So it is not just a question of opposing slow to fast, but rather of highlighting more important dichotomies, like carefulness and carelessness or attentiveness and haste: attentiveness to the selection of ingredients and the sequence of flavors, to how the food is prepared and the sensory stimuli it gives as it is consumed, to the way it is presented and the company with whom we share it."

The media-savvy Arcigola protestors came armed with bowls of penne pasta, symbolizing basic Italian food and they appealed to both the nationalistic and nostalgic elements of public opinion combined with an anti big-food business message. The timing of this protest was also propitious. It came in the wake of a major wine scandal that was responsible for the death of 19 people poisoned by wine adulterated with industrial alcohol. The impact of this scandal was immediate; Italian wine exports plummeted by a third. There was a rapid realization that the nation's reputation for food and wine could not be taken for granted and that the pursuit of profit regardless of the consequences could not be allowed to remain unchallenged.

Reports of the protest spread around the world but, for the time being, Petrini and his colleagues remained focused on Italy. The wine scandal prompted him to co-author a guide book to Italian wines, notable for its acrid criticism of some lower priced wines in the Italian market and carefully selecting a range of affordable wines which gained considerable popularity, as did the book.

The Italian-based campaign shifted to the international stage in 1989 when delegates from 20 countries, mainly European but including Argentina and Japan, met in Paris to issue the manifesto of the Slow Food Movement. Petrini was elected president and retains the position to this day. By 2011, the movement had spread to 150 countries and claimed over 100,000 members organized into 1,300 convivia or local chapters with a network of 2,000 food communities which practice the production of food on a sustainable small-scale basis.

At the 1989 meeting, the delegates adopted the snail as a symbol of their movement and declared: "Our defense should begin at the table with Slow Food. Let us rediscover the flavors and savors of regional cooking and banish the degrading effects of Fast Food." The objectives set out in their manifesto are wide ranging but focus on the ideas of sustainability in food production and developing the concept of an 'Ark of Taste' to preserve and promote local culinary traditions. There is also considerable emphasis on public education, mostly focused on the negative impact of agri-business, fast food and the introduction of non-organic elements into food production.

As the Movement has developed, it has spawned a number of initiatives such as the Slow Food Foundation for Biodiversity. This movement is principally aimed at developed countries with an emphasis on biodiversity and preserving local traditions and has spawned some 500 local food producing projects. The University of Gastronomic Science, founded in 2004, largely through the efforts of Petrini and Massimo Montanari, is another attempt to spread the good food message through an academic program in the science and culture of food. It has a campus in Pollenzo, in Petrini's home province of Piedmont and another in Colorno in Emilia-Romagna.

The Slow Food Movement organizes a great many meetings and programs at national level but also holds big international events, primarily the Salone del Gusto (Hall of Taste) and two specialist cheese and fish events, plus the big Terra Madre world meeting.

As the Movement grew, so did criticism of slow food as a concept and of Petrini as its leader. Perhaps, inevitably, he is accused of being egocentric and focusing too much activity around his hometown of Bra. Some criticize the organization for being too centralist while others say that its component parts, i.e., the local chapters, are of uneven quality, making the parts less impressive than the whole.

However, these criticisms can be dismissed as little more than sniping, the more substantive critique concerns the lack of viability of the concept. While slow food doubters are prepared to acknowledge that there is a niche for food produced in the way the Movement advocates, they argue that if the world's food production was conducted along these lines, it would create food shortages and raise the price of food to levels that would present real problems for the average consumer. Besides, convenience foods and yes, fast foods, are designed to match the pace and demands of modern society. Why, they argue, is it wrong to go out and grab a hamburger on the run? Who has time to get in the kitchen and produce food from scratch? Is it not the case that slow food is little more than an elitist movement with minimal relevance for most people? And then there's the criticism over what is described as the hopeless romanticism and nostalgia of the slow advocates. Surely, it is argued, they need to wake up and realize that we are in the– twenty first century where food consumption cannot revert to a supposedly golden era.

Petrini himself is an old hand at this debate and has a well-honed response to the criticisms. For example, here is his response to the criticism about slow food meaning little more than higher prices. "You need to be prepared to pay more for quality," he said in a *New York Times* interview in 2003. "We're too used to cheap food. We need to be eating better quality food but less of it. There are problems of obesity because people don't understand that. Slow Food believes you should eat less—eat more in moderation. That would help solve this elitist critique, and it would also improve the food that we do eat. So the goal is not to make it cost less. The goal is to eat less."

What about the charge of elitism? Here's his response in a British newspaper interview: "It's not only in England, but in Italy, too, and other parts of the world, that we associate the right to leisure, the right to enjoyment, with elitism, as though it is an elitist concept in itself. But excellent food does not need to be complicated or expensive. It can be very simple. It is true we will have to pay a bit more for our food. Food is too cheap now. We cannot expect such cheap food in the future."

Elsewhere, Petrini has spoken of refrigerators as being "halls of death" because they are repositories of waste. His point and his answer to those who question the cost and impracticability of slow food, is to focus on the question of food waste. He says, "We produce food for 12 billion, we are a population of 6 billion, yet 1 billion suffer from malnutrition… if you forget the value of food, you can easily waste it." Hence, the slow food slogan of: "Respetarre le rimanenze!" ("Respect the leftover!").

Petrini is, in many ways, an unrepentant romantic about the old days, but he tempers this romanticism with hard-headed arguments for why we should learn from the past. He says, "In the past 50 years, food has gone out of your daily life. This has brought about double thinking: I eat, but I don't know what I'm eating. I don't know how it was made or where it has come from. Slow Food's roots exist in pleasure – in reclaiming the conviviality of sharing good food. Eating is no longer about love, but about consuming fuel. A woman cooks some food, and no one smiles at her or says thank you. Neither is there any fascination with food. In Mediterranean Europe, there is still that fascination, still the conviviality, the ritual. The most important thing about eating is to enjoy the moment of affection between family members, or friends or work colleagues. A civilization that loses this ritual becomes very poor. It's especially important for children to learn again how to experience communal eating."

According to Petrini, society today is faced with the fetishization of food. "We're all full of gastronomy, recipes etc. Turn on a TV anywhere in the world and you will see an idiot with a spoon. And every newspaper and magazine has recipes and a photo of the dish taken from above like a cadaver. It's a form of onanism and is masturbatory. We must normalize food rather than put it on a pedestal far out of reach."

Petrini wants people to stop thinking of themselves as food consumers, "because the consumer is someone who steals from and destroys the planet. We want to say co-producer. To be a co-producer means to be responsible. It means to be rich in culture, education, understanding how food is made, understanding the necessities of farmers. Become active, not passive people. This needs to be a historic transformation."

It seems unlikely that the message of historic transformation will be taken on by everybody. Most people are likely to cling to their love affair with fast and convenient food but this does not mean that the Slow Food Movement is failing. Even those who are not prepared to embrace its entire message are likely to have been influenced by the essence of its belief in reconsidering ways we eat and ways that food is produced. And when they reconsider, they change their habits. This is going to be a very slow transformation but somehow appropriate for a movement that uses the snail as its symbol.

Chapter 16

The Pioneer Cookbook Writer

Bartolomeo Platina

The claim of Bartolomeo Platina (1421–1481) to be listed among the great food gurus of the world could easily be questioned because he was not a chef, or possibly even a cook, and his interest in food ranked alongside a gallery of other, mostly ecclesiastical interests for which he also gained fame. However, not only was he the author of the first published cookery book (this claim is disputed but other candidates for this title appear to be less credible) but he was also intensely interested in the modern preoccupation of the connection between food and health.

His landmark work, *De Honesta Voluptate et Valetudine*, written in Latin and generally translated as *On Honorable Pleasure and Health* (but arguably more accurately rendered as meaning *On Honorable and Wholesome Pleasure*) was probably written in 1468–9 but may have been started earlier and set aside. It is also incidentally probably the only major gastronomic work to have been written in prison. Fortunately, the book has been translated into a number of languages and anyone reading a cookery book today owes a debt of gratitude to Platina for creating this genre of food books and for devising a format which is used to this day. Alan Davidson, the compiler of the *Oxford Companion to Food*, says "one could claim on Platina's behalf that he was the very first scholarly writer on food and cookery."

Platina was born in 1421 at Piadena near Cremona and adopted the Latin version of his hometown's name, Platina, as his own. The original family name of Sacchi was abandoned, a common practice among Italian Renaissance scholars. His life is quite unlike that of anyone else mentioned in this work. He first became a soldier and was then taken on as a tutor to one of the sons of Marquis Ludovico Gonzaga. This marked the start of a controversial and prominent academic and ecclesiastical career. It also brought him under the patronage of Cardinal Francesco Gonzaga who was instrumental in getting him to Rome and securing the post of a secretary.

Platina showed an aptitude for this kind of work and was appointed to the College of Abbreviators by Pope Pius II. This was the department that drafted papal bulls and was the kind of job destined to have placed Platina on a strong career path in the Vatican. Unfortunately for Platina, he quickly fell out of favor following the pope's death. Pope Pius' successor, Pope Paul II threw Platina out of the college after he ill-advisedly challenged the pontiff in pamphlet form, leading to a four-month spell in the prison at St. Angelo Castle. On release, he joined the so-called Roman Academy, formed to revive the study of classical works. Platina seems to have had a skill for being in the wrong place at the wrong time since the Academy also attracted the Vatican's disfavor and along with other members, he faced trumped-up charges of conspiracy to kill the pope. As a result, he found himself back in jail. While in prison, he worked on his cookery book which was eventually completed in 1469 although it was not published until 1474.

In the interim before publication, Platina started work on a book for which he was arguably better known during his lifetime: *Lives of the Popes*. His fortunes in the Vatican turned when, in 1471, Pope Sixtus IV was elected and subsequently appointed him as a prefect of the newly formed Vatican library which replaced the existing unofficial collection of books belonging to the papacy. Platina was to retain this position until his death from the plague in 1481. By then, three printed editions of his cookery book had been published.

Platina's book contains recipes and a general treatise on the links between food consumption and healthy living. Remarkably some of these recipes are recognizable and close to the kind of food eaten today. This includes what would now be described as the humble poached egg as well as more complex pasta, fish and meat dishes. Platina's work is encyclopedic in scope and demonstrates the first attempt at systematic organization of the culinary art. Today, we expect cookery books to be neatly divided into sections covering various foodstuffs but in the Renaissance period this was revolutionary. Platina began his book with a chapter on meat dishes, followed by soups and pastas, then on to sauces and condiments, emphasizing the then novel discovery of sugar for seasoning, which was starting to replace traditional spices. There is a notable emphasis on butter-based cooking that was pioneered in Italy by Platina's chef mentor who is discussed below. By the time he finished, he had covered all the major components of a recognizably modern meal although when he was writing it would have been a meal which only the privileged classes would have eaten.

Platina is didactic about how food should be cooked, and had firm views set out in terms that defy contradiction. Writing about the preparation of meat he insisted that "Beef and cow's meat ought to be boiled, and breast of veal also, but the back . . . requires roasting. You will reduce their hams to small pieces. You will boil a whole sheep with no harm, and good roasting can be done with legs and hams." Indeed, there is a specified cooking method for all commonly consumed types of meat.

The recipes are not his own, a matter which has encouraged some commentators to question Platina's credentials as a food writer, but there is no artifice here as he clearly attributes all but ten of the recipes to Maestro Martino de' Rossi of Como. It appears that he met Martino while traveling to Rome in 1463 with his influential protector Cardinal Francesco Gonzaga, who in turn introduced him into the household of the renowned epicurean Ludovico Scarampi Mezzarota, the Cardinal Trevisan who was Martino's employer.

By the time Platina met him, the famous chef had written his own work, *Libro de Arte Coquinaria*, (*The Art of Cooking*) a technical guide to cooking. It contains 260 recipes and draws on the work of others, as have all cookery books. Besides undoubted technical competence Martino's work is credited as providing a bridge between Medieval and Renaissance cookery. It remained in manuscript form and was widely plagiarized although it was not printed. Nevertheless, whole sections of this work appeared in published works without the kind of acknowledgement made by Platina who described Martino as "the prince of cooks from whom I learned all about cooking."

The genius of the non-chef was to use Martino's work and other information, presumably gained by personal contact with the chef, to produce a useable handbook in Latin (thus accessible to a wider audience), enabling others to reproduce these recipes.

The recipes, some of which are not precise, form only part of the book. The rest is devoted to general nutritional issues, the impact of food on health and the creation of a general feeling of well-being. In addition, Platina had to grapple with the vexing contradiction of a church culture emphasizing asceticism while extolling the pleasures of a gourmet, which are very much pleasures of the flesh.

The Renaissance-period Vatican was hardly austere, yet there were matters of doctrine to be considered. Platina cleverly confronted this issue of pleasure by turning the emphasis onto the health benefits of fine cuisine. He drew a distinction between self-indulgence and what he described as "the pleasure which the intemperate and libidinous derive from self-indulgence and a variety of foods and from the titillations of sexual interests" and "honest" or "right pleasure." This kind of terminology was employed in debates over food up to the nineteenth century. Even when discussing specific dishes Platina tries to underplay the pleasurable aspects of the food, although he was not shy in discussing forms of presentation to make it more attractive.

As we have seen, Platina lauded Martino and cooks in general and says that it is the master chef who embodies the qualities of experience, cleanliness, patience and understanding of his subject. The chef, wrote Platina, should follow Martino's example in striving for splendor by which he means creating an attractive appearance for the food when it is served.

While lauding both complexity and design of dishes Platina goes to great lengths to emphasize an interest in food and its consumption to promote better health. He even argues, in a somewhat convoluted fashion, that good eating is comparable to military valor. He wrote: "Just as in the past he who saved a citizen in battle seemed to deserve civic honors, he ... who would save many citizens by asserting a rational plan for food is also deserving of honor." Platina insisted that if his rational plan for healthy and honest eating were to be followed, "We would not see today so many so-called cooks in the city, so many gluttons, so many dandies, so many parasites, so many most diligent cultivators of hidden lusts and recruiting officers for gluttony and greed." This was a call for moderation in consumption, something we hear a lot of nowadays.

When Platina argued the case for good food in terms of health promotion he described what to eat at which time of the year and described how to exercise, this being intimately connected with eating habits. He says, "As much care as runners habitually take care of their legs, athletes of their arms, musicians of their voice, even so it behooves literary scholars to have at least as much concern for their brain and heart, their liver and stomach."

Platina was a man of his time, drawing on Roman sources such as Apicus, Pliny, Cato and others who advocated the Four Humors theory of health. The so-called humors are black bile, yellow bile, phlegm and blood; their interaction and workings were said to control how the human body behaves. Platina's application of this theory concerned the interaction of food on these humors.

His book enjoyed considerable success, it remained in print well into the seventeenth century, there were at least 14 Latin editions and it was translated into French, German and Italian. The first English translation appeared in 1967, a rather unusual event as it was produced as a Christmas gift for customers of the Mallinckrodt Chemical Corporation in Saint Louis, Missouri. A more authoritative translation by Mary Ellen Milham was published 11 years later.

The case for others as cookbook pioneers is eloquently made for earlier cookery books, such as the Arabic language books of Al Warraq, which appeared in the tenth century as well as Roman cookery texts from the fourth and fifth centuries. By the thirteenth century, there were a large number of texts in circulation. Records remain of some cookery works from Denmark, Germany, France and Spain. However, none of them amount to the systematic work undertaken by Platina. He would be accorded a place in history for the organization of the recipes alone but once his more general treatise on food and health is added he is elevated to the ranks of pioneering food scholars.

Platina recipes adapted from the work of Chef Martino

Anyone expecting a precise cookery-book type recipe of the kind we are used to today is likely to be disappointed because Platina is often lacking in precision and does not provide a full methodology. However, it took until the late nineteenth century before the appearance of cookbooks in a form that would be considered as acceptable today. What follows is a mixture of the original recipes and a little added guidance on how they might be achieved. We start with something very basic, which Platina calls 'boiled eggs' but has more in common with what we would now describe as poached eggs.

Poached Eggs

Ingredients
fresh eggs
sugar
rosewater
sweet spices
verijuice (fermented juice of unripe grapes)
grated cheese
Substitute: Grape or orange juice can be used instead of verijuice

Method
Put fresh eggs into boiling water without the shell. When they harden, take them out right away; they should be tender. Pour over them sugar, rosewater, sweet spices and verjuice, which is the slightly fermented juice of unripe grapes. Grape juice can be used instead or orange juice. They can then be sprinkled with grated cheese.

Fried Broad Beans

Ingredients
broad beans
onions
figs
sage
pot-herbs
soft fat or cooking oil
spices

Method
Cook broad beans mixed with onions, figs, sage and several pot-herbs and either put them into a frying pan that has been well greased with soft fat, or else rub them with oil and then fry them. Place onto a wooden board or a flat surface, spread (or roll out) into the form of a pancake and sprinkle spices over it.

Macaroni

Ingredients
flour
egg white
rosewater
purified plain water

Method
Mix together well-ground white flour, moistened with the white of an egg, rosewater and plain water. Roll this into slender bits like a straw, stretched to the length of half a foot. With a very thin iron stylus (needle), scrape out the middle. Then, as you remove the iron, you leave them hollow. Then, spread out just so and dry in the sun, they will last for 2 or 3 years, especially if they are made in the month of the August moon. They should be cooked in rich broth

and poured into dishes and sprinkled with grated cheese, fresh
butter and sweet herbs. This dish needs to be cooked for two hours.

Saffron-flavored Sausage

This is the original Platina recipe which is more or less useless for
an inexperienced cook but provides a basic guideline for making
sausages:

Ingredients
ground veal or pork fat
grated cheese
rich, ground spices
2–3 eggs
salt
pork intestine
spices

Method
Into well-ground veal or pork fat, mix grated cheese which is not
only aged but rich, well-ground spices, two or three eggs, beaten
with a paddle, and as much salt as the batch requires, and saffron
so as to make everything saffron-colored. When they are mixed,
put them in a well washed intestine which has been drawn out
exceedingly thinly. Not good unless they have hardened for two
days, they require cooking in a pot. They can be kept, however, for
a fortnight or more, if you add more salt and spices or if you dry
them in smoke.

Lucanian Sausage

And here's another recipe subject to the same strictures as those above:

Ingredients
lean and fat pork meat
salt
fennel
half-ground pepper
pork intestine

Method
If you want good Lucanian sausages, cut the lean and fat meat from the pig at the same time after all the fibers and sinews have been removed. If the piece of meat is ten pounds, mix in a pound of salt, two ounces of well cleaned fennel, the same amount of half-ground pepper, rub in and leave for a day on a little table. The next day, stuff it into a well cleaned intestine and thus hang it up in smoke.

Roast Chicken

Well, this is another way of finishing off a chicken roast.

Ingredients
chicken
verjuice
rosewater
sugar
ground cinnamon
Substitute for verjuice: grape or orange juice can be used

Method

You will roast a chicken after it has been well plucked, cleaned and washed, and after roasting it, put it into a dish before it cools off and pour over it either orange juice or verjuice (see above). Grape juice can be used instead, with rosewater, sugar and well-ground cinnamon, and serve it to your guests.

Chicken Pie

Still on the chicken theme here is the original Platina recipe for a pie using chicken or other poultry, unlike some of the other recipes, other than the crust for which he provides no details, this is an easy to follow dish.

Ingredients

chicken or other poultry
lard or cooking oil
crust
plums, cherries and other sour fruits

For the juice:
verjuice
8 eggs
parsley
marjoram
mint

Method

If you want a crust with chicks and any sort of bird, first boil them. When they are almost cooked, take them out of the kettle, and when they are out, cut them in pieces, and fry in a frying pan with plenty of lard. Then pour them out into a pan or well-oiled earthen pot lined with a crust. Add plums and cherries or sour fruit to this mixture without harm. Then beat with a paddle verjuice and eight eggs, if you are having more guests, or fewer… moderate the amount of juice.

With this mix parsley, marjoram, and mint chopped as fine as possible with a knife, and place on a fire but far from the flame, for it must boil slowly. Meanwhile, it ought to be stirred with a spoon as long as needed until it covers the spoon with a thick coating. Finally, pour this juice over the crust and put it on the fire, even if it is a meat pie. When it is cooked, serve to your guests. It will be very nourishing, digest slowly, and leave little indigestible residue, repress bile, and irritate the chest.

Chapter 17

The Father of Modern
French Cuisine

Fernand
Point

$\mathscr{F}$ernand Point, who was born in 1897 and died at relatively young age of 57 in 1955, would have been greatly amused by an event held on 13 November 1978 to mark the month of his wife's 80th birthday. It was billed as "The Greatest Gastronomic Fete Ever Known" and was presided over by Marie-Louise Point. Gastronomes gathered at the 17th-century Chateau de Vizille near Grenoble to pay homage both to Marie-Louise Point, who carefully preserved her late husband's legacy by taking over his famous restaurant, and to the man who had personally influenced many of those present.

The focus was the fine food prepared under the direction of the chef Paul Bocuse (Chapter 5), who was apprenticed to Point and there was, of course, plenty of wine, especially Mumm's champagne, which Point liked to consume with considerable gusto. No expense was spared on the entertainment provided by military bands and there was no lack of extravagant decoration. The birthday cake, which resembled a pyramid, the trademark of Point's famous La Pyramide Restaurant, was placed in a small lake and brought in with the accompaniment of ballet dancers and a string orchestra. Chefs, politicians, ambassadors and other famous personalities were among the 700 guests who gathered for this tribute to the man credited with transforming twentieth century French cuisine.

Point was no stranger to extravagance, nor to the art of perfection and he definitely enjoyed flamboyance mixed with a degree of mischief, so this was a party he would have relished. But he was at heart very serious about food and prone to making wonderful sweeping claims about his art, such as: "If the divine creator has taken pains to give us delicious and exquisite things to eat, the least we can do is prepare them well and serve them with ceremony."

The influential American chef Thomas Keller said, "I believe Fernand Point is one of the last true gourmands of the twentieth century. His ruminations are extraordinary and thought-provoking. He has been an inspiration for legions of chefs." He was known as La Roi (The King), by his peers and hailed as "the world's greatest chef," a title bestowed on others appearing in this book but entirely appropriate for the time it was given, a time when French cuisine still ruled the world. That time has since passed but it can be argued that he came at the end of an enormously influential cycle that began with Antonin Carême (Chapter 6), moved on to Auguste Escoffier (Chapter 9) with Point taking up the baton, then followed by Paul Bocuse. It was around this time that chefs from other parts of the world began to lose their awe of French supremacy and became world leaders in their own right.

Like his predecessors, Point took on board some of this rich French heritage while specifically rejecting other aspects making him very much a man of his time. Fernand Point came to prominence after the First World War, which also marked the beginning of an era when most people in Western Europe were becoming accustomed to a greater variety of food. Vast improvements to transportation, especially by rail, meant that food could be more easily sent from one region to another and no longer had to be preserved before dispatch. People at this time began to travel more widely and were thus exposed to different cuisines. This created new opportunities and pressures for creative chefs who wanted to use the freshest food, even if it was not grown in their locality.

Point was among those who seized these opportunities with both hands and understood that the complexity and richness of the food associated with haute cuisine was a thing of the past. He preached simplicity, although nowadays what Point regarded as simple is likely to be thought of as rather complex. He is credited with advancing an idea that remains a cornerstone of modern cooking, namely the notion that each dish should be constructed around a single ingredient or dominant flavor. He eschewed what he saw as the unnecessarily elaborate composition and presentation of dishes that had been the hallmark of haute cuisine.

Point insisted on absolutely fresh ingredients, he wrote: "Every morning the cuisinier must start again at zero, with nothing on the stove. That is what real cuisine is all about." Point was also interested in the regional provenance of dishes, ensuring that the characteristics of the region were reflected in the food. He despised the haute cuisine focus on preparing heavy sauces in advance; favoring instead light sauces made-to-order. But he shared the insistence of his predecessors in aiming for perfection. "Success," he wrote, "is the sum of a lot of small things done correctly." He also liked to say: "I'm not hard to please, I'm content with the very best."

Like many great chefs, Point was no slouch, he followed a regime that he had adopted since 1914 when he was an apprentice at the Hotel Bristol in Paris. This involved rising promptly at 4:30 am, starting work at five in the morning and finishing at eleven at night, with a couple of hours rest in the afternoon. "Cooking demands complete dedication," he wrote, "one must think only of one's work."

Point stressed that great cuisine could not flourish if it was free of innovation; on the contrary the work of great chefs should be recognized but not clung to with a kind of fetishism. Although he stressed the importance of producing lighter, fresher food, this is the man most famous for his catchy declaration: "Butter! Give me butter! Always butter!" Butter aside, the pioneers of the 1970s nouvelle cuisine movement acknowledge Point as their inspiration. They took healthy and light cuisine to a new level and used his ideas and methods for dishes that characterized this movement. Indeed Point personally trained the leaders of this movement, including the chefs Paul Bocuse, Alain Chapel, Louis Outhier, Georges Perrier and Jean and Pierre Troisgros.

Point's influence also spread outside the realm of food preparation because he broke the tradition of remaining in the kitchen while his guests were dining. He, on the contrary, liked to stride into the dining room, greet his guests and discuss the food, a practice taken up with greater vigor by his apprentice Bocuse and which is now commonplace.

Point wrote: "As far as cuisine is concerned, one must read everything, see everything, hear everything, try everything, observe everything, in order to retain, in the end, just a little bit!" The idea that guests might be able to contribute to this process had evidently not occurred to his predecessors.

Not only did Point value the ideas of his guests but he insisted that the dining room and its settings had to be of the highest order. The crockery came from Limoges and the crystal glasses from Baccarat. He strictly limited the number of seats to fifty and laid down inflexible dining hours. The restaurant did not have a printed menu but offered a choice of dishes, never more than twenty, which changed daily. Even the most influential customers could not breach the rules of Point's restaurant. He created a sanctuary for fine food that followed his dictates and could only be sustained by an uncompromising regime.

Striving for perfectionism with a pronounced intransigence inside and outside the kitchen were the hallmarks of this man, who was a tyrant to his staff but in equal parts respected by them. To describe Point as larger than life is more than a figure of speech. He was enormous, six feet tall and weighing 370 pounds with a 66-inch waistline. As his size suggests, he loved to eat and drink. Philippe Troisgros, one of the chefs mentioned above who trained under him, recalled that he could eat three chickens and a pot-au-feu between breakfast and lunch. Once he was established as a successful restaurateur, he would employ a barber to shave him in the late morning while consuming a magnum of champagne.

Point, who came from the famous Burgundy wine region, was born into the restaurant business as his father, Auguste, ran a small buffet restaurant at the Louhans railway station. His mother and grandmother, reputed to be excellent cooks, worked in the kitchen and encouraged the young Fernand's interest in cooking. His father was ambitious for his son and realized that he could develop this interest but needed to look beyond his own restaurant to do so. In 1922, the restaurant closed because the railway authorities refused to place it on the list of recognized eating establishments.

The Points moved to Lyon but failed to find suitable premises for a restaurant. However, the following year, Auguste Point found a restaurant in Vienne, eight miles south of Lyon. It was called the Restaurant Guieu, established 20 years previously by Leon Guieu, a popular figure in the town and a successful restaurateur.

The Points moved swiftly to overcome skepticism over their accession. The location was good because it attracted both local trade and travelers making their way to their way from Paris to the Côte d'Azur. The town was also attractive, built on seven hills and situated at the confluence of the Rhone and Gere rivers.

When the restaurant opened, Fernand Point left the family business to become an apprentice in various well-known kitchens, a common practice which gave aspirant chefs exposure to the skills of great chefs in return for a pittance by way of remuneration. Point went to Paris to work at the famous Foyot restaurant and the Bristol hotel. He traveled south to the Majestic in Cannes and to Évian-les-Bains, where, at the Royal hotel, he worked alongside Georges Bocuse, father of Paul Bocuse (whose family background is remarkably similar to that of Point). This classic form of apprenticeship was cut short in 1925 when Point's father died and Fernand moved back home to take over the restaurant in Vienne. He renamed it La Pyramide in homage to a rather fine pyramid nearby built by the Romans. This magnificent structure built of stone had four columns and four arches. The pyramid became Point's trademark; it was on his menus and he used the symbol in a number ways including dishes molded into pyramids and pyramid-shaped butter molds placed on every table to accompany the bread.

Point was just 26 when he re-established the restaurant. In 1930, he married Marie-Louise who took over the business side and ran the dining room. It was a close business and personal relationship; Point called his wife Mado and insisted on making her lunch every day.

On the death of her husband, she worked hard to retain its reputation and became famous in her own right for her work.

However, Point had a rather dim view of female chefs. "Only men have the technique, discipline and passion that makes cooking consistently an art," he said echoing the prevailing misogynistic view in French kitchens of his time.

Now that leading chefs seem to have the status of rock stars, it is commonplace to see them as worldly figures who can happily mingle in A-list circles. But Point was very much a chef of the old school. He stuck close to his kitchen, rarely even traveling far from his restaurant. He was dismissive of any form of intellectual activity, never reading a book unless it was about food. Point was a fine craftsman, even a rather old fashioned one for his time. Yet he believed in innovation in the realm of food and although he would never have dreamt of expanding his restaurant empire in the way that modern chefs lend their names to establishments manned by others, Point was no slouch in expanding his own establishment. He rapidly acquired an adjacent piece of land which served as a formal garden, created a terrace providing additional dining space and added a second storey to the building.

Point ruled the restaurant with a rod of iron, terrifying, cajoling and educating both staff and customers. At the dawn of the new day, Point was to be found searching the kitchen's storerooms and shelves to ensure that none of his staff had hidden away food preparations to be used in the current day's cooking. They had to start from scratch and nothing less was acceptable. Point maintained standards with an unflinching insistence on freshness.

He became the epitome of the French restaurant tyrant which has since been frequently caricatured and emulated by those of infinitely lesser talent. Customers were never presented with an itemized bill, just a total amount. Few dared to quibble. Point fully expected his customers to behave according to his rules. "La grande cuisine," he declared, "should not wait for the customer; it is the customer who should wait."

He would not, for example, tolerate customers smoking during their meal. When he spotted this happening, he would dispatch a coffee and the bill to the table, regardless of whether the meal was finished. If challenged, he would declare with a straight face that he naturally assumed that the customers had finished their meal as they were already smoking.

In 1933, when the *Michelin Guide* started to rank restaurants, La Pyramide was among the first of 23 restaurants to acquire a three star rating. This was just seven years after his father's death. The restaurant retained its rating for 50 years. It was not just the *Michelin Guide* that recognized this establishment, there was a procession of famous gourmands heading to its doors and it became the fashionable stop-off point between Paris and the southern coast. Sacha Guitry, a celebrated French playwright and actor made a famous pun in French, "Pour bien manger en France, un Point c'est tout"—"To eat well in France, a Point (or full stop), that's it."

It was a remarkable achievement in a short space of time. Point's reputation for excellence rapidly spread but was brought to a juddering halt by the German invasion of France. Declining to serve the officers of the occupation force, he closed the restaurant for the duration of the rest of the war.

Jean Troisgros, mentioned above, said, "He knew how the old classic recipes were prepared but he was not especially concerned with following them 'to the letter.' He built on them and created his own recipes."

So the food was rich but not as elaborate as the heritage haute cuisine demanded. Troisgros and his brother were among the chefs who went on to become the pioneers of the 1970s nouvelle cuisine movement which built upon Pont's lighter style, using the freshest ingredients and employing stunning presentation.

Much of what is remembered and known about Point is contained in his seminal work *Ma Gastronomie*, the product of his conscientious scribbling in a cream-colored notebook he kept with him at all times. The book, first published in 1969, contains his ideas and thoughts but was not written by Point, although he is credited as the author. It is the painstaking work of an editor who also assembled the 200 recipes it contains.

In 1974, the book appeared in English. This version was the work of Frank and Patricia Shannon Kulla who persuaded Charles Flammarion, the French publisher to sell them the English language rights. But their edition is more than a translation. The Kullas interviewed Point's widow and a number of his disciples, who are not mentioned in the French book. As a consequence, they fleshed out more of Point's methods and, as Frank Kulla later said, "We thought to give people a feeling of the day-to-day operation of the restaurant . . . from the viewpoint of chefs who absolutely loved this man; they would do anything for him, really. They had such tremendous admiration for him."

New generations of chefs study this work almost religiously. Thomas Keller insists that "if someone said to me I could only have one cookbook, this is the one." He wrote an introduction to a later edition saying "through Chef Point's words I finally understood and discovered a higher sense of purpose."

"Cookbooks are as alike as brothers," Point wrote, "the best is the one you write yourself." Point, the larger than life chef, was faithful to his own words. The large man died at a relatively young age, pausing only for illness to depart from his kitchen. His legacy is his food and, although it was not apparent at the time, it was the end of an era when French chefs were pre-eminent in the culinary world.

Point Recipes

Fernand Point's only published repository of recipes is *Ma Gastonomie,* however, this work does not contain recipes in the form that modern cookbook readers expect to see them. They assume a significant amount of knowledge and do not fill in the gaps between processes; so what appears here is one of the book's recipes which is presented in modern form and, a recipe provided by one of his disciples and Point's widely quoted views on the preparation of eggs.

Eggs

Sometimes it is the so-called simple things that distinguish mere cooks from great cooks. Legend has it that Point would test applicants for his kitchen by asking them to fry an egg. He had firm views on this matter, insisting that there was only one way to accomplish this feat. This involved melting some unsalted butter in a pan over a very low heat without allowing it to sizzle, carefully placing the already unshelled egg into the pan, covering the pan and then cooking slowly until the egg white set, a point that can be identified by a mild steam emanating from the egg, while the yolk remained perfectly liquid.

Similar principles were applied to the preparation of a "simple omelette" which, according to Point, should be made as follows:

Whip the yolks and white of the eggs separately. Add the beaten egg yolks, salt and pepper to sizzling butter in a skillet.

When the eggs begin to set, add a good spoonful of *crème fraîche* and the beaten egg whites. Keep the pan moving over a high heat to avoid having the omelet stick to the pan.

Marjolaine
(Multi-layered chocolate cake)

This is one of Point's most famous dessert recipes. The version given here has been elaborated from the chef's typically less precise published instructions that assume knowledge of certain things.

Ingredients
125 grams (4.5oz.) butter
4 eggs, separated
250 grams (9oz.) caster sugar
125 grams (4.5oz.) plain chocolate
125 grams (4.5oz.) plain flour

For the frosting:
180 grams (6oz.) bittersweet chocolate
180 grams (6oz.) butter
180 grams (6oz.) icing sugar

For the chocolate curls:
1 bar plain chocolate
icing sugar

Method
Preheat the oven to 180°C/350°F/Gas 4

1. Butter a round cake tin of 20 centimeters (8 in.) and line the bottom with parchment paper, butter the paper
2. Put the butter in a bowl and the bowl in a saucepan half filled with hot water on a low heat, stir until the butter is soft enough to pour, remove from the heat
3. For 5 minutes beat the egg yolks with two-thirds of the sugar, or until the mixture is light and form ribbon trail
4. Coarsely chop the chocolate
5. Stir the chopped chocolate into the egg mixture

6. Whisk the egg whites until stiff, sprinkle in the remaining sugar and whisk until very stiff and glossy

7. Sift one-third of the flour into the chocolate mixture, spoon one large spoon of egg whites, fold them gently together then add the remaining flour and egg whites in the same manner

8. Spoon the mixture into the prepared tin, bake for 60 minutes, or until the cake shrinks from the sides of the tin, insert a thin knife blade into the cake, the blade should emerge clean

9. Remove from the oven, run a knife blade round the edge of the cake, place a wire rack on the top of the cake and tin and then turn both over together to unmold the cake, remove the tin

10. Put a piece of baking parchment over the cake and turn the cake over on the wire rack, leave to cool on the paper

11. Cut a card round slightly smaller than the cake, or use a cake board

12. When the cake is cold, place the card on top of the cake and reverse

To make the frosting:

1. Chop the chocolate, put the chocolate in a bowl and the bowl in a saucepan half filled with hot water on a low heat, until melted, remove from the heat, allow to cool slightly

2. Beat the butter until soft and smooth, sift and stir in the icing sugar until light and creamy, stir in the melted chocolate in the butter mixture, mix quickly because it sets quickly, pour the frosting on top of the cake, spread it evenly over the top and side of the cake, use a palette knife to make sure that the cake is evenly covered

To make the chocolate curls:

1. Chocolate bar at room temperature, shave the chocolate with a vegetable peeler

2. Sprinkle the curls on the cake, sift icing sugar evenly on the curls.

Fernand Point

Veritable Gratin Dauphnois
(potato gratin)

This is Paul Bocuse's memory of the dish

Ingredients
1 clove finely chopped garlic
2.75 pounds (1250g.) peeled and thinly sliced potatoes
2 large eggs
0.75 liter cup (3 cups) of whole milk
2–3 tablespoons of heavy cream or creme fraiche
pinch of freshly grated nutmeg
salt and ground white pepper to taste
3.5 tablespoons butter

Method
Preheat oven to 350°F/180°C. Rub the sides of a large enameled or cast-iron ovenproof dish with the garlic clove and butter liberally. Lay thin layers of potatoes on the dish. In a separate bowl, combine the eggs, milk, cream, grated nutmeg, salt and pepper in a mixing bowl and whisk. Spread a thick coating of this mixture over the potatoes in the dish, adding some knobs of butter. Bake for around 45 minutes, or until the potatoes are slightly brown. Open the oven door ajar and let the dish set for a few minutes. Serve very hot.

From *French Chefs Cooking: Recipes and Stories from the Great Chefs of France* by Michael Buller, Wiley, 1999.

Chapter 18

Making Food Entertaining

Gordon Ramsay

𝒢ordon Ramsay is far from being the first chef to have appeared on television but is arguably the chef who has done most to use television as a way of propelling interest in food to a level where it competes with other forms of entertainment. The Scottish-born Ramsay who has made his name into a brand, and hates being described as an entertainer, insists that he is a serious award-winning chef. Yet he spends more time out of the kitchen than within, indeed much of this time is taken up with making television programs, presumably for the purpose of entertainment. But this is not the only contradiction in this volatile man's life: Ramsay states that he hates the kind of schmoozing of restaurant guests favored by some chefs and resolutely remains in the kitchen.

Yet he is more than happy to appear in millions of homes schmoozing like mad with television audiences. He is frequently dismissive of French restaurants, French chefs and France in general yet his primary culinary influence is most definitely French. And while Ramsay is famous for shouting at people and securing his reputation as one of the most offensive people to have come out of a kitchen, he insists he swears only in the kitchen and is a mild mannered person at home.

"At the end of the day," Ramsay said in an interview, "I'm not the only person who swears. I get it off my chest and move on. I've got four amazing kids –I don't go round the house swearing." He carefully nurtures a brash self-centered persona but is also an avid charity worker and continues to give considerable support to his brother who is a drug addict.

So Gordon Ramsay is clearly not a simple person and it is not even simple to explain his status as a food guru without getting caught in the dazzling spotlights of a television studio where even the most complex things can be reduced to caricature.

The idea that a chef could be the star of a television show, as opposed to being an anonymous person who prepares food for a living, is relatively new. When Marguerite Patten (Chapter 14) and Delia Smith (next chapter) appeared on television they both regarded themselves as culinary educators.

Previously, TV bosses might have featured a chef as some kind of novelty item for afternoon scheduling aimed at female viewers interested in cooking. However, we are now entirely comfortable with the idea of chefs as mainstream television performers, on a par with people with skills such as singing and dancing who obviously thrive in the world of entertainment.

No chef has more effectively parried his prowess in the kitchen with an ability to entertain than Gordon Ramsay. The simple fact of the matter is that were it not for television and Ramsay's considerable on-screen talents, he would still be regarded as a first-class chef but almost certainly not as a guru with considerable influence on the way people think about food, restaurants and even eating. Purists will sniff and say that this is nothing more than the product of showmanship and they would be right, although their pejorative views on showmanship are misguided. They fail to recognize that Ramsay has stimulated interest in food even among those who never thought they would exceed the culinary skills required to boil an egg. He has succeeded in making the whole subject about as populist as it can possibly be.

The big question mark hovers over how Ramsay has achieved this level of interest. He has a personality which personifies drama and he milks it for all its worth. In case there is a scintilla of doubt over whether his famous swearing and tantrums are being employed to attract television ratings, the titles of two of his TV programs say it all; one is called *The F Word* and the other *Kitchen Nightmares*, the central drama being, of course, Ramsay "effing" and blinding away at hapless restaurateurs whose businesses are failing.

Readers of the London-based *Radio Times* voted Ramsay as the most terrifying television personality and the issue of his temper frequently makes an appearance in interviews, alongside a series of highly publicized brushes with other chefs, food critics, members of his staff, members of his own family and well, more or less everyone who crosses him in some way. In one of the most publicized incidents, Ramsay threw out of his restaurant the British food critic A.A. Gill who was dining with the film star Joan Collins. Ramsay claimed he had been insulted by Gill. After the event, Gill, who is also no stranger to the acerbic tongue, described Ramsay as "a wonderful chef, just a really second-rate human being."

His views were returned in kind: "Gill," said Ramsay, "writes about chefs as if they're idiotic little run-around dumb boys that have never had a proper education. And I suppose in many ways, kitchens are built on huge insecurities and so you're constantly scrapping for pole position, and you're far happier cooking than you are sitting down and trying to study (for) an O-level (examination). Fine, I suppose your security is your success and your key to success is your fine palate. But there's a journey to get there and a huge price to pay for it. So - would I kick him out again? I think I'd ask him to be constructive." These comments give a rare insight into the insecurities which surround the lives of professional chefs.

Ramsay alludes to the lack of a formal professional structure for the work of chefs compared with many of the professions or other trades which have a universally recognized structure.

Chefs, on the other hand, may well have received some vocational training and will probably have served an arduous apprenticeship, followed by a long climb up the kitchen ladder. This process is largely informal and, unfortunately, where formal qualifications exist, as in the case of chef's vocational training at colleges, they are not highly regarded. Being a chef is one of the few remaining trades where a young entrant to the industry is almost entirely dependent on his or her mentor. Even when a young chef is installed in a kitchen, there is constant pressure and constant danger because kitchens are filled with hazards. It is rare to meet a chef who has not been cut, burned or possibly suffered more serious injuries at work. Moreover as Ramsay has previously observed, "You become stubborn because you have to. Kitchens are hard environments and they form incredibly strong characters."

Added to these perils is the pressure to perform or, as Ramsay puts it, to scrap "for pole position." No wonder chefs tend to lack some of the social graces expected by people who think that working in a professional kitchen is even vaguely similar to preparing food at home. Here's an example of a Ramsay rant which exemplifies the way he approaches criticism and other challenges to his way of doing things. Fittingly, this example shows his response to objections to his swearing by Raymond Blanc, owner of Le Manoir aux Quat'Saisons in the British Midlands. Blanc, like Ramsay, has a considerable television following.

"I don't want to bang on about Raymond Blanc but that guy is full of s***," said Ramsay. "When Raymond was carving out his reputation at the Manoir, he was a talented, full-on compulsive, swearing, tough chef, in his kitchen. Now he is in his late fifties, he starts to philosophize. Which is bullshit! F*** off; you French twat."

Ouch! Chefs are notoriously bitchy about each other but few have gone out of their way to be as publicly offensive about their colleagues as Ramsay. Talking about two of Britain's best-known chefs he was quoted as saying: "From an early age, I understood that cooking was never going to be a job, it's a passion. Poor old Antony Worrall Thompson, poor old Delia Smith, I don't think the penny's dropped yet!"

Ramsay has become the public face of the conflicts, insecurities, and high levels of aggression found in working kitchens everywhere in the world. Instead of retreating behind a polite façade to assure the public that chefs are really rather charming people dedicated to the art of producing fine food, Ramsay instinctively seized on the drama of the situation and has used it to create a narrative of his own which has become compelling viewing for millions of people.

Unlike some of the other gurus in this book, Ramsay has simulated interest in the entire business of serving food commercially. His television shows often focus on restaurants and how they work, injecting a sense of drama into this essentially didactic exercise. Although he is probably the most famous television restaurant "doctor," wading around yelling at failing restaurateurs and telling them how to fix their business, his own business empire has had mixed success.

Nevertheless, with a slew of Michelin stars, he retains a high reputation for the food produced on his premises. There is no particular Ramsay style of cooking, but his food is generally French-influenced, albeit with a reasonable amount of respect for foods from Britain and a self-professed desire to keep things simple. Ramsay sees himself as an obsessive, perfectionist in food and service, and there is no doubt that he is driven by a strong competitive streak.

He was born in Johnstone, Scotland in 1967 and the family moved to the wrong end of Stratford-upon-Avon when he was five. Ramsay describes his childhood as being "hopelessly itinerant." This was largely because of the restlessness of his hard drinking and womanizing father who moved between a series of menial jobs in search of the big time that never came.

The only thing about young Gordon's life that apparently interested his father was his talent for football. When he was at school, his competitive nature propelled him towards a career as a professional footballer. At the age of 12, he was chosen to play for the under-14s side at Warwickshire and shortly afterwards had a trial at Glasgow Rangers, the much more famous home team of the town where he was born. Ramsay was understandably excited about this and by the age of 16 his family moved from Stratford-upon-Avon back to Glasgow so he could qualify to play for the team.

The following year, he was offered a place in the youth team. He then suffered two serious injuries, smashing a cartilage while playing football, followed by another injury incurred while playing squash. Ramsay was determined to play on after the first injury but after the second, when he was only 19, the football club told him they could not have him on the team. According to Ramsay, the shock and disappointment of being kicked off the team was not assuaged until he received his third Michelin star.

Rangers had in fact offered to try and find Ramsay a place with a third division club but even at the age of 19 he was unprepared to settle for second best. Instead, he took his mother's advice and signed up for a hotel management course at the North Oxfordshire Technical College, physically close to Oxford University but many miles away in all other respects. It was here that he discovered cooking and gravitated towards the culinary aspects of the course. His father, who was determined that his son should be a football player, was furious, declaring that "cooking's for poofs."

He never forgave his son for the disappointment of abandoning a football career and deserted his family soon afterwards. Gordon Ramsay was hardly passionate about a food career until, according to him, he came across a lecturer yelling at the students. Something clicked and he realized that the kitchen could be as boisterous and tough as the football pitch. And then he realized that this was something he could do rather well.

Like many catering school graduates, Ramsay quickly embarked on a career involving a succession of jobs. One of the first was as a commis chef at the Wroxton House Hotel. He must have been good because his next job involved heading the kitchen at the Wickham Arms, a post that he had to relinquish after an affair with the owner's wife. He then went to London, moving from kitchen to kitchen until being taken on by the mercurial and already very famous chef Marco Pierre White who ran the kitchens at Harveys.

Ramsay stayed at the restaurant for just under three years and said he put in 17 hours a day while focusing on acquiring a refined palate.

Later, he claimed to have left because he was tired of "the rages and the bullying violence" in White's kitchen. Many of Ramsay's employees have found that this description of working with White compares closely with their experience of working under Ramsay.

However, it was White who introduced him to a higher level of restaurant cooking with standards he had not previously encountered. Clearly, Ramsay had the talent to seize on this experience and make full use of it. White advised him to continue his training in France but Ramsay was not keen; however he made full use of his mentor's introduction to Albert Roux at La Gavroche in London's classy Mayfair district. The restaurant and its chef de cuisine were among the most highly rated in Britain at the time. Although Ramsay's relationship with White was clearly strained, it was amicable enough for them to have parted in a civilized way. It was only later that Ramsay became bitter about White and pursued a long lasting feud with him. He appears to have got on better with Roux who was instrumental in helping him embark on what became a three-year stint in France.

Ramsay often refers warmly to his formative culinary experiences in France, seemingly ignoring his frequent rants against the French and their cooking. In France, he joined Roux as his number two in the Hotel Diva restaurant in the French Alps and from there went to Paris where he worked with the famous and highly-rated chefs Guy Savoy and Joël Robuchon.

Ramsay recalls that he was exhausted after his three years in France and spent the next year working as a personal chef on a yacht based in Bermuda. In 1993, he was back in London and took up the post of Head Chef at La Tante Claire restaurant in Chelsea. Under Ramsay, the restaurant's reputation soared. Despite the difficulties he had with White, his former mentor offered him the opportunity to become the Head Chef at a new restaurant he was opening which was subsequently renamed as Aubergine.

For the first time, Ramsay was given a 10 percent equity share in the restaurant, alongside White and his business partners. With Ramsay in the kitchen, Aubergine was awarded a Michelin star followed by its second star 14 months later. In 1996, he was awarded the Order of the British Empire (OBE) medal in recognition of his services to gastronomy. The award was significant recognition for someone at the starting point of an illustrious career and, among things, acknowledged the growing public interest in all things concerning food.

Ramsay was moving close to his goal of winning three Michelin stars and was anxious to do so in his own restaurant. His relationship with White and the other partners at Aubergine soured to the extent that they ended up suing him, a matter finally settled out of court. After this bruising experience, Ramsay embarked on plans for his own restaurant and ended up buying Tante Clare, which was not far from Aubergine. He renamed it as Gordon Ramsay at Royal Hospital Road. The ego of the title said a lot, as did his almost maniacal determination to get it right. The opening came two years after Ramsay's first cookbook, *Passion for Flavour*, was published putting him on the map of chefs to watch. By now, he had reached the grand old age of 26.

The backing for the restaurant came from his father-in-law Chris Hutcheson with whom he went on to form his restaurant empire until, perhaps inevitably, the partnership ended with some well-publicized acrimony in 2010. Together they created a company that became Gordon Ramsay Holdings Limited, in which Ramsay held the majority of the shares. It embraced all his business interests including the restaurants, the media work and the consultancies that flowed from Ramsay's fame.

The first restaurant opened in 1998 and by 2001 Ramsay finally gained his third Michelin star.

It is no exaggeration to say that the Royal Hospital Road restaurant was an instant success that quickly spawned new restaurants. In the same year, Ramsay made his first television appearance in a fly-on-the-wall documentary called *Boiling Point*. So, by the age of 32 he had become a Michelin-starred chef, successfully opened his own top-of-the range restaurant and written the first of many books.

The next restaurant was called Petrus, closely followed by a failed restaurant in Glasgow called Amaryllis. But failure did not hold Ramsay back; in the space of just 12 years, he opened over 20 restaurants, most of them with him as Head Chef for at least a short period. These restaurants are not all owned or wholly owned by Ramsay's company but he retains control over their operations. In this mad scramble to extend the restaurant empire Ramsay's company spread its wings to New York, Dubai, Tokyo, Florida, Prague, County Wicklow, West Hollywood, Los Angeles, Versailles, Montreal, Capetown and Melbourne.

Many of Ramsay's restaurants are in famous hotels, such as the Connaught and the refurbished Savoy in London. He has a mixed record of getting on with the management of these hostelries but they clearly recognize his pulling power.

Some of Ramsay's critics have seized on the failure of some of these restaurants, including the South African venture, which opened in a hail of publicity and was then quickly forced to close. However Ramsay's failure rate is well below that of the industry as a whole and in between the failures have been a string of success. He has also brought on protégés such as Marcus Wareing and, despite his often stated misgivings about female chefs, Angela Hartnett. This is in the best tradition of nurturing new talent. Despite the mixed bag of success, the restaurants have all been widely recognized for their quality. Ramsay has also won a dozen Michelin stars and became one of only three chefs in Britain to hold three at the same time.

A more valid criticism of this avid restaurateur is that he is spread too thinly and that he cannot possibly keep a close eye on so many restaurants while also pumping out books and television programs and acting as a consultant to companies such as Singapore Airlines.

Then there's the not so small matter of his food factory in South London, which he bought from Albert Roux. There was a flurry of controversy in 2009 when it was revealed that the factory was supplying food for reheating at his upmarket Foxtrot Oscar restaurant in Chelsea, alongside three of his gastro-pubs. Ramsay claims this is standard practice even in the best restaurants but his claim sits uncomfortably with his well-publicized insistence on making food from scratch.

While the restaurant chain was building, Ramsay's television career was also taking off. He appeared in another documentary called *Beyond Boiling Point* in 2000, but it took four years before his own TV show started airing and crashed into the public consciousness. The show, *Kitchen Nightmares,* went from strength to strength and in 2005 crossed the Atlantic under the name *Hell's Kitchen*, using the same reality television format as the British show. Each program follows a well-established pattern in which Ramsay arrives at a failing restaurant, tastes the food, declares it to be inedible, looks around and finds the décor to be appalling, probes the kitchen and explodes as he describes its lack of hygiene before telling the restaurant management how utterly useless they are. Then Ramsay moves in his team, redecorates the restaurant, seemingly overnight, changes the menu and introduces a raft of improvements. Although the format hardly varies, the drama is compulsive viewing for millions of people who are presumably enthralled as they watch the shouting, crying and run of walkouts. This is reality television at full blast and although it can be enjoyed as simple drama the series also conveys a vast amount of information about running restaurants and preparing food.

In case any viewers were left in doubt about Ramsay's facility with foul language, he subsequently hosted a program called *The F Word* in which there were indeed some F words, not all of them about food. This somewhat bizarre show showcases Ramsay's cooking, mixes in some competitions, gets him out and about doing physical things that are connected with food, provides an opportunity for celebrities to get in the kitchen and generally constructs a shrine of homage to the Great Chef.

Setting the mood for being offensive, the first series of *The F Word*, saw Ramsay mockingly naming his turkeys after a number of Britain's best-known television chefs: Antony (Worrall Thompson), Ainsley (Harriott), Jamie (Oliver), Delia (Smith), Gary (Rhodes) and Nigella

(Lawson). This show is extremely popular as are his other shows in Britain, the United States and beyond.

Then there are the books, over 20 of them, including the ironically titled autobiography *Humble Pie*, published in 2006. In one year, 2008, four Ramsay books were published. This would be a remarkable feat for even a fulltime cookbook writer. If indeed the author named on the cover is really writing all these books and newspaper columns, alongside a punishing schedule of television work and running a global restaurant chain and consultancy, then Gordon Ramsay must have acquired Superman-like powers of productivity.

Ramsay's response to criticisms of his diverse activities is typically boisterous. He told the journalist Rosie Millard: "Some silly cow in Japan turned round and said, 'Yeah well if he's such a hands-on chef, who does the cooking?' " says Ramsay witheringly. "She was wearing a fantastic pin-striped $1,000 suit. I said to her, 'Who made your suit?' She said, 'Armani'. So I said, 'Did you ask whether f****** Giorgio Armani had stitched it?' Of course not! Too many people are focusing on me."

But the signs of strain are showing: in 2009, Gordon Ramsay Holdings was reported to have encountered severe financial problems following some defaulted payments and a critical audit by the accountants KPMG.

Commenting on these troubles Ramsay said: "We were told to go into administration, that it would be smoother for everyone. I thought of selling some of the company. My wife and I discussed selling our house. It's taken several million of my own money with several more million to come but I'm still standing." The company was subsequently forced to close restaurants in France and the United States.

This, incidentally, was also the year in which the food factory controversy blew up. The following year Chris Hutcheson, Ramsay's father-in-law and CEO of the company resigned, or according to Ramsay was fired, in a blaze of publicity. Ramsay subsequently wrote a bizarre open letter to his mother-in-law telling her that he had hired a private detective to investigate suspicions he had about the way her husband was running the company. Hutcheson was not about to go quietly and said of his son-in-law: "I have dealt with his breakdowns for years. It is like a tsunami when he gets going. He is schizophrenic... sometimes he is calm and sometimes he is absolutely manic." As ever, there is little but drama in Ramsay's affairs.

But Ramsay still maintains that it is cooking which gets him up in the morning. In an interview with the *Irish Sunday Tribune* he said, "I maintain standards and I strive for perfection. That level of pressure is conveyed in a very bullish way and that's what cooking is all about." This could serve as a suitable epitaph except that Gordon Ramsay is far from finished, merely pausing between explosions.

Ramsay Recipes

*The following recipes are taken from the website:www.
gordonramsaysrecipes.com*

Herb Crusted Rack of Lamb

This recipe showcases Ramsay's use of fresh herbs in a relatively
simple dish that at first glance appears to be complicated.

Ingredients
For the lamb:
2 large racks of lamb cut in half with 3 bones per serving
salt
pepper
olive oil

For the crust:
4 slices of stale bread made into crumbs.
7 tablespoons grated Parmesan (roughly ½ a cup)
sprig parsley
sprig thyme
sprig coriander
sprig rosemary
2 tablespoons English mustard
splash of olive oil

Method

Preparing the lamb:

Pre-heat the oven to 400°F (200°C/Gas 6). It should actually be 392 degrees, but don't worry about getting that technical unless you have a digital oven.

Place lamb on cutting board fat side up. Lightly score the fat layer with a sharp knife. Next, generously sprinkle the lamb with salt and pepper. Mop up the excess seasoning with the rack of lamb, ensuring it's thoroughly coated.

Heat some olive oil in an oven safe pan. Seal the lamb by holding each side in the oil long enough to develop color (careful not to burn your hands). Gordon Ramsay says, "it's simple mathematics, no color, equals no taste." Make sure you brown that lamb.

Transfer the pan with the lamb into the oven and bake for 7–8 minutes. Prepare the crust while the lamb is cooking.

Preparing the crust:

Place all of the ingredients for the crust except the mustard into a blender and pulse several times until it looks nice and green. Make sure you don't over do it with the olive oil, just a splash. Pour the mixture into a deep dish (bowl or plate) and set aside.

Putting it all together:

Remove the lamb from the oven and brush generously with mustard. Dip the lamb into the crust mixture coating it completely. Dip several times to ensure an even coating. Allow meat to rest for a bit. Place it back into the oven for 3–4 minutes when you're ready to serve.

This recipe featured in *The F Word*, Series 1

Gordon Ramsay's Mayonnaise

Ramsay emphasizes the preparation of food from scratch and avoidance of pre-prepared ingredients. This recipe provides a simple guide how to make a basic sauce.

Ingredients
3 egg yolks
teaspoon of Dijon mustard
pinch of salt
pinch of pepper (freshly ground if possible)
1 lemon
1¼ cups (300ml.) of flavorless cooking oil

You can whisk this by hand, but it will take quite an effort, use a food processor if you have one.

Directions
Put the egg yolks in a food processor with the Dijon mustard and turn the food processor on. The first 30 seconds of making mayonnaise is the most crucial, so be careful during this period and go slow with the oil. SLOWLY begin pouring the oil into the food processor while it's on. After 30 seconds or so you can start pouring faster. Turn off the food processor when you've added all the oil.

Add the salt and pepper, then cut the lemon in half and squeeze the juice into the mayonnaise mixture. Give the mix a quick burst with the food processor and done!

Store the mayonnaise in the fridge.

This recipe featured in *The F Word* series

Sea Bass with a Sweet and Sour Pepper Sauce, Citrus Pilaf and Braised Endive

This is a more complicated Ramsay recipe that is essentially French-influenced in its cooking method but encompasses some ingredients less typically found in French cuisine.

Ingredients
For the sea bass:
3–3.5 pound (1.3-1.6kg.) sea bass fillets, skin on sea salt
1 sprig thyme, leaves removed from stems

For the sauce and rice pilaf:
2 red peppers, cored, seeded and thinly sliced
2 yellow peppers, cored, seeded, and thinly sliced
4 shallots, thinly sliced
2 star anise
2 sprigs basil
1 tablespoon white wine vinegar
3 tablespoons Vermouth (approx.)
¾ cups (180ml.) water
citrus rice pilaf
1½ cups (300g.) Basmati rice, rinsed
1 large onion, finely chopped
3 tablespoons olive oil
1 sprig thyme
1 small cinnamon stick
peel of ½ orange
peel of ½ lemon
2½ cups (625ml.) chicken stock or broth
2 large endives
1 shot Grand Marnier (1½ oz.)
⅔ cups (170ml.) orange juice
4 tablespoons (about ¼ cup) butter
icing sugar for dusting
olive oil

salt and pepper
extra butter

Method
Preheat oven to 390°F/200°C/Gas 6.

Trim the sea bass into neat fillets and score the skin with a sharp knife. Season with a pinch of salt and the fresh thyme leaves.

Pan-fry the sea bass, skin side down in hot olive oil, gently holding the fillets down for 30 seconds with your fingers to stop the sides curling up. Season the top of the fillets and leave to cook from the bottom up. The fish will begin to turn white as it cooks. When the fish is about 80% cooked, flip it over and cook it the rest of the way through. Spoon some of the cooking oil over the top to add an extra crispness to the skin.

Sweat the peppers and shallots in a pan of hot olive oil until softened. Season, then add the star anise, basil and vinegar. Pour the vinegar in around the side of the pan so that it gently heats up before reaching the center. Add the vermouth – enough to come up to just under the layer of vegetables. Keep over the heat and allow the mixture to reduce until almost all the liquid has evaporated and you can hear a little sizzling and crackling. The vegetables should look rich and glossy. Add the water and reduce for 15 minutes. When the water looks like a syrupy sauce, remove the star anise and basil stalks and transfer to a blender. Blend until smooth. Taste and season if necessary, blend again. The consistency should be of a smooth, thick soup.

For the pilaf, sauté the onion in oil until soft. Add the rice, thyme, cinnamon, star anise and citrus peel. Season and cook for about 30 seconds to infuse the flavors – the rice should begin to look translucent. Add the boiling stock, bring back to the boil and cover with a cartouche (circle of greaseproof paper). Cook at 200°C (440°F) for 20 minutes.

Once cooked leave to stand for 5 minutes and remove the thyme and cinnamon before serving and mix through a knob of butter.

Cut the endive in half lengthways and dust all over with icing sugar.

Melt the butter in a pan and caramelise the endive all over until golden brown.

Deglaze the pan with the Grand Marnier and add the orange juice. Braise gently until the endive is soft and liquid is almost a glaze.

Serve the sea bass skin side up on a bed of rice with the pepper sauce and braised endive along side.

This recipe is featured in *The F Word* series.

Gordon Ramsay

Chapter 19

Let's Have a Delia

Delia
Smith

*H*aving a Delia may not sound too flattering but in many households it is shorthand for cooking one of the many recipes contained in books written by Delia Smith. The name Delia is instantly recognizable, in the way that first name familiarity only works for the truly famous. Unlike other famous personalities who populate television cookery shows, she is not flamboyant; on the contrary, she makes a virtue of being as ordinary as possible and never shouts or screams on screen. It seems that she deliberately sets out to cultivate a slightly dowdy appearance; her 'stardom' rests on giving sound, down-to-earth advice and ... that's more or less it!

Delia's sage advice is eagerly sought by the many households in Britain, and elsewhere for that matter, who would not dream of preparing the Christmas dinner without following her instructions. Indeed her followers have become dependent on her wisdom for everything from boiling an egg to baking a cake. She has single-handedly inspired a great many people to get into their kitchens and cook everything from simple dishes to recipes that they never thought they would be able to produce. Even quite experienced cooks turn to Delia for guidance, albeit often without admitting that she is the source of their recipes. Why this reluctance? It has something to do with the immense amount of snobbery that surrounds the culinary art (an extraordinarily pretentious phrase only used here to emphasize the gap between Delia Smith's determined practicality and the higher reaches of food pretension).

Delia Smith

Delia can live with the sarcasm and criticism she receives; indeed it seems to underpin her connection with followers who identify with her as a comforting alternative to the pretention that can surround the subject of food. "Cooking," she said in an interview with the *Times*, "is used as a statement, it needs to lighten up, it's a bit poncey. The food snobs were up in arms about tinned mince – well, caviar comes in tins; foie gras comes in tins. They'll use a tin of puy lentils or chickpeas, no problem. But if you cook mince with onions and spices and put it in a tin, there's something wrong, even though it's as nutritious as if you made it yourself."

So Delia is clearly not on a mission to impress foodies. "I think food lends itself to snobbery," she said in an interview, "I've always upset people." The TV chef Gary Rhodes said that when she dedicated a television program to how to boil an egg she insulted viewers' intelligence. However, in the wake of the program's broadcast egg sales in Britain rose by 10 percent.

A fellow television chef, Anthony Worrall Thompson, famously described her as the "Volvo of the kitchen," equating her with the sturdy, unexciting Swedish cars much loved by staid families. He now denies that this is an insult, insisting that he "called her a Volvo because her recipes work and she's the safest cook on TV. She was a schoolmarm. With fewer and fewer people able to cook, she had a great purpose. I really admire her."

On another occasion, he called her the "coldest woman on television." Worrall Thompson was referring to her determinedly plain appearance, a marked lack of ostentation and a dress sense suggesting a desire to be in a classroom rather than on the TV screen.

Moreover she unfashionably decided to convert to Catholicism at the age of 22, after having been baptized in the Church of England. Delia takes her faith seriously and has written three religious books, one of them, *A Journey into God*, is an ambitious work on the subject of prayer. It is therefore unsurprising that in cynical Britain, where religion is often regarded as something of a joke, she is often described as "Saint Delia."

It may be imagined that none of this troubles her but she is quite sharp with critics like Worrall Thompson and in a September 2000 interview she said, "I am not some prim Brownie pack leader. In fact, I am a bit of a bitch."

A 1995 *Observer* newspaper profile of Delia had an anonymous food critic saying, "She has the great gift of the popularizer, of being exactly one step behind. That's how you make a fortune." This shrewd observation is spot on. Delia Smith is not an innovator, certainly not a trend spotter but she has the particular gift of recognizing what ordinary people want when they enter a kitchen and she does her best to ensure that they will not be disappointed. "I found," she said, "in my whole career the best thing that can happen to you is that you hear what people want."

"Her critics," she says, chastise her for being boring, "people probably think I'm a bit old-fashioned. But I think that is me, really, I wouldn't want to be anything else." Delia sticks to basics and freely admits that she is not really at home with modern food. "Certain aspects are too cheffy," she said in an interview, "all the foam, and the drizzle, and the towers, and the sprinkles. Italian food is perhaps the only food that isn't poncey nowadays."

In her website, *Delia Online*, her official biography states: "Wondering why English food was so awful in the 1960s set Delia off on a quest to learn about it and educate people in how to cook their traditional dishes." This emphasis on English food is however misleading even though she is widely considered to be a quintessentially English cook. Her interest in the food of her own country appears to have been prompted by a reaction to the highly effective popularizing of Italian and French food by Elizabeth David (Chapter 8) at the time she started working in the food industry. However, as her career developed she has used a lot of Italian and French techniques and dishes, often in skillful adaptations. Her genius then does not lie in a certain type of cuisine but in an ability to make many kinds of food accessible to home cooks.

Significantly her famous *Delia's Complete Cookery Course* series started in BBC television's continuing education department where programs, as the name suggests, are supposed to be educational. Nigella Lawson, who is firmly on the glamorous side of the TV chef spectrum, recognized this in a positive way when she told a television interviewer that, "she's like a home-economics teacher who wants her class to do better."

It is hard to precisely quantify Delia's influence over home cooking but there are indications suggesting that it is massive. A hitherto obscure English company producing a particular aluminum frying pan she recommended for making omelettes was suddenly thrust into prominence when its product was mentioned on a Delia program and it was besieged by a surge of demand. Sales rose from 200 per year to 100,000.

A similar thing happened when she mentioned a lemon zester, previously absent from most household kitchens but suddenly elevated into a sellout product. This extraordinary impact on sales became known as the "Delia Effect." According to her literary agent Deborah Owen, "There is this wonderful quirky side to her that just doesn't understand how famous she is. That's a very attractive quality."

Like some of the other hugely influential cookery writers in this book, Delia Smith is not a trained cook. She makes no bones about this and says, anticipating criticism, "I'm not a cook"; this is a point she has made on a number of occasions. And, just to confirm some of the very worst suspicions that trained chefs have about her she says, "I sometimes think the chef end of cooking is not the real end of cooking. Cooking is all about homes and gardens, it doesn't happen in restaurants."

However this does not mean she does not take cooking seriously, she claims that thinking about food and recipes is her constant preoccupation, "Even if I'm not publishing recipes I'll still be thinking 'I'd like to try that' or 'I wonder if that will work?' because it's in my blood now."

The inventor Thomas Edison's famous adage about genius being one percent inspiration and 99 percent perspiration certainly seems to apply to Delia Smith who works like a demon to get her recipes right and has a profound distrust of ad-hoc creativity. She says, "There are people who claim to be instinctive cooks, who never follow recipes or weigh anything at all. All I can say is they're not very fussy about what they eat. For me, cooking is an exact art and not some casual game."

Delia Smith does not come from a background that suggests any kind of special interest in food. In the exquisite precision of the British class system, she can be said to be of lower middle class origins. Born in 1941 in none-too-fashionable Woking and growing up in equally unfashionable Bexleyheath, Delia appears to have had an unhappy childhood with little motivation from her parents. She left school at the age of sixteen without any qualifications and went to work as a hairdresser; then she tried her hand as a shop assistant and a travel agent before moving to London in 1960.

There were some early stirrings in the direction of food and there is a widely repeated story of how her interest deepened when she believed her boyfriend Louis Alexander to have been attracted to women with superior culinary talents. As it turned out, he was more attracted to the Catholic Church and was about to abandon all contact with the opposite sex to become a priest.

Somewhere round this time in 1962, Delia found herself in a restaurant called *The Singing Chef*, located near the large railway station at Paddington, and applied for a job. The chef, Leo Evans, did in fact sing but Delia was more interested in his soufflés. At first she was little more than a kitchen helper, doing the washing up and then acting as a waitress. However, the owner could see she was keen and allowed her to start cooking. For the first time Delia had a job that really interested her. Again, according to her website biography, "She began to wonder why, if French food was so good, English food was so awful. This curiosity encouraged Delia to read English cookery books in the Reading Room at the British Museum, trying out the recipes on the Harley Street family with whom she was lodging."

Delia was hooked on cooking but when she was later asked if she ever dreamed of cooking as a career, she answered: "No, I didn't. It happened when I started going out to restaurants in the '60s: the whole idea of eating out and learning about cooking was suddenly something I wanted to do. Initially learning to cook was to get me through life, not a career."

She was a keen student and in working hard to improve her cooking skills, Delia followed a clear method, the kind of method she was later to impart to her followers. By the end of the decade, this young woman, entirely lacking in academic qualifications and without being trained as a chef, was sufficiently confident to approach the literary agent Deborah Owen about writing a book on eighteenth century English food. Owen recalls that, "she was really angry at this postwar laughing at British cuisine." And "she's always been passionate. She thought 'I'm going to show people how to boil an egg. It's boring, but it's needed.'"

The book did not materialize but in 1969 Delia secured a cookery column in the big selling tabloid newspaper, the *Daily Mirror*. At the paper, she met the deputy editor Michael Wynn Jones and within two years they were married. Wynn Jones subsequently became an essential part of Delia Inc.

Within two years, the first of Delia's many books appeared. As if to confirm the worst suspicions of food snobs, the book was entitled *How to Cheat at Cooking*. It contains 400 recipes with all sorts of tricks for readers anxious to impress beyond the boundaries of what they may have imagined to be their cooking abilities. Among the recipes, which attracted considerable derision was one for boiling an egg, yet this proved to be extremely popular. "Fill your kitchen with serious-looking accoutrements and have lots of intriguing jars for your herbs and spices," she advised. "They'll look very phony if they're chockfull, so never quite fill them up."

Despite the critics, the book was a success and in 2008 she produced an updated version, which was even more successful, instantly becoming a number one bestseller. Meanwhile in 1972, Delia embarked on what would become a twelve year-long column for the London *Evening Standard* newspaper.

She then began writing a steady flow of books; many of the earlier ones are now forgotten, such as a book on recipes from country inns and restaurants, published in 1973 and *The Evening Standard Cookbook*, published a year later. This was followed by a work unenticingly called *Frugal Food* and then a cake recipe book in 1977.

Like many 'overnight' successes, Delia's climb to fame was therefore not sudden at all but presaged by considerable groundwork. However it was through the medium of television that she became famous starting with regional appearances in East Anglia. Delia finally found a national niche in a show called *Family Fare*, which she started hosting in 1973. The unassuming Delia quickly established a no-nonsense persona on the screen. But she admits that television was daunting, "Looking at a camera and speaking to imaginary people for the first time and cooking at the same time, with no editing, was terrifying," she recalled. "The program was 24 minutes, 30 seconds and you had to do it in that time. If you made a mistake in the middle you had to start at the top. It was very good television training, but I did look a bit shy."

When asked what prompted her to go into television, she replied, "I'd have people come up to me and say, 'Oh, I really enjoyed your column yesterday,' and I'd ask 'Did you make the recipe?' They'd say 'Oh, no, I can't cook'. I realized there was still a long way to go in teaching people to cook. At that time, people had to go to evening schools to learn to cook. I thought, wouldn't it be wonderful if they could learn in their own homes."

Family Fare was a success but the program that catapulted Delia Smith into national attention began in the unlikely BBC Continuing Education Department. She presented them with an idea of a show that focused on basic cooking techniques and dishes likely to be familiar to an audience with no specialist knowledge. *Delia Smith's Cookery Course* quickly became a success, a success that appears to have taken her bosses at the BBC by surprise. The program became a three-part series generating literally millions of sales of books that accompanied it. Not only have these books been repeatedly republished, but in British homes they are likely to be the most thumbed and most prominently used of the cookbooks on a great many kitchen shelves.

Delia has largely stuck with the BBC for the rest of her television career, which has spanned some 18 shows and series, including two programs, *Delia Smith's Summer Collection,* followed by a *Winter Collection* series which both broke all her previous records. In 2004, she announced that she was "retiring" from television declaring that food programs were increasingly becoming about entertainment rather than food. However, by 2008 she was back with a new show and in 2010 hosted a highly successful retrospective called *Delia through the Decades.* Her more than twenty books are estimated to have sold in excessive of 21 million copies. The biggest selling of which, the *Winter Collection* book, sold a staggering 2 million copies in hardback.

Controversy struck again when Delia signed up as a behind-the-scenes consultant for the Sainsbury's supermarket chain in 1993. Together with her husband she created a company called New Crane Publishing which, among other things, became the publisher for *Sainsbury's Magazine.* The magazine had a readership of 2.3 million and won awards but critics wondered why Delia was becoming so commercial and whether this undermined her status as a national icon. It is the kind of criticism that is unlikely to have much resonance in the United States but in Britain there is a greater ethos of separating so called "commercial" activity from the kind of work undertaken by those who appear on the public broadcaster, the BBC.

Delia Smith does not apologize for her commercial work and indeed went on to work for another supermarket chain, Waitrose, after ending her deal with Sainsbury's in 1998. New Crane Publishing was sold in 2005 for a reported US$11 million, but this did not include the *Delia Online* website which generates considerable web traffic. Delia insists that she was blunt in advising the supermarket chain on its products and that she never used her position to endorse its products.

However when her second how-to-cheat book appeared and started recommending specific stores for buying foodstuffs, the controversy reignited. Her response was: "We debated long and hard whether to mention products but at the end of the day this book is for people who are either in a hurry or are afraid to cook. The more information you can give them the easier it is."

This failed to satisfy many of her critics who then seized upon another issue that found Delia posed against more fashionable opinion: battery-reared chickens. She told a radio program that while she didn't particularly like battery-reared chickens this form of production was necessary to feed those who are not so well off. She also declared that "she didn't do organic" but was quite happy to use raw materials produced in other ways. All this seemed to confirm that "Saint Delia" was not on the side of the angels but she maintains that she is not in business to be a food politician. "I'll stick to the kitchen," she said. "I'm about helping people to cook, not saving the nation from battery chickens."

It is a little strange that someone who almost makes a virtue of being non-controversial manages to attract such a high level of criticism but such is the price of fame. To put this in some perspective, her critics, albeit some of them being very high profile, pale in comparison to her loyal followers. Among them are universities who have given the woman, without a single academic qualification, four honorary degrees for her work and she has been honored twice by the Queen with an MBE in 2009 and an OBE in 1995. Indeed, according to her biographer, Alison Bowyer, she was offered a peerage by Prime Minister Tony Blair, but turned it down.

Turning down a peerage seems to be part of Delia's determined efforts to retain the common touch and this nestles comfortably alongside her other great passion: football. She has been an avid supporter of the Norwich City Football Club for three decades and was made a club director in 1996. There is nothing manufactured about her enthusiasm for football or the considerable effort she has devoted to the club. Perhaps her major contribution has been in improving its catering services to a stage where they now form a profit center as opposed to the embarrassing catering in other clubs. It is cruel but accurate to point out that Norwich City is not one of England's finest football clubs, nor is it one of the worst, it rumbles along somewhere in the middle, the sort of place where Delia appears to be most comfortable.

"She remains a symbol of Middle England values," said a *Times* profile of her in 2009, "what sets her apart from the new generation of celebrity chefs is that, where they are selling their personalities, she has always been all about the cooking".

Jamie Oliver (Chapter 13) who must surely count among those chefs "selling their personalities," has been effusive in paying tribute to her, he said, "Whatever anybody else says about her, Delia is the Guv'nor. She's spent years making food accessible and building up trust with the British public and for that alone she's a treasure."

Typically Delia Smith sets the bar quite low in describing her mission. She said, "I think I will have performed a great service if I can make it possible for families to sit round and eat a meal together."

Smith Recipes

All these are can be seen at *DeliaOnline.com*

Eggs Mayonnaise

Here is a classic Delia, something every would-be cook should know how to make and is interestingly different from the Gordon Ramsay recipe for the same thing given above.

This is her introduction:
"Not the kind you get in help-yourself salad bars and cafés – this is the real thing. Eggs, boiled – not hard, but with a bit of squidge at the centre – anointed with a shimmering, golden emulsion laced with a little garlic. I have to admit, this is probably my most favourite starter. I like to serve it with sliced cornichons or pickled cucumbers and tiny black Provençal olives."
Serves 6

Ingredients
9 large eggs
18 medium cornichons (baby gherkins), sliced lengthways
about 18 small black olives

For the mayonnaise:
2 large egg yolks 10 fl. oz. (284ml.) groundnut or other flavorless oil
1 clove garlic, crushed
1 heaped teaspoon mustard powder
1 teaspoon white wine vinegar
freshly-milled black pepper
1 teaspoon salt

Method

First, place a medium-sized mixing bowl on a damp tea cloth so it will remain steady and leave you both hands free to make the mayonnaise – one to drip the oil, the other to hold an electric hand whisk. Next, measure out the oil into a jug. Now put the egg yolks into the bowl, adding the garlic, mustard powder, salt and a little freshly milled black pepper and mix all of these together well. Then, holding the jug of oil in one hand and the whisk in the other, add just a drop of oil to the egg mixture and whisk this in. However stupid it may sound, the key to a successful mayonnaise is making sure each drop of oil is thoroughly whisked in before adding the next drop. It won't take all day, because after a few minutes – once you've added several drops of oil – the mixture will begin to thicken and go very stiff and lumpy. When it gets to this stage, you need to add the vinegar, which will thin it. Now the critical point has passed, you can begin pouring in the oil in large drops, keeping the whisk going all the time. When all the oil has been added, taste and add more salt and freshly milled black pepper, if it needs it.

If you'd like the mayonnaise to be a bit lighter, add 2 tablespoons of boiling water and whisk it in. Mayonnaise only curdles when you add the oil too quickly at the beginning. If that happens, don't despair. All you need to do is put a fresh egg yolk into a clean basin, add the curdled mixture to it drop by drop, then continue adding the rest of the oil as though nothing had happened. Now place the eggs in a pan in cold water. Bring them up to the boil and boil for 6 minutes, then cool them rapidly under cold, running water and leave them in the cold water for about 2 minutes. Next, remove them from the water, peel off the shells, cover the eggs with cling film, and leave them in a cool place until needed. Now cut the eggs in half, arranging three halves on each plate, top with a heaped tablespoon of the mayonnaise and garnish with the cornichons and olives. Any leftover mayonnaise should be stored in a screw-top jar in the fridge, but for no longer than a week. Note: You could also serve this with a couple of anchovies per person draped over the mayonnaise in a crisscross pattern.

From *How to Cook Book Three* by Delia Smith, BBC Books, 2001 and *Delia's Vegetarian Collection,* BBC Books, 2002.

Coq au vin

This is a personal favorite and, for many amateur chefs, it is recipes like this that have encouraged them to venture into territory which they hitherto deemed as being too difficult.

Delia's introduction says:
A truly authentic coq au vin is made, obviously, with a cock bird, and some of the blood goes into the sauce which, by the time it reaches the table, is a rich, almost black colour.

In Britain we make a less authentic adaptation, but it makes a splendid dinner-party dish. The results are different but every bit as delicious if you use cider instead of wine, but it must be dry cider. I also like to give this dish half its cooking time the day before, let it cool, then refrigerate and give it the other half of the cooking time before serving. At the half-cooked stage, turn the chicken pieces over so that they can absorb all the lovely flavors overnight.

Ingredients
1 x 5 pounds (2.27kg.) chicken, cut into 8 joints
1 ¼ pints (710ml.) red wine
1 ounce (28g.) butter
1 rounded tablespoon softened butter and 1 level tablespoon plain flour, combined to make a paste
1 tablespoon oil
8 ounces (227g.) unsmoked streaky bacon, preferably in one piece
16 button onions
2 cloves garlic, crushed
2 sprigs fresh thyme
2 bay leaves

8 ounces (227g.) small dark-gilled mushrooms
salt and freshly milled black pepper

To garnish (optional):
chopped fresh parsley

Method
Melt the butter with the oil in a frying pan, and fry the chicken
joints, skin side down, until they are nicely golden; then turn them
and color the other side. You may have to do this in three or four
batches – don't overcrowd the pan. Remove the joints from the pan
with a draining spoon, and place them in the cooking pot. This
should be large enough for the joints to be arranged in one layer
yet deep enough so that they can be completely covered with liquid
later. Now de-rind and cut the bacon into fairly small cubes, brown
them also in the frying pan and add them to the chicken, then
finally brown the onions a little and add them too. Next place the
crushed cloves of garlic and the sprigs of thyme among the chicken
pieces, season with freshly milled pepper and just a little salt, and
pop in a couple of bay leaves.

Pour in the wine, put a lid on the pot and simmer gently for
45-60 minutes or until the chicken is tender. During the last
15 minutes of the cooking, add the mushrooms and stir them into
the liquid. Remove the chicken, bacon, onions and mushrooms
and place them on a warmed serving dish and keep warm.(Discard
the bay leaves and thyme at this stage.) Now bring the liquid to a
fast boil and reduce it by about one third. Next, add the butter and
flour paste to the liquid. Bring it to the boil, whisking all the time
until the sauce has thickened, then serve the chicken with the sauce
poured over. If you like, sprinkle some chopped parsley over the
chicken and make it look pretty.

From *Delia Smith's Complete Cookery Course*, BBC Books, 1992; *Delia
Smith's Complete Illustrated Cookery Course*, BBC Books, 1989; *The Evening
Standard Cookbook* by Delia Smith, Book Club Associates, 1975; and *The
Delia Collection: Chicken,* BBC Books, 2003.

10-Minute Raspberry Cheesecake

This is a prime example of the kind of recipe that gets Delia into trouble with food snobs: first it shortcuts a few basic preparation methods and secondly, it also contains a specific product endorsement. It also happens to make a rather nice cheesecake.

Delia's introduction says:
Well actually it does take 30 minutes to cook but all you have to do is throw it together in lightning fashion. You can then top it with any soft fruit you like, but my favourite is with fresh raspberries and our hero ingredient for the week – The English Provender Company Raspberry Coulis. This, as it happens, is also good poured over a bowl of hulled strawberries (which have been sprinkled with a little caster sugar) and a huge dollop of D'Isigny crème fraîche or, if you're feeling good, from the same supplier – fromage frais.

Ingredients
2 ounces (56g.) butter
8 digestive biscuits
12 ounces (340g.) cream cheese, such as Philadelphia
2 tablespoons caster sugar, plus one extra teaspoon
2 large eggs
3 drops vanilla extract
142 milliliters (¼ pint) tub soured cream
5 ounces (141g.) raspberries
200 grams jar ready-made raspberry coulis (I used The English Provender Co. Raspberry Coulis)

Method
First, pre-heat the oven to gas mark 4, 350°F (180°C). Melt the butter, then crush the biscuits to fine crumbs using a rolling pin and combine them with the melted butter. Now, press the biscuit mixture evenly over the base of a lightly oiled, 8-inch (20cm.) springform tin. Then in a mixing bowl, beat the cream cheese and 2 tablespoons of caster sugar together until smooth and free from lumps.

Next, beat in the eggs and vanilla extract. Then spoon the mixture into the tin, spreading it out evenly, and bake on the center shelf for 25–30 minutes or until the mixtures feels firm in the middle. The cheesecake will shrink slightly from the sides of the tin but this is normal.

Now turn the heat up to gas mark 8, 450°F (230°C). Spoon the soured cream over the cheesecake, sprinkle on the teaspoon of sugar and bake for 5 more minutes. Remove from the oven and leave to cool. To serve, loosen the base from the side of the tin, and decorate the top of the cheesecake with the fresh raspberries and drizzle over a little of the raspberry coulis. Pour the rest of the coulis into a small jug and serve separately.

How to Cheat Hero Ingredient

1 x 200 grams jar The English Provender Co. Raspberry Coulis

This recipe first appeared in *You* magazine.

Chapter 20

The Ethical Chef

Alice
Waters

$\mathcal{A}$lice Louise Waters, born 1944, has been described as "the mother of American cooking" and "one of the most important figures in the culinary history of North America." These are sweeping and extravagant claims, justified in many ways by the extraordinary impact she has had on the way Americans view food. Moreover, she is self-consciously a political activist who has campaigned vigorously and effectively to support sustainable local agriculture, to improve the eating habits of children and in general to use food as a vehicle for social change.

Some food critics have identified Waters as the successor to Julia Child (Chapter 7), who had a similarly profound impact on American food in the 1960s and '70s, although her influence lingered long after that. Child brought a warm gust of European, especially French food appreciation to the United States and gave it a meaningful American twist. Waters, on the other hand, has her feet firmly embedded in American soil. She is credited with having founded the Californian cuisine movement which emphasizes local produce and focuses on simple, flavorsome dishes. These often turn out to be fairly complex but are nevertheless stripped bare of the kind of ornate presentation favored by Julia Child. There is another way of looking at this comparison, one cited in a *New York Times* profile of Waters in which the San Francisco food critic Patricia Unterman argued that Child "set the stage for the culinary boom in America by teaching people how to cook, and then Alice Waters took everyone to the next step by teaching about ingredients."

The parallels and differences between the two women are interesting in other ways. Waters is not a trained chef but an incredible enthusiast who is virtually self-taught and achieved a level of proficiency sufficient to direct the kitchen of an award winning restaurant. Child avidly took cooking lessons in France and labored over the production of a voluminous French cookery book but only in her later years ventured into a professional kitchen but, seemingly, without conviction.

At the heart of Waters' world lies the Chez Panisse restaurant in Berkeley, California, which she opened in 1971, at the age of 27. She has famously and often described its origins as being "a simple little place where we could cook and talk politics." It became a lot less simple and has since hauled in a shawl of top restaurant awards, spawned other food enterprises and seen a parade of chefs passing through its doors who have become famous and set up their own wonderful restaurants. The restaurant has also provided the inspiration for a dozen books written and co-written by Waters, giving those who have never been to her restaurant a figurative taste of what they would find.

Unlike a great many other food gurus of the modern age Waters has eschewed television cooking shows and has never had her own show, although she is quite prepared to appear on television programs advocating her food philosophy.

Waters insists that she had no idea how influential she would become or that she would spawn what can be described as a movement: "When I opened up Chez Panisse, I was only thinking about taste," she told an interviewer. In another interview she said, "I want to know where everything comes from, I don't want to have to choose between local and organic. I want both. I don't want to live a half-good life."

Her customers clearly share her views and expect to be served what the restaurant itself describes as freshly picked fruit, vegetables just out of the soil and fish straight out of the sea. It is no hyperbole to say that when Chez Panisse started it was creating a new eating experience. And yes, there was a lot of political talk among her friends from the Free Speech Movement and others from the milieu which influenced Waters in the heady 1960s. This was a time when American campuses were in

turmoil protesting about the Vietnam War and many were joining the civil rights movement and promoting an alternative lifestyle.

Some of that lifestyle focused on drugs, sex and rock and roll but for Waters it was food that mattered most. She has explained why food is central to her politics: "I really believed you could change the world," she said in an interview, "politics was more than just voting, we thought. Politics was how you lived your life." Elsewhere she has elaborated on what food politics means: "When you make a decision about what to eat, it affects the quality of life of our planet. In other words, if you buy food from people who are taking care of the land, you are supporting sustainability for future generations. Buy from people who care about our nourishment, people who care about our children, people who care about food for the right reasons. If you buy food from people who are growing it in an irresponsible way, from people who are destroying communities around the world and destroying our natural resources, then you are supporting a whole other system. I think it's a very political act to make the right decisions about what you put in your mouth." And there is more to this in Water's view, "Communities are brought together when people care about what they eat, I continue to believe that the very best way to bring people together is by changing the role food plays in our national life."

Most Americans still eat a great deal of processed food and buy food originating from factory farms. But there has been a sea change in awareness of the kind of produce advocated by Waters; certainly the mood has swung in her direction in recent years. Nevertheless, Waters seems to epitomize many things that are vastly unpopular in the United States. She is seen as a radical liberal, a charge she would not dispute, but she does dispute the frequent accusations of elitism and lack of realism in her approach to food. She told the CBS' *60 Minutes* program: "I feel that good food should be a right and not a privilege and it needs to be without pesticides and herbicides. And everybody deserves this food. And that's not elitist."

Elsewhere she has said, "Fresh, nourishing food need never again be stigmatized as elitist. Wholesome, honest food must be the entitlement of all Americans, not just the rich." She is acutely aware of the contradictions in her position but argues: "Often somebody will complain that it is all very well for me - the owner of an expensive restaurant with a sophisticated clientele located in a mild climate - to prescribe this kind of eating, but for most Americans it is a luxury that is all but out of reach."

Among her critics is James McWilliams, a food historian at Texas State University, who is basically sympathetic to her views but has argued that Waters' campaign for better food is a great example of the perfect being the enemy of the good. He added, "There is a kind of elitism about it, which isn't necessarily a bad thing. If you have the time and the resources to support the local food-shed, that's great. But there are some who see her as having boutique concerns that are out of touch with where our food worries should be - like how we're going to globally produce 70 percent more food in the next 40 to 50 years." This is the nub of the problem because even the most strident advocates of organic and non-factory produced food question whether the planet has the resources to feed all of its people without resorting to factory farming methods.

Waters argues that her solutions are not new but drawn from deep rural traditions. She does not acknowledge that even in times when food was produced in more traditional ways there was widespread starvation and malnutrition. These problems are hardly likely to be lessened as the global population grows and there is a major shift away from employment in agriculture. Waters, as we shall see, has chosen to focus on specific projects that make a real difference while leaving these bigger questions to one side.

Alice Waters came from a middle class family in Chatham, New Jersey. Her father was an insurance company executive and she had three sisters. It was, by all accounts a conventional family that produced a very unconventional offspring. Alice Waters has been married twice, first to the French filmmaker Jean-Pierre Gorin, and then to Stephen Singer, an Italian olive oil importer who also became Chez Panisse's wine buyer. She has one daughter, Fanny, whose name was given to the café that opened after the restaurant.

Waters challenged her comfortable –middle-class background as
a student at Berkeley University where she was a political activist,
primarily in the Free Speech Movement, formed in response to a campus
ban on political activity. She also worked on the congressional campaign
of Robert Scheer, an anti-Vietnam War politician. Unlikely as it may
seem this marked her emergence as a cook who beguiled other members
of the campaign team as she cooked for them on the campaign trail.
Waters has suggested that her interest in food was kindled when she was
19 years old and living in France, absorbing French food culture and the
centrality it had in family life. From a young age she had been what she
calls a "picky eater." In fact, she has keen taste buds and this has served
her well as a chef.

Although her interest in food was clear when Waters graduated with
a degree from Berkeley in French cultural studies in 1967, she went
to London where she trained as a teacher in one of the progressive
Montessori schools. Her Montessori experience later provided the basis
for her edible education and edible schoolyard programs that echo the
school's method of giving children hands-on experience in learning.
From London she traveled first to Turkey, which she said inspired her
enthusiasm for hospitality and respect for local communities. From
there she went back for a year to France, a seminal experience which
convinced her that she was not going to be a teacher but a chef.

Interestingly, the main influences she credits for her interest in French
food are not French, including Elizabeth David (Chapter 8), who
influenced many other people's interest in French food in the 1960s.
On a personal level, she credits Richard Olney, a prominent American
authority on French food, who like David preferred France's rustic
tradition to that of the haute cuisine, more commonly associated with
French food. He in turn introduced her to Lucien and Lulu Peyraud,
owners of the Domaine Tempier vineyard in Provence, who she later
described as being her "second family." Lulu Peyraud became a major
influence on her Chez Panisse menus.

Back in the US, she got together with Lindsey Shere who was to become
the restaurant's pastry chef. Waters described what followed: "We had

this little fantasy, 'Oh, let's have a little cafe,' we said. I wasn't worried about paying for it. I just knew if I did the right thing, people would come. We opened the restaurant with US$10,000. My father mortgaged his house (he was paying the rent on the building which Waters and her colleagues bought three years later). We had 50 employees and paid them each US$5 an hour."

This was back in 1971 and the style of the restaurant was based around Provence dishes from the south of France. In fact there was a general mixture of non-pretentious French country cooking. The restaurant was named Chez Panisse, not after the deep-fried chickpea flatbread typical of Nice but in homage to Honoré Panisse, a character in the movies of Marcel Pagnol, set in Marseilles in the 1930s. Waters, in addition to her other interests, is deeply interested in films. She has a number of prominent film people as regular patrons and, in 1980, was featured cooking in a movie by the German filmmaker, Werner Herzog, called *Werner Herzog Eats His Shoe.*

David Goines, a long-time friend of Alice Waters and illustrator of two of her cookbooks, recalled his impression of why she opened the restaurant: "Alice wanted to have her friends to dinner every night," he said. "The only way to do that was to open a restaurant." The restaurant was far from being an immediate success. Some of the cooking was disastrous and Waters seemed to have little grip on the financial end of the business, mainly because she was intent on using the highest quality ingredients, regardless of cost. It quickly went into debt to the tune of US$40,000. Then a white knight materialized in the shape of a cookware shop owner called Gene Opton.

Waters recalled what happened next, "Gene Opton picked up all the receipts off the floor and paid the bills, and pretty soon she became an owner, but she became disenchanted with my business practices, and the other restaurant owners bought her out, and I continued my wanton ways." It took eight years for the restaurant to turn a profit but its reputation was spreading and Waters' insistence on perfection was getting noticed.

By 1980, the restaurant had reached a level justifying expansion and she opened the upstairs Chez Panisse Café. Paul Aratow, its first chef de cuisine, who also helped build the premises, played a key role in the restaurant's development. He is also, in his own right, a considerable expert on French and Italian food.

In 1982, the restaurant was almost destroyed by fire but was largely saved and rebuilt. Two years later, Waters decided to open a more casual café a few blocks from the original restaurant, naming it Café Fanny, after her daughter. The Chez Panisse website says, "The restaurant has always served a set menu that changes daily and reflects the season's bounty. Monday nights at the restaurant generally feature more rustic or regional dishes, such as a lamb tagine or fisherman's stew, in addition to a first course and dessert. Tuesday through Thursday, the restaurant serves a 4-course set dinner menu, including dessert. On Friday and Saturday evenings, a more elaborate 4-course meal is served."

The restaurant sources its food from some 85 suppliers, most of which are local small scale enterprises. Vegetable waste from the restaurant goes back to the supplying farms that use it for compost heaps.

Waters says that the similarity of the climate in California and Southern France helps to explain the enormous influence of Provencal cuisine on her cooking. She is famous for creating dishes like the California-style pizza which emanate from Italy and an equally famous goat's cheese salad that has some resonance with the famous feta cheese salads from Greece. Essentially what characterizes her food is the way the taste of the fresh ingredients is preserved. Rich sauces definitely have no place here but adroit seasoning and often complex but resolutely light sauces reign supreme.

The restaurant and Waters have won an impressive clutch of awards including the naming of Alice Waters as the Best Chef in America by the James Beard Foundation (Chapter 3) in 1992; a lifetime achievement award from the San Pellegrino *50 Best Restaurants* panel; recognition by a number of academic bodies as well as a seat in the California Hall of Fame.

Perhaps most remarkable among the achievements of Chez Panisse is the way in which it spawned so many other restaurants and food producers as chef after chef passed through its doors and left to found their own establishments. Among them was Dianne Dexter, a former pastry chef who went on to found the Metropolitan Bread Company. The restaurant's alumni founded the even more famous Acme Bread Company. Another alumni, Lindsey Shere, founded yet another well-regarded bakery, and Peggy Smith, who worked at the café went on to establish the leading cheese-making Cowgirl Creamery. Jeremiah Tower, who learned his trade as a chef at Chez Panisse, has now become one of America's most famous chefs. Mark Miller and Paul Bertolli, who both served as head chef for the restaurant, have gone on to lead some of America's most famous kitchens.

The list of Chez Pannise alumni goes on and on. Some of these chefs have fallen out with Waters but all of them have carried the influence of this remarkable restaurant across the United States.

Waters no longer works in the restaurant kitchen on a day-to-day basis but remains actively engaged in menu planning. Her attention has largely switched to food campaigning. One of her earlier endeavors was supporting the Garden Project, established at the San Francisco jail for prisoners to work on the land and continue to do so after release. Waters full-time job these days, if this can really be said to be her occupation, is as head of the Chez Panisse Foundation, established in 1996. This coincided with the restaurant's 25th anniversary. The aim of the foundation is to "transform public education by using food to teach, nurture, and empower young people".

It focused on the Berkeley Unified School District where, even before the foundation was established, Waters was helping schools integrate the curriculum with the dinning services; this means getting children involved with growing, cooking and sharing food.

Her pioneer project was the Edible Schoolyard program at Berkeley's Martin Luther King, Jr. Middle School, where an organic garden and kitchen classroom was established. This was followed by a wider School

Lunch Initiative, providing 10,000 students with wholesome food at lunchtime, eliminating processed food and stressing organic fruit and vegetables. Water's work is very similar to that of Jamie Oliver (Chapter 13) in Britain, and more recently in the United States.

Edible Schoolyard affiliate programs have since been established in New Orleans, New York, Los Angeles, San Francisco and Greensboro. In various ways they echo the pioneering work in Berkeley where the foundation's follow-up studies found that children's food awareness had risen and their eating habits improved.

Waters has campaigned on a broader national level to raise awareness of organic food and extend the free meals program. In 2003, Waters was among the founders of the Yale Sustainable Food Project, making sustainable food part of the university curriculum. She urged President Clinton, to plant an organic garden at the White House. Although this project never came to fruition under President Clinton, he became an enthusiast for Water's food and wrote, "I know how passionate Alice is about fresh foods and the importance of Americans living healthier lives." Clinton added, "Alice and people like her, along with my own weight and heart problems, inspired me to take on the issue of childhood obesity." The White House organic garden project finally materialized in 2009 under President Obama where its inauguration formed part of the anti-obesity *Let's Move* campaign of First Lady Michelle Obama

Waters told the *Vegetarian Times* that once people "come in contact with real food, it's hard to go back. If we can just get them all connected at the farmers market or in their own backyards with growing things and picking them when they have that irresistible flavor, there's just no going back."

At an international level, Waters has served as a vice president of Slow Food International, the organization devoted to preserving local food traditions and many of the other ideals, which she has promoted in America. Arising from this movement Waters helped organize the first American Slow Food Nation event in San Francisco. It is a festival of food and politics that looks set to grow and attract even more attention. Her involvement in Slow Food led the French government to give her a Legion of Honor award. The founder of this movement, Carlo Petrini, is featured in Chapter 15.

There are people who wonder how the whole business of food managed to get so politicized but this is to view world history with a set of blinkers, ignoring the vast changes in economic development, social development and all that goes with it. To say that food was "never" political in the old days is to ignore how, as we saw in Chapter 6, the revolutionary forces sweeping France had a profound impact on the way food was cooked and served.

What has happened in the later part of the twentieth century is that food has become a bigger topic and makes consumers more active participants in the whole food process. However, in some ways, life has come full circle because it was not that long ago, the vast majority of people were either food producers themselves or very close to the source of production. Waters has emerged from this new milieu as being one of the leaders of the socially conscious food-consumption movement and, as she told the *New Yorker* magazine, she sees delicious food and concern over its origins as inexorably intertwined. She said, "The sensual pleasure of eating beautiful food from the garden, brings with it the moral satisfaction of doing the right thing for the planet and for yourself."

Alice Waters is too uncompromising to ever be really mainstream. Yet much of what she advocates and her insistence on focusing on the origins of food are concerns shared by a much wider circle of people than ever seemed possible when Chez Panisse was founded in the 1970s. "I always knew it had to happen," she said in an interview, "I just didn't know it would happen so soon. These are not my ideas… it's the way people have been eating for hundreds of years."

Alice Waters Recipes

The recipes which follow show, in the first instance, how Alice Waters approaches a simple dish and in the second instance how she has a adapted classic Provençal dish which appears to be simple but has a complex set of ingredients. The third example is her take on a classic French salad dressing.

Carrot Soup

Serves 6 to 8

Ingredients
4 tablespoons butter
2 medium onions, sliced
1 sprig thyme
2½ pounds (1kg.) carrots, peeled and sliced (about 6 cups)
salt
6 cups (1440ml.) chicken broth

Method
In a heavy-bottomed pot, melt the butter. When it starts to foam, add the onions and thyme and cook over medium-low heat until tender, about 10 minutes. Add the carrots, season with salt and cook for 5 minutes. Pour in the broth, bring to a boil and then simmer until the carrots are tender, about 30 minutes. Season to taste with salt. For a smooth soup, use a blender and purée until smooth.

Variations
Garnish with crème fraîche seasoned with salt, pepper and chopped herbs.

Add ¼ cup (41g.) basmati rice with the carrots, use water instead of broth, add 1 cup (240ml.) plain yogurt just before puréeing and garnish with mint.

Cook a jalapeño pepper with the onions, add some cilantro before puréeing and garnish with chopped cilantro.

From: *The Art of Simple Food* by Alice Waters, Clarkson Potter, 2007

Soupe Au Pistou With Lamb Shanks

Serves 6 as a main course

Ingredients
6 small lamb shanks
salt and pepper
olive oil
2 medium onions, sliced
1 large carrot, peeled and sliced
1 celery rib, sliced
14 garlic cloves, peeled and crushed
2 medium tomatoes, quartered
10 cups (2400ml.) basic chicken stock
bouquet garni: thyme, parsley, and bay
2 pounds (907g.) fresh shell beans, shelled

For the soup:
1 pound (450g.) romano beans, cut in ½ inch pieces
1 pound (450g.) green beans, cut in ½ inch pieces
1 large bulb fennel, diced
2 carrots, diced
2 medium potatoes, diced
extra-virgin olive oil
3 large onions, diced
2 small zucchini (courgette), diced

4 medium tomatoes, peeled, seeded and chopped
2 tablespoons chopped parsley
2 teaspoons chopped thyme

Optional:
1 cup (118g.) cooked pasta, such as orzo, mezzi tubetti,
    conchiglie or orecciette

For the pistou:
2 tablespoons toasted pine nuts
3 garlic cloves
salt
2 cups basil leaves
½ cup (120ml.) extra-virgin olive oil
pepper

Method
Season the lamb shanks generously with salt and pepper, and
refrigerate for several hours or overnight. Heat 3 tablespoons olive
oil in a large, deep skillet over medium heat and brown the shanks.
In a large enamelware Dutch oven, heat 2 tablespoons olive oil
over medium heat and lightly sauté the onions, carrot, celery and
garlic. Add the tomatoes, chicken stock and bouquet garni. Season
to taste and bring to a boil. Add the lamb shanks in a single layer,
cover and reduce to a gentle simmer. Cook on the stovetop or in a
350°F/180°C/Gas 4 oven for 2 hours, or until quite tender.

While the lamb is braising, bring about 2 quarts of salted water
to boil. Add the shell beans and cook until just tender, about 30
minutes. Remove the beans and let them cool at room temperature.
In the same boiling water, replenishing as necessary, one vegetable at
a time, parboil the romano beans, green beans, fennel, carrots and
potatoes until just done, and spread them out to cool.

When the shanks are done, remove them from the broth and set aside. Strain the broth, discarding the braising vegetables. Let the broth settle, and skim away any fat from the surface. Measure the broth, and add chicken stock, vegetable cooking liquid, or water to bring the quantity to 10 cups (2400ml.). Return the shanks and broth to the Dutch oven. Set aside.

Heat 3 tablespoons extra-virgin olive oil in a large sauté pan over medium heat and sauté the diced onion until soft and translucent, about 5 minutes. Add the zucchini and continue cooking for 3 or 4 minutes. Add the parboiled romano beans, green beans, fennel and carrot and potatoes, stirring well to coat with the oil. Add the tomatoes, shell beans and chopped parsley and thyme. Season everything with salt and pepper, and cook for 2 minutes more.

Bring the broth and lamb shanks to a simmer. Stir in the sautéed vegetables and cook gently for a few minutes. Taste the broth, adjust the seasoning, and stir in the pasta if using. (The soup can be cooled to room temperature at this point, refrigerated, and reheated the next day.)

To make the pistou, pound the pine nuts and garlic with a pinch of salt as mortar. Add a few basil leaves and continue to pound. Alternating basil and olive oil, continue pounding until a smooth paste is achieved. Stir in any remaining oil and season with salt and pepper. You will have about 1 cup of pistou.

To serve, heat the soup and ladle into deep, wide soup plates, with a lamb shank in each. Swirl a heaping tablespoon of pistou into each serving.

From: *The Art of Simple Food* by Alice Waters, Clarkson Potter, 2007

Potato Gratin

This recipe makes for an interesting comparison with that of the same dish by Fernand Point
Serves 4

Ingredients
butter
4 large yellow potatoes (about 1-½ pounds)
salt and fresh-ground black pepper
1 cup (240ml.) milk
3 tablespoons butter, cut into pieces

Method
1. Rub a 9- by 12-inch (23x30cm.) gratin dish with butter.
2. Peel and slice about ⅟₁₆-inch (0.15cm.) thick the potatoes.
3. Make a layer of potato slices in the gratin dish, overlapping them slightly, like shingles.
4. Sprinkle with salt and fresh-ground black pepper.
5. Continue to layer the potato slices, seasoning each layer, until the potatoes are used up. You should have two or, at the most, three layers. Carefully pour the milk over the potatoes.
6. The liquid should come up to the bottom of the top layer of potatoes. Add more if necessary. Generously dot the top of the potatoes with butter.
7. Bake in a 350°F/180°C/Gas 4 oven until browned and bubbling, about 1 hour. Halfway through the baking, take the gratin dish out of the oven and press the potatoes flat with a metal spatula to keep the top moist. Return to the oven and keep checking. The gratin is done when the potatoes are soft and the top is golden brown.

Variations
- Peel and smash a garlic clove and rub it all over the inside of the gratin dish before buttering it.

- Use duck fat instead of butter.
- Use heavy cream or a mixture of half-and-half and cream. Omit the butter.
- Substitute celery root, parsnip, or turnip slices for up to half the potatoes.
- Add chopped herbs such as thyme, parsley, chives, or chervil between the layers.
- Sauté mushrooms, sorrel, spinach, or leeks, and layer them between the potato slices.
- Sprinkle grated Gruyère or Parmesan cheese on each layer and sprinkle more on top for the last 15 minutes of baking.

From: *The Art of Simple Food* by Alice Waters, Clarkson Potter, 2007

Acknowledgments

A number of people have generously provided valuable assistance and support in the preparation of this book and I am most grateful to them. Some prefer not to be mentioned here but know that I greatly appreciate their help.

The original idea for this work came from Nick Wallwork and so it is unlikely that it would have been produced without this inspiration. I would also like to warmly acknowledge the work of Michael Hamlin and his team in designing and producing the book. Graeme Still's sharp eyes were deployed to proof read this manuscript. Other contributions, ideas, and support came in, alphabetical order, from: Michael Duckworth, Humphrey Hawksley, Heather Holden-Brown, Rody Kwok, Kees Metselaar and last but not at all least, from Jenny Stevens.

A number of recipes have been included in this book; I am most obliged to the copyright holders who have given their permission for their inclusion. Every effort has been made to contact other copyright holders but not all have responded.

I should add that while writing this book I have frequently referred to Alan Davidson's incomparable *The Oxford Companion to Food.*

As ever none of the above are responsible for any errors which may be found in this book, I am quite capable of making these mistakes all by myself.